Lesser Crossroads

Lesser Crossroads

Edited by Hubert G. Schmidt *from*

THE STORY OF AN OLD FARM

by Andrew D. Mellick, Jr.

RUTGERS UNIVERSITY PRESS

1 9 4 8

F
142
.S6
M715

10/28/48 Personal 3.36

29238

Preface

In 1889 there appeared, under the title *The Story of an Old Farm*, a seven hundred and forty-three page volume best described in the words of its own prospectus as a "new semi-social, semi-historical work" in which "an attempt has been made to survey New Jersey history from the human rather than the civic side, thus filling in many interstices left by greater historians, and producing pages attractive from their biography, gossip and local color."

Had the fates been kind to its author, Andrew J. Mellick, Jr., he would not, in all likelihood, have had the time or inclination for so ambitious an undertaking, for in his early life we find little indication of future authorship. His father, a New Jersey farm boy become merchant, moved to New York City just before Andrew's birth in 1844, and to Bergen Point, New Jersey, during his boyhood. It is probable that it was from his mother—whose lineage went back to the Mayflower and whose ancestors for several generations had been respectable rural and small-town folk—that he inherited a pride in family and locality and an intellectual outlook which eventually inspired his writing endeavors.

The second of eight children, Mellick received only a common-school education, and at sixteen went to work for his father, who had by this time turned to real estate.

For more than twenty years thereafter Mellick was an extremely energetic man of business. In 1870 he and a brother attempted a development of lands along the route of the New Jersey Central Railroad, a venture which might well have made him a rich man. The depression of the mid-seventies, however, wrecked him financially, and in 1878 he accepted employment with a New York firm interested in lands in the Far West. It was while he was in New Mexico in behalf of his employers four years later that he was thrown from a horse and received the injury which was soon to result in a creeping paralysis and eventually his death in 1895.

A lesser man would have been hopelessly disheartened by the doctor's verdict and his own increasing infirmity. Mellick seems to have accepted his fate with equanimity. He worked at a desk job in his particular field as long as it was possible and then took to the invalid's couch which was to be his for the rest of his days.

During his travels before his accident he had been a facile letter writer and had published in minor magazines a number of articles about places which he had visited, including Cuba, Niagara, and Ohio. A trip to France, the Low Countries, the Rhine Valley, and England in 1880, had especially quickened his intellectual curiosity. Confined now to a life of physical inactivity, he began to devote his time to writing. Unable to grasp or wield a pen, he had to depend entirely upon dictation for putting his ideas on paper. One of the first tasks which he undertook was the dictation of a long account of his European travels. Other articles followed, and eventually the plan for *The Story of an Old Farm* took form.

The necessary research in numerous libraries was done by friends and relatives; many interested persons lent or donated original manuscripts or copies; and the help of many relatives was enlisted in gathering data for the genealogy of the Moelich and allied families. But it was Mellick himself who synthesized and organized the materials. A letter to a friend in Iowa after publication of the book well describes the problems involved:

> [The book] was undertaken to enliven what would otherwise have been dreary hours. It has brought to a sick man that best of all medicine—content; has satisfied vague longings for emotion and excitement, and has been an incentive for him to gladly welcome each coming day. During the entire time the writing of the book was under way no visits could be made to localities, libraries, the rooms of historical societies, or to individuals. Information not obtained from books was only to be had by extensive and prolonged correspondence, necessitating the dictating of over two thousand letters. In addition, not only did the body of the work grow by dictation, but the copious notes, covering two thousand folio pages . . . were preserved in like manner. This was the more difficult because of it never being possible to foretell what possible pains or ailments each day would claim for its own. Consequently the regular services of an amanuensis could not be made available, reliance being had on the kind, but chance, offices of parents, sisters, and friends, when they had the necessary time at their disposal.*

Mellick's unmarried sister, Abigail, was his devoted slave, and probably more than any other helper was responsible for the successful completion of the book. It is amazing that in its pages, we find so little reflection of the mechanical difficulties which the preparation of the manuscript presented.

Printed in 1889 at Somerville, New Jersey, *The Story of an Old Farm* had a surprisingly wide sale, though not a large one. As a successful author and corresponding secretary for a local historical society, Mellick's energies for some time were taxed by the demands of his correspondence. He then turned to a projected history of Plainfield. Although he had been able to see little of this New Jersey town to which he had moved with his family in 1885, he had come to look upon it as home. Unfortunately he did not live to complete the writing of its history.

* Quoted in *Somerset County Historical Quarterly* (Somerville, N. J., 1912), I, 28.

Preface

Mellick did not consider himself a historian in the ordinary sense, and we cannot apply the usual rules in judging his work. Although it sometimes leans heavily upon individual sources of information and in other ways shows certain technical weaknesses common to the work of untrained persons, it also shows surprising points of strength. Among these are a very sincere love for his subject, a seldom-equalled charm, and an understanding of human nature, one of his greatest qualities. To these must be added his intellectual honesty, his seldom-erring memory for detail, his capacity for painstaking labor, and, despite his lack of training, an intuitive feeling for authenticity. Fortunately these qualities were applied to a far wider field than his title would seem to indicate, and *The Story of an Old Farm* is a book of far greater significance than might be at first evident.

There are, undoubtedly, some critics who will damn Mellick as "antiquarian" (whatever this term may mean when exactly defined) and he, himself, would have been the first to acknowledge the truth of the charge. The editor is one of those who question whether it is necessarily a weakness to appeal at least occasionally to the natural love of the curious and different, and to the very human interest in the small details of life of another place and time. In the particular case of Mellick, his story is given additional character and charm by his very love for quaintness and for homely virtues, by his sentimentality and unfailing romanticism, by his pride in family and locality, by his nostalgia for a good life which was perhaps never really lived, by his respect for the accomplished and for those who held position, by his revelation of the prejudices and virtues of his own day, and even to some extent by the Victorian floweriness of his phrasing. The qualities of a tale, like those of the product of the vine, may well differ; the essential in each case is the giving of pleasure.

These characteristics are partly the result of Mellick's

personality, partly a consequence of the period in which he wrote. His work is fascinating for the picture of the 1880's which he presents, as well as for that of the eighteenth century with which he was chiefly concerned. An artist at heart, he saw the gaucheries, the callowness, and the hypocrisy of his own time in their true light, but portrayed them with an understanding and tolerance possible only in a contemporary. It is true that he shared the moral code and some of the prejudices of his own day. But, unlike the self-righteous of any age, he comprehended that an earlier century naturally had viewpoints and standards different from his own. So, though lecturing his readers on the benefits of temperance—meaning teetotalism—he openmindedly, sometimes almost mischievously, tells us of the drinking habits of an earlier era. He might not condone the moral lapses of a Franklin, father or son, but he understood them. Though vigorously patriotic himself ("electric with patriotism," according to the prospectus of his book), he was able to speak objectively about those who accepted British "protection papers" during the Revolution, admitted that certain of the Loyalists were "to some extent justified," and went out of his way to defend the Hessians, who were so universally hated in New Jersey. Irreligious conduct, cruelty, and unfaithfulness found him less forgiving, but these were no more condoned at the earlier period than in his own. And in his dual approach to the matter of position and caste, he was typically American. His essential democracy caused him to praise endlessly the "honest, simple, God-fearing folk" and their "homely virtues of industry, integrity, frugality, and hospitality." At the same time he had a certain awe for title, position, and wealth, especially as they concerned persons of an earlier day when class lines were less hidden by self-deception.

The central theme of *The Story of an Old Farm*, the migration to America of a not untypical German middle-class family and its adjustments to a new land, could be told in far less space than that used; and the secondary motifs, such as the development of a community from wilderness to settled countryside and the course of the War for Independence in New Jersey, could be narrated more briefly. It is also true that the "gossamer thread" which supposedly ties together dissimilar parts of the book becomes at times rather thin. But standards of brevity and consistency must not be applied to Mellick. He is a true story-teller, willing at any time to be diverted and to ramble off on some side path. A story occurs to him, so he tells it; if the reader is not interested, so much the worse for him. As Mellick says in an aside, a book should be, in part at least, written for the pleasure of the writer. After a side excursion, he comes back in due time to the main story. Perhaps in final analysis Mellick's greatest claim to fame is his ability as a story-teller, a narrator who willy-nilly carries his audience along with him. But any reader except the most impatient will find himself too charmed and interested to resent the interludes.

Although never reprinted, *The Story of An Old Farm* has had a constant reading public; the misfortune which made Mellick an invalid has been the good fortune of thousands of readers. Very few copies, however, of the original work are now available. In bringing this informative and heart-warming chronicle to a contemporary reading public, the original book has been subjected to a present-day editorial perspective. Under the new title, *Lesser Crossroads*, this classic is being made available to the audience it justly deserves.

In the Preface to the original edition, Mellick tells us:

When the writing of the *Story of an Old Farm* was undertaken, it was not anticipated that the completed volume would find readers beyond a limited circle. The narrative, it was supposed, would prove interesting only to the descendants of the founder of the homestead which had been the inspiration of its pages, and, perhaps, also to a few local readers. But as the work progressed, its scope broadened until the compilation gradually assumed a character calculated to interest lovers and students of general history. Finally, valuable material accumulating, the author found embodied in the chapters so much fresh information relating to Colonial and Revolutionary times in New Jersey as to warrant his seeking readers beyond the realm of kinsfolk and township residents. It was still necessary to preserve the original plan of the narrative, but it is hoped that the general reader will take in good part, and not find objectionable, the slight filament of family annals that runs through the successive chapters. After all, it is but a gossamer thread, and one that has served an excellent purpose—now as a silken clue to the labyrinth of historical research, and always as the continuous cord upon which has crystallized a mass of interesting facts, traditions, and incidents illustrative of times and customs now long bygone.

The editor's task, in general, has been an attempt to preserve all that which "the general reader will take in good part" and to eliminate all that "which would prove interesting only to the descendants of the founder of the homestead."

Because of the unusual methods it was necessary for Mellick to use in the preparation of his manuscript, it has been found impossible to run to earth all of the explicit sources upon which he based much of his writing. Fortunately it is evident that Mellick's standards of truth-finding were high and, despite some minute errors, his work can stand on its own feet. Under such circumstances the editor's contribution to the text becomes a small one.

The handling of certain technical problems should have a few words of explanation. Mellick had a Victorian love for punctuation, and was not always consistent in this regard or in his capitalization and spelling. Therefore, many small changes have been made in order to conform to modern practice. Typographical errors have been rectified, *errata* corrected, and inconsistencies ironed out. On the other hand, the author's phraseology has been almost entirely retained, since to do otherwise would take away something of Mellick's style. Considerable rearrangement of the text has been made at times in the interest of coherence. Because of the frequency of changes, no mechanical devices for showing them have been used.

At this late date it seems scarcely relevant to retain Mellick's personal acknowledgements as written in his original preface. The same is true of his bibliography of nearly two hundred items, many of them manuscripts, obscure pamphlets, and articles of his own day. Those interested in this bibliography are referred to the original book. Eighty-seven pages of genealogy of the Moelich and related families have likewise been deleted.

Decisions on what should be retained and what expunged were difficult indeed. Some deletions, such as chapters on Germans and Germany, were made because of lack of essential unity; but in other instances passages nearly as far astray were retained simply because of their interest or charm. Some sections, such as his detailed tracing of the history of various land grants, and those of more purely genealogical significance, which were included in *The Story of an Old Farm* because of Mellick's particular interest in them, will not be found in *Lesser Crossroads*. In general, decisions on deletions have been made on the basis of interest, historical value, or relationship with other parts of the book. The editor realizes that no decision will please all readers.

Hubert G. Schmidt

Middlebush, New Jersey
June 1948

xii

Contents

Lesser Crossroads

Introduction

THE TRAVELER by the old highway leading from Somerville to Peapack, in Somerset County, New Jersey, will remember the village of Lesser Cross Roads, perched on the southerly side of a sloping eminence some eight miles on the journey.

> *"One of those little places that have run*
> *Half up the hill beneath the blazing sun,*
> *And then sat down to rest, as if to say,*
> *'I climb no farther upward, come what may!'"*

Just here is located the Old Farm. Let us visit the little hamlet and learn something of its history, and of the generations that have lived, toiled, and died amid the cheerful hills and smiling valleys of the rolling country north of the village; it is the gateway of Somerset's quiet beauty and pastoral loveliness, unsurpassed in this portion of New Jersey.

We will choose one of those generous June days when early summer has veiled its youthful bloom in a maze of leaf, mystery, and shade. That our approach to this secluded village may be in harmony with the rural calm of its homely atmosphere, we will journey by the travel-stained stage wagon that for so many years has lumbered out of Somerville every afternoon about three o'clock. Squeezing in on the front seat by the driver's side, our legs and feet are soon seemingly inextricably entangled with mailbags, bundles, whiffletrees, and the horses' tails. The stage is "loaded up," three on a seat—twelve inside—with a mountain of luggage piled up behind. As we rattle down the main street and turn on the Peapack Road, the town, with its outlying villas standing amid parterres of flowers and shaded gardens, is soon left behind. Pounding over a wooden bridge that spans a little stream, the team settles down to its regulation jog of five miles an hour over the pleasant levels of Bridgewater Township. On either side lie well-tilled fields, rich with the promise of bounteous harvests. Barn swallows twitter in a farmyard hard by; a kingfisher, with a loud cry, sails away at our approach. From over the fences come the sound of whetting scythes, the rattle of mowing knives, and the talk and laughter of the haymakers; while the breeze for miles away is fragrant with the perfume of freshly tossed clovercocks.

Stop after stop is made at farmhouses and cottages by the roadside; now to leave a morning paper—twelve hours from the New York press—now a bundle or package which has to be fished from under the seats, calling forth nervous giggles from the women. Now and then someone is "taken up," or "let down," the last stop for that purpose having been to discharge a stout farmer's wife from the rear seat of the stage; the intervening passengers must crouch, half-standing, holding down the backs of the seats while she wades to the door dragging after her a large newspaper parcel, a spreading turkey-feather fan, and a huge paper handbox encased in blue checked gingham. This impedimenta carries in its wake several hats and belongings of her fellow travelers. The stout woman receives a warm welcome from two buxom girls and a sunburned farmer, who wait behind a paling fence with a background of well-swept, rusty clapboards, and porch o'erclambered with honeysuckle and June roses. The wide-open brown eyes of the shorter and plumper girl take in with lively interest each occupant of the stage. While leaning gracefully over the gate, the sunlight burnishing her rich waves of chestnut hair, the maiden's glances rest a little longer, perhaps, on the younger men of the party. But her glimpse of the traveling world is transitory, for soon our Jehu, having collected his fare, has returned a fat wallet to his trouser leg and climbed over the front wheels to his seat. The stage rattles on, and reaching a short incline bounces over a "thankee-marm," [1] sending the trunks on the shackly rack behind springing in air, and the rebound almost bumping together the knees and chins of those of us on the front seat.

We are now on the new road—so the driver tells us. There is certainly nothing in the highway peculiarly applicable to newness, but, like the New Forest in England or *Harper's New Monthly Magazine* in New York, having once been new it never can grow old. It must be new —you can see for yourself the old road meandering off toward the foothills on the east, taking in on its way an ancient weather-beaten tavern that once did a flourishing business. But this "cutoff" was opened some thirty years ago, leaving the old hostelry stranded in the shallows of deserted traffic. Should the ghost of its former proprietor, the genial Bill Allen, ever walk its crumbling porches, he could easily discern across the fields the tide of travel setting along the new road, which once paid tribute in a silvery stream to his now decaying till.

By and by the horses are tugging and straining up the long ascent of a spur of the "Blue" range of New Jersey hills, which the people hereabouts delight in calling "the mountains." Reaching the crest, we pause for a breath and enjoy an extended view of a landscape rich with the variegated hues of the luxuriant June vegetation. In the foreground lies the Revolutionary village of Pluckamin; church spires rising above the dense foliage of the cluster-

---

[1] A surfaced depression across a roadway for the passage of water.

ing trees mark the hiding places of other little villages that dot the undulating western plain; while far north, binding the horizon, are billows of verdure—the swelling hills and green valleys of Bedminster and Peapack. On descending the hill and crossing Chambers Brook, which is the line between Bridgewater and Bedminster townships, we pass one of the oldest houses of the neighborhood. It was built in 1756 by an Irishman named Laferty, who afterwards became unpleasantly notorious as the father of a very beautiful and profligate daughter who brought upon more than one prominent family in this part of Somerset much shame and grief. Her son, hanged in Somerville in the early part of this century, is the only white man who has suffered capital punishment in this county since the Revolution.

Presently the stage is clattering through the main street of Pluckamin and draws up in front of the tavern door, offering to the village loungers who adorn the empty dry-goods boxes in front of the several stores their daily ten-minute dose of mild excitement. Here the mails are changed, and we embrace the opportunity to stretch our legs on the tavern porch. Some of the party, "athirst with breezy progression," disappear inside in search of what a jocose Californian would call "interior decorations," but in the vernacular of this part of the country is known as "a leetle apple." This is historic ground. On the open space facing us, where the roads converge, Washington, Knox, Greene, and the conquerors at Princeton have stood about, and talked over the needs and plans of the Revolutionary Army.

The next point of interest on the route is the North Branch of the Raritan, which the road crosses where it flows through a shady glen. The banks are fringed with forest trees whose interlacing branches form over the devious stream a roof of almost impenetrable foliage. At times the waters brawl over the shallows, offering to thirsty cattle a convenient and picturesque ford; but now, owing to early summer rains, the river is brimming. Rumbling over the bridge, we hear the musical sound of falling waters, and looking under the overhanging boughs discover the torrent plunging headlong over the dam in an impetuous flood. The cool afternoon breeze blowing down the river comes to us laden with delicious, woodsy, watery odors which quicken our youthful remembrances. Again we are boys with cork dobbers, buckshot sinkers, and hickory poles angling in the pond above for slippery catfish, the darting dace, or the elusive sucker. Featherbed Lane is what they call the bit of road beyond the bridge. Successive years have brought successive loads of stone until the roadway has risen above the lowlands on either side, and travel is no longer impeded by the annual spring freshets. Time was when just here and beyond stood a fine forest of over four hundred acres; but that was during the life of that eccentric genius, Doctor Henry Van der Veer, who was blessed with the good old English prejudice against the felling of timber.

At the next turn of the road we are suddenly confronted by the venerable church of Bedminster, standing with dignity overlooking an attractive little green. No bewildering maze of tower, transcept, clerestory, gable, or rich ornamentation impresses the beholder. It is an oblong wooden structure painted white, with green blinds covering its double rows of square-capped windows and with an octagonal tower which supports a round-topped cupola. It is not, however, without good architectural proportions or a general effect which is imposing; in fact, it is an excellent example of what Emerson calls the only original type of American architecture, the New England meetinghouse. But to appreciate what a religious and social factor is Bedminister Church in this well-ordered community, it should be visited on a pleasant Sunday morning, when a quiet spirit broods over field and wood and nature seems at rest and filled with calm repose. The world awakens when, with gentle swell, over the valleys

7

and echoing hills sounds the sweet music of the swinging bell, pealing from the belfry windows the old, old invitation, "Come to prayer! Come to prayer!" They come, these country worshippers, from farm, from village, and from mill; they come on foot, in wagons, on horseback; some by the dusty highways, some over the peaceful meadows, some through the shady lanes.

Not the least interesting features of a Sunday morning at this old church is the motley array of vehicles standing at the fences and trees on both sides of the road for a quarter of a mile or less. A strange collection, indeed, embracing every kind of trap in use for the past half century. Here is a sulky, to which the spruce young farmer has driven his favorite colt to "meetin' "; there a long-bodied, black-covered Jersey wagon, with a rotund old lady backing out over the front wheel and whiffletrees, aiding her descent by clutching at the cruppers of the horses, who are passive enough after a week at plow and harrow. More modern equipages are not wanting, and occasionally can be seen the old-time, white-covered farm wagon, carpeted with straw, with splint chairs from the farmhouse for seats.

An old country church like this, which draws its people from miles around, means much more than one located near populous towns and cities. It is the beating heart around which all the neighborhood interests and hopes circulate. It is the place for a weekly interchange of news and gossip, and the people on Sunday morning lay in a store for the coming six days not altogether confined to uses of religious and spiritual comfort. As the hour for service approaches, the men gather about the door or under the trees, discussing their horses, the crops, and whatever may have been of interest during the past week, and on entering we find the wives and daughters in animated conversation over the backs and partitions of the pews. When the sexton has rung the last bell by stoutly pulling two ropes depending from the belfry to the vesti-

8

bule floor, the men come clattering through the doors, which face the congregation on either side of the pulpit. The elders and deacons, first depositing their hats on the sides of the tall pulpit stair, seat themselves to the right and left of the minister, their faces settling into the dignified composure due their official position. Gradually a hush pervades the audience, preceding the solemn invocation. The blessing over, a stir and bustle in the rear gallery proclaim the large choir to be standing. The cherry-cheeked girls are shaking out their frocks, the stalwart youths are clearing their throats; now the ear of every child in the assemblage is alert to hear the first twang of the tuning fork, following which comes the long concerted "do–mi–sol–do" of the choir. They have the pitch, and break away into a loud psalm of praise or song of thanksgiving, the large congregation taking up the refrain till the old church rings with that most jubilant of all music, hearty congregational singing.

And so the service continues, with prayer and praise, and sermon and doxology, not forgetting the collection taken up in funny little black bags poked down the pews at the end of long poles. I must acknowledge it is many years since I have been in this time-honored church; but how well I remember the pleasure with which a certain small boy in a roundabout brass-buttoned jacket and nankeen trousers looked forward to a summer Sunday morning at the old church. His seat was well up toward the pulpit, and, did the service grow wearisome, through the open door could be seen the horses biting at the flies, the leaves stirring in the soft south breeze, and the butterflies floating in the sweet sunshine over the close-knit turf of the green. Will the delightful old lady who sat in a great pew immediately in front of the one occupied by that same small boy ever be forgotten; the one who, when he, lulled by the monotone of the sermon or the droning of the drowsy bees that circled in and out the open door, nodded with sleep, would surreptitiously pass back little

9

bunches of pennyroyal or other fragrant herbs, and on rare occasions—ah, happy day!—a store-bought peppermint lozenge?

All this time our stage wagon is still rolling on, not very rapidly it is true. Presently our goal is in plain sight, facing us as we drive along the straight road which stretches over a level country, 'twixt meadows, orchards, and comfortable homesteads. The attractive parsonage with its surrounding glebe is behind us on the left; beyond on the right, down a tree-embowered lane, a glimpse is obtained of a substantial farmhouse and its old-fashioned garden. On we roll, passing the forge with its waiting horses, loud-breathing fire, and dusky interior, until the stage creaks and strains as it mounts the side hill and comes to a standstill at the Bedminster Tavern, which rests on the edge of the first terrace of the incline. Here ends our ride, Bedminster and the Lesser Cross Roads being one and the same.

Perhaps you do not like my village? I must confess it has an air rather unkempt and forlorn: it can hardly be called a village—just a wayside hamlet. In the last century when these four roads met here, or rather the two highways crossed each other, the natural consequence was that industrial germ of all new settlements—a blacksmith shop. Later came the store and tavern. Little houses have since dropped haphazard along the roadsides, but the village has long since been finished and now seems quite in the decadence of age. Its most pleasing aspect is along the north road, where the rusty old houses with their gable ends fronting the highway picturesquely cluster in patches of white and gray on the successive terraces that form the ascending hillside. Trees and generous shade were evidently not considered adjuncts to rural beauty by "the forefathers of the hamlet"; yet, notwithstanding the bareness of the place, it has a quaintness of its own due to the antiquated houses with their old-fashioned gardens.

The small structure on the corner opposite the tavern is that magazine of wonders, a country store. Is it not a funny little shop? Just like one of the wooden houses that come in boxes of toy villages. Its interior is odd enough to satisfy the most diligent searcher for the queer and old. The counters are worn smooth by the dorsal extremities of the neighborhood Solons, who have gathered here for sixty years of evenings to settle the affairs of the nation and comment on the gossip of the country for miles around. Many an ancient joke has here over again won a laugh—many a marvelous tale has been listened to with open-mouthed wonder by country lads who have tramped miles for the pleasure of an evening in general society. Although it is a wee store, here can be found everything from a fishhook to a hayrake, from a quart of molasses to a grindstone. Dress patterns and calicoes—fast colors—rest on the shelves; nail kegs and sugar barrels offer seats for waiting customers; boots, pails, and trace chains decorate the ceiling; while dusty jars tempt the school children to barter eggs for sticks of peppermint and wintergreen, or the succulent Jacksonball.

Of the roads focusing here, the one from the south we have traveled, and with the one towards the north we shall soon grow familiar. The west road leads to Lamington, New Germantown,[2] and the pleasant agricultural lands of Hunterdon; while the one on the east stretches away beyond the North Branch of the Raritan River, over the historic hills on which rest Liberty Corner, Basking Ridge, and Bernardsville, villages rich in Revolutionary reminiscences.

Down the east road a little way—you can see it from the corner—stands the schoolhouse. Your guide has been soundly thrashed more than once in that little building, or in one on the same site; but that was more than a

---

[2] Renamed Oldwick during the First World War.

quarter of a century ago, when he, a brown-cheeked, barefooted boy, trudged over these hills each morning before half past eight, carrying his dinner in a tin blickie. Surely the boys of that time have not forgotten the Cross Roads pedagogue who never spared the rod, or rather rods, for he had two. With one, a young sapling cut fresh each morning, he could plant a welt on the shoulders of a boy six feet away. This was but the admonitory gad. When serious business was meant, the luckless culprit must mount the back of a larger boy, who, gathering the victim's legs under his arms, tightened the trousers over the point of attack; then would "the teacher" lay on with a short, sharp switch. The office of underboy was no sinecure, for did the descending birch miss its shining mark, it must fall upon the coadjutor's legs, to the great amusement of his comrades. I wonder do the girls still have standing in the corner of the school lot the stone playhouse, filled with broken bits of china; and the old stone fort in the opposite corner, is it still intact and well supplied with pebbles to resist assault? I will go bail that the boys of the present know as well as did we old fellows the short cut across lots to the Mine Brook Hole, a deep hole guarded by gnarled oaks and overhanging sycamores. A plunge in its cool depths must at any time be the *ultima Thule* of delight in a schoolboy's summer nooning.

The day wears on. The stage has long ago lurched and jolted eastward, and is now creeping along the road that stretches over the bottom lands beyond the river, thus avoiding the hills which we must proceed to climb. You are forgiven for not falling in love with the village —perhaps it was hardly to be expected—but, now that we approach the Old Farm, I shall be disappointed indeed if you fail to appreciate the singular beauties of its grassy hillsides interspersed with ancient orchards, its broad meadow spaces, its groves of oaks, and its streams of sinuous course.

He who loves his fellow man, and he who loves nature, must be fond of a country road; it appeals in tones both human and divine, for it is the bond connecting the works of the Creator with the productions of humanity. The road running north from Bedminster, up which we now bend our steps, is in happy accord with such a suggestion, and gives promises of rural loveliness as it leaves the village and wanders over the hills, hedged in by banks from which outcrop the shale forming the foundations of this part of the world. The reddish-brown roadway lies on the sunny rise in pleasing contrast to the flushed, time-stained grays of the gables of the bordering houses, which peer down over the banks from their settings of sweetbriar, marigolds, and snowballs. We mount for a quarter of a mile or less and soon see, beyond, the rounded tops of a brave bit of timber. It is the confines of the Old Farm, which lies to the right, on the east side of the highway. Before reaching it we pass a neglected "God's Acre." It is the simple burial place of slaves and their posterity, who once formed an important element of the workaday world of this township. The headstones, if there ever were any, have long since disappeared; the decrepit fences are covered with a rambling growth of weeds and creeping vines, and the rains of many years have beaten level the humble mounds of the dusky toilers.

But the hoary trees of the deep green wood beckon us on. Venerable oaks have thrown their shade over the slopes, glades, copses, and leafy recesses of this royal grove since the days the Indians roamed at will over these fair lands. Looking far in the timbered acres to where the shadows and sunlight alternate, and "one leafy circle melts into another," does it not suggest Sherwood Forest? Free from underbrush, with the majestic trees standing at stately distances, one can well imagine seeing, where the sunshine darts through yon sylvan bower, Robin Hood and his merrie men kneeling on a soft bed of green moss at the base of a sacred oak, while jolly Friar Tuck invokes a blessing on some new marauding enterprise.

Let us push on over the breezy uplands. The road scales a small ridge, then lies along a short level, and sinks into a little dell, only to mount higher on the farther side. Its trend is now eastward, and the flanking banks are surmounted by rusty gray rail fences, whose straddling posts rise from a tangle of milkweed, sumac, wild blackberry, and alder bushes. The eye rambling south and west overlooks a charming prospect for miles away. The ebbing sunshine, flooding down wide streams of light, intensifies every shade of color in nature's mosaic of tillage and fallow, of level sweeps of pasture and waving fields of grain. On the other side of the road the hillsides of the Old Farm fall away abruptly in great, grassy cascades till they blend with the meadows that stretch to a line of waving trees, marking where a winding silvery stream hastens to join the Raritan. The peaceful atmosphere of such a landscape possesses what someone has called "the quality of gracefulness." The face of the country is buoyant and rolls away in billowy undulations, now subsiding into quiet valleys, now gently ascending woodland slopes, the deep soil of the green fields lying in continuous, lawn-like surfaces, presenting between the eye and the horizon in every direction a panorama of symmetry and beauty.

From here the main road runs due east over a high level, and soon has on both sides the broad upland acres of our ancestral plantation. Walking on, we reach the edge of a long, steep descent known for a century past as the Melick Hill. Here the road plunges down over a series of plateaus until, nearly two thousand feet away, it disappears around a graceful bend, where it crosses the brawling Peapack Brook, in this direction the boundary of the farm.

One may journey many miles in many countries without finding a lovelier outlook than from this hilltop. Perhaps you think that the fertile valley below, luxuriant with the freshness of gentle summer showers, smacks too much of utilitarian beauty? True, nature does not here present herself in a grand or majestic aspect; precipitous rocks, bold declivities, and long ranges of serrated peaks are not features of the landscape. But nature in its various phases fits all moods, and it has other charms than those of the wildly picturesque; those unveiled in the homely and restful scene of these peaceful hillsides have a quiet fascination, far more satisfactory than if emanating from gorge, chasm, or upheaved rocks. As you watch the slanting sun illume the meadows with their meandering brooks, the orchards, farmsteads, and great barns, emblems of plenty; as you watch the afternoon shadows settling in the valley and slowly creeping upward and backward on the opposite slope, you are reminded of one of those lovely vales in midland England, vales which Henry James describes as mellow and bosky, and redolent of human qualities.

We are told that one born with a soul for the picturesque finds in American landscapes naught but harsh lights, without shade, without composition, without the subtle mystery of color. Standing here overlooking this countryside, do you discover anything garish, any tones that offend? Color—why, here is the very essence of the mystery of color. See yonder that little island of cloud-shadow float over the field of bending grain, a field of a most delicious green interspersed with suggestions of yellow, the promise of golden harvests soon to come. Observe, beyond the river how in those broad acres of young corn the tender green stands out against the rich dark loam from which it draws its lusty strength. See, too, the luxuriant verdure of the woodland, topping the undulating rise beyond yon sloping pastures. Here are light, shadow, form, and color, and all that go to make a picture of quiet, restful beauty with an atmosphere of sweet content. Bear with my enthusiasm. I love these hills and all that can be seen from their kindly sides.

Come! We will go down into the valley. The terraces give pleasant breaks to the steep incline of the road. As we proceed, the faint sound of millwheels and brooks comes up from below, and the air is fresh and cool with the palpable breath of the waters pouring over the dam. Presently, across the fields on the left are to be seen the large barns, hovels, and farm buildings, and not far beyond, a little lower down, wreaths of blue smoke curl above the long brown roof of the old homestead. Just before reaching the foot of the hill we come to a grand old maple, whose spreading branches have for a century of summers waved a leafy welcome to comers to the Old Farm. To you, perhaps, it is but a fine tree, but I would be devoid of all sensibility if deaf to the music of the leaves stirring amid its branches. Their sound awakens memories of the many happy, youthful days that have witnessed my return to the refreshment of this old maple's shade, and to all the pleasure that invariably followed a visit to this cherished homestead. Here we leave the highway and, turning to the left up a short incline, are in front of the Old Stone House. Facing an antiquated dooryard and shaded by elms, it rests lovingly against the side of a sunny bank of turf, springing from the grassy slope as if part of the geological strata rather than a superstructure raised by the hand of man. They builded well in those old days, and now the walls of this sturdy dwelling, humanized and dignified by five generations of occupants, are as staunch and apparently as well preserved as when laid in 1752; as firm as when Johannes Moelich erected here in the wilds of Colonial New Jersey a home like those ancient houses of masonry he had always known, bordering the banks of the winding Rhine in the far-away fatherland.

There is nothing pretentious about this dwelling, nothing suggestive of the fine mansion; it is just a quaint low house with a comely old-time presence. Almost a cottage in size—it has but nine or ten rooms—the white-washed walls, massive enough for a citadel, are pierced in a haphazard sort of way with odd little windows, from which twinkle queer diminutive panes of glass. At the west end it is one and a half stories high, but the slope of the hill gives another story at the eastern gable. Formerly the roof was thatched with straw, and among my many treasures prized as souvenirs of this old farm is a pair of the original thatching needles, made of iron and shaped like a sickle. Buildings, like people, have facial expressions peculiar to themselves. This homely house bears on its aged face a gentle and benign expression of invitation and welcome.

There is an air of comfort and repose about this farm-house that renders it distinctive among dwellings. The open door ushers us into an ample hall. An ancient time-piece ticks at the foot of the stair and the cool evening breeze draws through the upper half of the rear door, beyond which there is a view of a pleasant stretch of meadow disappearing down a steep bank into a belt of trees bordering a millpond. From the back porch you can see at the foot of the hill on the east the buildings of Schomp's gristmills and sawmills. Together with their contiguous dwelling, the dam, and the beautifully shaded stream below, they present a charming rural picture. Formerly the bottom lands on this side of Peapack Brook were checkered with square vats, for the owners of the Old Farm have not only been farmers, but for four generations were tanners of leather and grinders of bark. But the tan vats have long been filled up, the bark mill is a picturesque ruin, and the waters that once turned its busy wheel now run to waste in their sluices and raceways.

But to return to the Old Stone House. You see it is only a plain farmhouse after all, with no remarkable stair-cases or ancient tiles to interest the visitor. It is true quaint cupboards with curious little panes of glass peer out from the corners of some of the rooms, and those extraordinarily complicated locks on the doors are of German manufacture and were put on at the building of the house. The incline of the floors is not due to the old age of their supports or the weakening of the walls. When this old house was new, carpets were unknown among farmers, and these floors were laid on an incline in order that each morning, before they were freshly sanded, the old sand and dirt could be more readily swept into the hall. By far the most interesting room is the farm kitchen, or living room, downstairs. There is an outer kitchen resting against the east gable in which is built the great Dutch oven. What batches of rye and wheaten loaves have browned in this capacious salamander! On opening the furnace door the savory fumes of baking cake seem in the air; you almost see the plethoric pans drawn from the heated vault, the rich crusts puffed with the pride of their own sweetness till they burst in golden crevices. Picture to yourself in all the years of generous living the endless procession of pies, puddings, creature comforts, and dainty delicacies that have been discharged from the mouth of this broad oven. Both tradition and memory bear witness that there have been good cooks in the Old Stone House.

To the east of this outer kitchen is a neglected garden begirt by a crazy fence of ancient construction. Clambering hop and other straggling vines partially hide the weakness of the aged inclosure, while a luxuriant growth of currant and gooseberry bushes, intermingled with all sorts of weeds and creepers, give to the fence an air of substantiality which it is far from possessing. The black loam, enriched with years of rotting leaves, plants, and vegetables, feeds patches of hereditary lilies and old-time flowers grown from seeds brought from Germany. Several ancient plum and twisted quince trees cluster in one corner, their trunks gray with the lichen of time, though still thrifty from the long drinking of the rich juices of exuberant vegetation. Were it later in the season a few choice yellow pumpkins and crooked-necked summer squashes would be seen turning their ripening backs to the warm sun, and pale green cucumbers, fattening on the black soil, would sprawl among the beds. But now the narrow paths are bordered with pinks and sweet williams; between them stand early beets in sober rows and young bean vines just reaching for their rusty poles, while blossoming potato and tomato plants contribute their bit of color.

The threshold of the farm kitchen even in my time was guarded by a double Dutch door, but the demon of improvement has replaced it with a more modern entrance. We can step directly from the grass and trees of the dooryard to its interior, and at once are in a bit of the Old World. As we come out of the daylight, the room seems dark, with mysterious corners and outlets, for it is lighted by small windows set deep in the thick stone walls. As for the outlets, I know well that the corner one farthest from the door leads into the large cool cellar, where are firm yellow pats of butter and pans of rich cream, where stone crocks stand on the earthen floor filled with moist pot cheeses, nut cakes, and all manner of good things, while corpulent jars distended with sweets and rows of pies stuffed with lusciousness adorn wooden shelves hanging from the ceiling.

Most of the furniture of this room dates back to the last century. The huge press standing against the west wall was built in Germany before 1735 and is a curiosity in its way. Though the wood is of walnut it is black with age, and its height is so great as to preclude the use of its round black ball legs, which for years have served as children's playthings in the garret. This massive piece of brass-mounted furniture is capped by an overhanging cornice that projects some twelve inches, and has stood in its present position since the house was built.

While these oaken beams were growing dark with the

mellowing hand of time, golden-haired children have sat about this ancestral hearthstone, building in the glowing embers pictures wrought of their budding fancies. These same beams, still unbent by the burden of age though brown with the deposits of years, have seen those same children, now old men and women, picturing in the ashes of the lighted logs the memories of their past lives. And so the generations have come and gone, and so they have moved "gently down the stream of life until they have slept with their fathers."

And who was the German immigrant who felled the forest of this Bedminster valley? And who were his children and his children's children who have wrestled from these sunny slopes their treasures of grain and abundant grasses, and have dotted the pastures below with glossy cattle? You do not find their names emblazoned on the pages of the nation. Neither have their vices or profligacies distinguished them as subjects for memoirs, plays, or novels. An honest, simple, God-fearing folk, with the homely virtues of industry, integrity, frugality, and hospitality, they have tilled the soil, tanned leather, built churches, supported schools, occupied modest positions of public honor and trust in the community, and fought the battles of their country. Quietly have many of them passed their uneventful but well-ordered lives, and quietly at life's close have they lain down in Pluckamin or Bedminster churchyard, their memories embalmed in the respect and affection of their fellows. It is the character and virtues of just such plain people that have constituted the bulwarks and strength of the American nation. The annals of families and communities are the real basis of all history. We are told that the history of a nation is to be read in its political life. An obviously true proposition, but to present to the mind the complete progress of a people, it is not only necessary to understand the superstructure of politics and civil life,

but that substratum of society as well which cultivates the
arts of peace and gradually develops the country, that
substratum of living men and women whose acts and the
daily routine of whose existence form the true foundation
of history.

The Crooked Billet Wharf

THE STORIED BEAUTY of the winding Rhine is nowhere more famed than in the vicinity of the ancient city of Coblenz. Here have nature and man combined in forming a scene of rare and picturesque loveliness. On reaching this quaint settlement it is not the old town with its massive walls stretching along the banks of the Rhine that first impresses one; nor is it the Moselle, whose waters here swell the flood of the greater river. It is the majestic fortress of Erhenbreitstein, crowning the almost perpendicular rocks on the farther shore, four hundred feet above the stream, that dominates the scene and dwarfs every object within its frowning presence. This vast fortification, the Gibraltar of the Rhine, is inaccessible on three sides and dates back to the Franconian King Dagobert in the seventh century. From its extensive glacies, fosses, and towers the eye ranges over a charming and varied landscape storied with legends, and green valleys filled with the romance of the Middle Ages. Immediately below are the palaces, turrets, and red roofs of the second city of importance on the river. The old basilica of St. Castor elevates its hoary towers above an angle in the town wall where the rivers join, and beyond it the massive arches of a bridge of heavy blocks of stone take fourteen huge strides across the Moselle. On the south in plain sight are the stately, gray stone battlements of the royal château of Stolzenfels, capping a timbered eminence, while down the river can be seen a succession of picturesque villages, whose long Rhine streets almost form one continuous settlement. About four miles away in this direction the convent island of Niederwerth splits the current of the stream. A little beyond and a mile or so back from the right bank of the river, in a valley surrounded by apple orchards, rests the ancient village of Bendorf.

With us a place of over four thousand inhabitants would feel entitled to be considered a town, but on the continent of Europe a settlement requires more than population to attain such dignity. Bendorf has the appearance of gray antiquity common to most of the old settlements along the Rhine. Its narrow streets, without sidewalks, are lined with low, two-story stone houses, though the continuity is occasionally broken by a tall, steep red roof studded with odd dormers, or an overhanging gable which casts a deep shadow across the contracted roadway. The stroller over the rough cobbles of the ill-paved streets comes again and again upon an antique turret protruding from the upper story of some time-stained structure, or upon picturesque wooden houses with their blackened constructive timbers exposed, enclosing panels of white plaster. Often the quaint façades are curiously carved with heraldic devices, grotesque conceits, and odd German lettering.

Here in Bendorf, in the early part of the eighteenth century, lived a sturdy burgher—a tanner and a freeholder of good repute—Johannes Moelich, who was born on the twenty-sixth of February, 1702. His family comprised four children, equally divided as to sex, and his wife, Maria Catherina, a rotund German matron who prided herself upon being the daughter of Gottfried Kirberger, the burgomaster of Bendorf. Having been born on the sixth of January, 1698, she was nearly four years the senior of her husband, to whom she had been married on the first of November, 1723. She is familiarly known in family annals as Mariah Katrina. The children were Ehrenreich (Aaron), Veronica Gerdrutta (Fanny), Andreas (Andrew), and Marie Cathrine.

One morning, while the year 1735 was yet young, Johannes gathered together his family, his household goods and effects, including considerable furniture, and taking with him his youngest brother Gottfried (Godfrey), departed through the *Bach*-gate of the town wall to the bank of the river. Here he embarked on one of the clumsy barges of that day and floated away, borne by Father Rhine to Rotterdam, where he took ship and sailed for America. This emigrant was the son of Johann Wilhelm and Anna Katherine Moelich, who came to Bendorf in 1688 from Winningen, a town on the Moselle four miles west of Coblenz. They had many relatives and friends in both places, and we can well fancy that the departure of Johannes and his family was an important event for these communities.

It would be interesting to learn just what cause led to his emigration. It could not have been poverty, as was the case with many of the thousands of his countrymen who had preceded him across the water, for we know that he owned property in Bendorf and had ready money for investment in the new country. Perhaps he appreciated the responsibility of his little family and hesitated to bring up his children under a government that had brought much misery and distress to its subjects. He had already established relations beyond the sea, his younger brother Johann Peter having landed in Philadelphia in 1728 from the ship *Mortonhouse*. Doubtless he had received letters from this brother and from friends among the many emigrants who had found an asylum in America, drawing an enticing picture of the liberal government of William Penn, which had secured to them in the fruitful valleys of Pennsylvania peaceful retreats where they no longer feared religious persecution or political oppression.

24

The Crooked Billet Wharf

In early Colonial days King (now Water) Street in Philadelphia lay close to the edge of the Delaware. A low, one-story, rambling tavern-house stood fronting it near the corner of Chestnut, its creaking sign bearing in dull paint the legend of a crooked stick of wood. It was here that Benjamin Franklin ate his first dinner in the Quaker City. This inn gave to the short dock facing it the name of the Crooked Billet Wharf, often mentioned in old-time Philadelphia annals. Anyone loitering on this dock on the morning of the twenty-ninth of May, 1735, could have heard the splash of a right bower, and on looking up could have discovered the ship *Mercury* swinging round to the tide. As she lies in the stream the vessel shows repeated marks of her weeks of battling with the fierce waves of the Atlantic, and her sides are streaked by the salt spray of many a weary gale. The log of this ship has not been preserved, so we know nothing of the particulars of her voyage or of the date of sailing. She was without doubt a small vessel, and many days must have elapsed since the yellow arms of Dutch windmills had waved farewells to her passengers from behind the dunes of the low Holland coast.

Among the one hundred and eighty-six sunburned, weather-beaten Germans and Swiss who leaned over her taffrail, looking with curious eyes upon the little entry port of Pennsylvania, were Johannes Moelich and his family. The aspect of this provincial town in its setting of dark forests must have presented a strong contrast to the animated quays and the spires, belfries, lofty pin-nacled houses, and dark windmills of the quaint old city from which they had embarked. It would be pleasant to be able to narrate Johannes' impressions and experiences on landing. Had he known that one hundred and fifty years later many of his posterity would be glad to read of his movements in Philadelphia, he doubtless would have kept a faithful journal. In the absence of such forethought on his part, we must draw upon our knowledge of the

25

Quaker City in those early days, and, with the help of Watson,[1] that delightfully garrulous Boswell of old Philadelphia, we shall be able to see with Johannes' eyes as he and his family make their way up into the city.

It was now over fifty years since the little ship *Welcome*, of only three hundred tons burden, had landed William Penn in Pennsylvania, and its capital had grown in population to some eight thousand souls. Thomas Lawrence was mayor, Philadelphia having been a chartered city since 1701. It was a compact little town of about one thousand houses, nearly all of brick, one and two stories high, with double-hipped roofs, although occasionally a more pretentious dwelling elevated its dormers above a third story. The area was not very extensive; a very short walk would bring one to the outlying commons and woods. Beyond Fourth Street the houses were but scattering; of course there were no pavements, and westerly there were no streets marked out beyond Seventh. The highway leading out of town followed the line of High, now Market, Street, and after it crossed the location of the present Eighth Street the forest commenced and extended to the Schuylkill.

Did you ask was there anyone to welcome Johannes? Though no message had announced the coming of the *Mercury*, without doubt the arrival of the ship was soon noised through the city; let us hope that the immigrant was expected and that when he landed on the Crooked Billet Wharf he found awaiting him some warm-hearted compatriot, who seized his hand and bade him a hearty welcome to America. In fancy, at least, we will picture him so greeted.

We will constitute ourselves one of the party as they leave the wharf and make their way along King Street, the children hanging back to look into the shop windows,

---

[1] John Fanning Watson, *Annals of Philadelphia, Being a Collection of Memoirs, Anecdotes, & Incidents of the City and Its Inhabitants.* . . . (Philadelphia, 1830).

26

for in the year 1735 that street was the center of the retail trade of the city. They are going to the State House to fulfill the first duty of all newly arrived foreigners, the registering of their names with the secretary of the province. What is more delightful than the first few hours spent in a new country, where everything is totally different from one's ordinary surroundings? Weeks of pleasurable experiences may be passed later, but the peculiar charm of the first uprolling of the curtain will never return. Though their country had been rich in the picturesque, the Moelichs found much to excite both interest and wonder, and in the short time occupied in reaching the State House they received many new and strange impressions.

An American on visiting England or the Continent for the first time finds himself attacked by a strange illusion. As he feels himself surrounded by an atmosphere of antiquity while wandering from one ancient town to another, his whole nature saturated with the charm of quaint architecture and picturesque effects, imperceptibly there steals over him a faint impression of a prior acquaintance, as if he were revisiting scenes familiar in some previous existence; and he finds himself almost doubting that the retina of the eye is actually receiving the impression of a picture seen for the first time. He recognizes the illusion and fully appreciates that what he sees is really new because not viewed before—he recognizes, also, that to him at least it is truly old and familiar; old in a thousand impressions and desires, born of books and the talk of travelers; consequently, he is rarely if ever confronted by the entirely unexpected. Johannes and his party were not troubled by this double vision. They had read no books descriptive of America, nor had they listened to the oft-told tales of returned travelers. To them all the panorama of the Quaker City existence was novel and interesting.

Proceeding westward along Chestnut Street, they are

met by such a procession as has never been seen on the highways of Europe; a drove of Negroes coupled two and two, recently imported from the Guinea coast and probably just landed from Barbadoes, which at that time was the distributing mart of the English slave trade. When they reach the next corner they see an even sadder phase of this barbarous institution. In front of the tavern, from a rude platform resting on two upright hogsheads, a slave auction was being held. "Likely Negro boys" and "breeding wenches," as the placarded bills announced, were being knocked down at a few hundred dollars a head.

As the Moelichs walked along the street the bordering detached houses had a kindly, domestic presence, due to their comely little porches with penthouse roofs shading wooden seats, seemingly extending to the passer-by a hospitable invitation to tarry. This air of hospitality was further enhanced by the attractive balconies that faced even the smaller dwellings, on which their occupants were wont to gather to enjoy the air at the cool of the day. Occasional glimpses of quaint interiors were obtained through open windows that swung on hinges inward, with small panes of glass set in their leaden-framed lattices. In some of the finer houses the best rooms were wainscoted in oak and red cedar, but in most instances the walls were plainly whitewashed. No carpets were to be seen, the floors being covered with silver sand drawn into fanciful figures by a skillful use of the sweeping brush, in which the housekeepers took much pride. Lofty chests of drawers, with round black balls for legs, extended nearly to the ceiling, and all the family china was to be seen through the diamond lights of odd little corner cupboards. On the massive Dutch dresser were displayed brightly polished porringers and platters of pewter, the dinner plates of that day being nearly altogether of that metal, though the use of wooden trenchers was not entirely out of date. Sometimes, through farther doors opening into the kitchen, our party was much amused at the sight of a peculiar feature of household economy. Before cavernous fireplaces, often girt with ancient Dutch tiles, were set baking-ovens, whose spits were turned by little bow-legged dogs trained to run in a hollow cylinder like squirrels, by which means was the roasting meat kept revolving. "Mine host" Clark, of the State House Inn, advertised about this time in Andrew Bradford's *Weekly Mercury* and in Benjamin Franklin's *Pennsylvania Gazette* that he had "for sale several dogs and wheels, much preferable to any jacks for roasting any joints of meat."

But what means this turmoil and uproar, and from whence comes this advancing crowd, enveloped in dust? Johannes' party quickly leaves the street and takes to a little footpath that runs diagonally from the corner of Third to High and Fourth Streets. Standing there, they see surge by an unfragrant rabble, in the center of which, tied to the tail of a cart, a poor wretch is bellowing with pain as stroke after stroke from a constable's whip falls on his naked back. The Germans look stolidly on the scene; they are too familiar with despotic punishments to be surprised or affected thereby. Following the cart are a number of petty criminals surrounded by constables. It is the weekly market-day parade of evildoers. After their tour of the city and their suffering from the turbulence of the populace, they will drift into no quiet eddy within the seclusion of the jail. They must take their places on the pillory and in the stocks that have been set up for their reception opposite the prison on High and Third Streets. This day addled eggs will sell as well as those freshly laid, for many a passer-by will deem it a virtuous action to have a fling at the culprits, for the pleasure of seeing them dodge their heads in the endeavor to avoid the noxious missiles.

Benjamin Franklin in his *Autobiography* says that the position of a Philadelphia constable was at that time one of a considerable profit. The management of the city watch was in their hands. It was the duty of the officer of each ward to summon a certain number of resident householders to attend him each night to aid in patrolling his district. This service could be avoided by paying six shillings, which was supposed to go for hiring substitutes. The number who paid for the exemption was much greater than those hired by the constables to walk the rounds; consequently, the officers put much unlawful money into their pockets. This system resulted in the night watches being largely composed of irresponsible persons who undertook the duties for a little drink-money, but quite neglected to fill their obligations.

Returning to Chestnut Street, our party, rambling on, is soon in front of that noted structure which the events of later years baptized as Independence Hall. The Philadelphian of the present day who halts for a moment in the sturdy presence of this time-honored, historic building looks with veneration on its homely façade. To him it bears amid the surrounding turmoil a dignified expression of peace and rest, as if emanating from the consciousness of a deserved repose after a great work nobly performed. Very different was the aspect it presented to the newly arrived Germans. No throbbing tide of humanity ebbed and flowed beneath its shadows; Chestnut Street, not yet the artery of a great city, did not pulsate at its portals. At this distance out it was but little better than a country road, and the State House, just completed, faced it square and prim, bright from lintel to rooftree with red bricks, fresh paint, and white mortar. There was then no beautiful park as a rich setting; the unkempt grounds extended but half across the square, and several small detached brick dwellings fronted Walnut Street at its rear.

Upon the original book of record in the Department of State of Pennsylvania, there is still to be seen the signature made by Johannes on that day; it is evidently the writing of a man of intelligence, as it is not only

30

legibly inscribed, but would stand as an example of good penmanship. Most of the arrivals by the same vessel, being unable to write, made their marks. The names are preceded by the following entry:

At the Court House, Philadelphia, present the Honorable Patrick Gordon, Esq., Lieutenant-Governor Thomas Lawrence and Charles Read, Esquires. The Palatines, whose names are underwritten, imported in the ship Mercury of London, William Wilson, master, Rotterdam, but last from Cowes, did this day subscribe the oaths to the Government, May 29, 1735.

The grounds about the State House, on this May morning, framed an interesting picture. Johannes, on leaving the building after registering, was a good deal surprised by the sight of an encampment of Indians, who happened that day to have taken possession of that open space. For a long time after this it was the practice of bands of red men to occasionally make excursions to the city for the purpose of purchase and barter. Generally they would remain for a week or more, and it was their custom to establish themselves with their squaws and children in the State House yard. While the young bucks roamed about the streets, shooting coins off posts with their arrows and visiting the stores for trade, the squaws and old men occupied themselves in camp by making and selling plaited baskets, beaded moccasins, and porcupine-quill work. The aborigines of this portion of the British colonies were known as "Delawares" because first found in the vicinity of that river, though they called themselves the *Lenni-Lenape*, which means "the original people." The great mass of this tribe had moved toward the setting sun in the year 1728, but at this time there remained several thousand in Pennsylvania, who were much dissatisfied with the sale of their lands, a discontent which was greatly increased a few years later by what was known as the "Walking Treaty," they claiming to have been swindled by the English in the great area of territory

31

acquired by the Europeans in that famous bargain. It was not till ten or fifteen years later that the Pennsylvanians, by calling to their aid the Six Nations of the North, induced these remaining Indians to depart for the "Sweet Waters of the West."

Again we find ourselves deploring the fact that Johannes neglected his journal. Where did he go on leaving the State House? After so long a voyage he must have desired to stretch his legs by a more extended walk, but perhaps Mariah Katrina and the children were not so eager for exercise. We will suppose that he established them comfortably at the Indian-King Tavern on High Street, where, before sallying out for a prowl about the city, he refreshed himself with his first glass of West India rum, at that time the only liquor imported in quantity into the colony, or with a foaming tankard of ale, which was then in such common use that most dwellings had small brew-houses connected with their kitchens. Johannes could not have been put to a very great expense at the tavern, as only modest charges for board and lodging were known in those early days. Professor Kalm,[2] the Swedish botanist, narrates in his account of his travels that, when in Philadelphia in 1748, he lodged with a Quaker, in whose house he met many honest people. "I and my Yungstraem, the companion of my voyage, had a room, candles, beds, attendance, and three meals a day for twenty shillings per week in Pennsylvania currency." Two dollars and eighty-eight cents!

On leaving the tavern, Johannes' friends carried him to see Christ Church, then nearing completion, and at once both the pride and the wonder of the people. It reared its impressive bulk on an open square adjoining a pond which reached from Arch to High Streets, once a noted place for shooting ducks.

Of course the mysterious friend with whom we have

---

[2] Peter Kalm, author of *Travels in North America*, the first English version of which appeared in 1770.

generously supplied Johannes insists upon a pilgrimage to the house of William Penn at Second Street and Norris' Alley, for that is a shrine at which newly arrived foreigners earliest worshiped. Penn's reputation was a cherished heritage to all oppressed Europeans, and his memory as the father of Pennsylvanian immigration was especially revered by the German heart. As our visitors strolled in that direction, the streets were enlivened by numerous and varied odd costumes. It seemed very singular to meet so many long-drawn Quakers, moving at measured pace with solemn visage, clad in lengthy shad-breasted drab coats adorned with horn buttons, their flapping waistcoats extending far down over the small-clothes that covered their sober strides. The long, straight hair of these peripatetic monuments of sedateness was covered by broad-brimmed felt hats, looped at the side with strings. These Quakers offered an excellent foil to the brilliantly arrayed young gallants, who tripped jauntily by under gold-laced cocked hats, with their gaily embroidered coats cut low at the neck behind so that the great silver buckles fastening their plaited stocks might be displayed. It was the fashion for young gentlemen to wear short, straight steel rapiers, often with jeweled hilts, which gave them quite a martial appearance, though not altogether in keeping with their clocked silk stockings, paste-buckled shoes, and ruffled wrists and throats.

Gay apparel was not confined by any means to the younger men. Old gentlemen met on the way were frequently resplendent in plush breeches, vests of various hues, and skirts stiffened with buckram till they stood out at an angle. Often double rows of solid silver buttons extended down their coats, and it was not uncommon to see suits decorated with conch shells set in silver. A brilliant sight they presented in all the glint of polished metal as they stamped along, shaking their powdered wigs, striking the pavement with their long silver-headed canes, stopping occasionally to greet some old friend and extend

33

a pinch of snuff, not so much because of generous pro-
clivities as the desire to display their chased silver and
gold snuffboxes, which were generally carried in the
hand.

The kaleidoscopic changes of colors to be noted
among the people thronging the streets this bright May
day were not all to be attributed to the well-to-do of the
populace: body servants contributed their full share to
the brilliant hues of the Colonial costumes, and as they
minced over the pavements at a respectful distance behind
their masters and mistresses often presented a gorgeous
appearance. An absconding one is described in an advertisement of that year as wearing damask breeches, copper-
colored cloth coat trimmed with black, and black stockings. A barber's servant, who ran away a few years before
that time, wore, according to the notice in the *Weekly
Mercury*, a light wig, a gray kersey jacket lined with
blue, a white vest faced and lined with red and having
yellow buttons, a pair of drugget breeches, a pair of black
stockings, and a red leathern apron. This last feature of
his dress was at that time a distinguishing badge of social
standing, being worn not only by workingmen but by all
apprentices, clerks, and employees of shopkeepers. It was
also the custom for the wives and daughters of tradesmen,
who assisted them in business, to wear short skirts of
green baize.

On reaching Penn's house, they found it to be a sturdy
edifice with bastions and salient angles. Its flanking gables
fronted on the street, but the main portion of the building
was set well back, so that the house faced three sides of a
small court. At the rear were the beautifully shaded
gardens, extending halfway to Front Street and nearly to
Walnut Street. This edifice was built in the earliest days
of the city by one of its greatest improvers, Samuel Carpenter, and it was fitted up for Penn's occupancy on the
occasion of his second coming to America. In 1704
Samuel Carpenter sold this house to William Trent for

eight hundred and fifty pounds. This was the same Trent who in 1719 established mills on the Delaware, thus founding Trenttown—now Trenton.

Meanwhile the day is wearing on, and the Moelichs have still a journey before them, for it is not to be supposed that newly arrived Germans will remain in Philadelphia when but a few miles beyond is a thriving settlement composed entirely of their own countrymen. The good Pastorius,[3] the faithful pastor, magistrate, teacher, patriarch, and friend of German folk, had died fifteen years before, but he left behind him at Germantown, seven miles away as the road then ran, a sturdy German community and a firmly established Lutheran church. It was the pole toward which the needles of all Rhenish emigrants turned, and we must conceive of some means of transporting Johannes and his party to that prosperous place. The human imagination is quite capable of bridging centuries and of creating situations, so there is no reason why we should not be equal to this task, especially as we feel confident of the assistance of Thomas Skelton, who advertised in the *Gazette* that he had "a four-wheeled chaise, in Chestnut street, to be hired." This was the only public conveyance in the city. It was twenty-five years later before Jacob Coleman began running the first stage "with an awning" from Philadelphia to the King of Prussia Inn at Germantown.

In 1735 the city boasted of but eight four-wheeled coaches, one of which belonged to Deputy-Governor Gordon. The streets were singularly clear of vehicles of every description. There were but six four-wheeled, one-seated chaises drawn by two horses besides the one that Skelton had to hire. The few carriages to be seen, if they could be so called, were two-wheeled, one-horse chairs, a cheap sort of gig with a plain painted body, ornamented with brass rings and buckles, resting on leathern bands for

---

[3] Francis Daniel Pastorius, who had established Germantown in 1683.

springs. The general means of conveyance both for goods and people was by horses; farmers' wives came to town on pillions behind their husbands, and stout market-women rode in from Germantown, their panniers, filled with produce, flanking their horses' sides. Much of the freighting of the province was done by pack horses, and it was a common sight to see a long line of them entering Philadelphia laden with all manner of merchandise—some so enveloped in fodder as to leave exposed only their noses and hoofs, others bearing heavy casks suspended on either side, whilst still others staggered along beneath the weight of bars of iron, bent so to hang as to escape the bordering trees of the contracted trails and roadways. There were but few carts; the man who brought the silver sand to the different doors each morning owned one; and we have seen to what base purpose another has been put by a town constable.

That peculiar Pennsylvania institution, the big blue-bodied wagon, had not yet made its appearance, though it was not many years before the prosperity of the province was such as to result in every farmer having a wagon. Their first introduction caused great indignation among the owners of pack horses, who feared that their business would be ruined. In 1755, when Postmaster General Franklin found Braddock fretting and fuming at Frederick, in Maryland, because his contractors had failed to provide means of transportation, he at once agreed to furnish one hundred and fifty wagons with four-horse teams from Pennsylvania, and to have them at Will's Creek within ten days. Franklin fulfilled his agreement, and thus was Braddock's army enabled to move on to its disastrous overthrow.

We will impress one of the carts into the service of aiding Thomas Skelton in moving our party. Johannes must return on some other day for his heavy luggage and furniture, as the *Mercury* will hardly as yet have commenced discharging from her hold. The Germantown

36

road left town at the upper end of Front Street, and after following the river for a short distance wound in a north-westerly direction and plunged into a dense forest, the haunt then, as it had been for centuries, of bears, wolves, deer, and wild turkeys. The wolves seemed to have proved the most annoying to citizens, as we find bounties for their extirpation offered for many years after. The high-way was not much more than a trail, the branches of the giant trees, that stood in solid phalanxes close to the wheel tracks, forming over the travelers' heads a roof of impenetrable foliage. Occasionally the shade was broken by the sunshine of a clearing, in the center of which stood a log house having a long sloping roof of thatch—the harbinger of the future greatness of suburban Philadelphia. Some of the clearings were already green meadows in which no sign of trees appeared; others were studded by stumps showing the recent marks of the pioneer's ax. On nearing Germantown the road traversed a swamp, the wheels of the cart and chaise jolting over the rough logs of the corduroy roadbed that made the bog passable.

Our friends, listening to the tales of their guides as they moved slowly through the woods, must have been filled with the most agreeable anticipations on approaching the end of their journey. They found Germantown to be as thoroughly German, in language and in the appearance of the people, as any of the villages they had left perched on the picturesque banks of the river of the Schoppen in the mother country. With its one long street bordered by straggling houses, it still presented much of the aspect of a frontier settlement. Many of the dwellings were the primitive structures of the early comers. They were built of logs, the interstices filled in with river-rushes and clay, and covered with a thin coat of plaster; their gables confronted the street, and a man of ordinary size could easily touch the eaves of their double-hipped roofs. The more modern houses were of dark glimmer-stone, with little windows set deep in the thick walls and

37

with huge chimneys rising at the corners. These low substantial buildings, with their steep roofs and protecting eaves, were planted well back from the highway and surrounded by fruit trees. The comfortably rotund matrons of these dwellings, who looked out at the new arrivals from the open upper half of their Dutch doors, were all busily knitting, for the Germantown housewives had already acquired an intercolonial reputation as the manufacturers of superior stockings.

The first German newspaper in Pennsylvania, and the first in the English colonies printed in a foreign language, was issued in Germantown the year of Johannes' arrival. This place retained all its German characteristics down to the year 1793. Until that date all the public preaching was in German; it was the language of business and society, and even that of the boys playing in the streets. The outbreak of yellow fever in Philadelphia in the year 1793 caused the offices of the general and state governments and of the city banks to remove to this suburban town. This introduced an English-speaking element and a population which proved to be, in part, permanent. Germantown, thus becoming favorably known to Philadelphians, rapidly increased the number of its English-speaking people.

And now we must bid Johannes a many years' farewell—here he and his family fade for a time from our sight and knowledge. By the aid of a lively fancy we have been able, for one day, to clothe him with all the attributes of existence and experiences, but to continue that for a decade would be to tax the powers of your scribe beyond his capabilities. Family tradition asserts that he remained in the vicinity of Philadelphia for ten years. We will leave him there to acquire the language, educate his children, rub off his foreign characteristics, and gradually to assimilate himself and his family with the manners and customs of the people of the new country of his adoption.

Purchase of the Old Farm

JOHANNES EMERGES from the mists of the years in December, 1747, in what is now Warren County, New Jersey, where he appears as the purchaser of four hundred and nine acres of land fronting on the Delaware River and Pohatcong Creek. This investment was made for the joint benefit of himself and his youngest brother Godfrey, who continued to be a member of Johannes' household until he was twenty-one years old. On growing to man's estate he settled on this land bordering Pohatcong Creek and the Delaware. In May, 1748, he took unto himself a bride of fifteen summers, Margaret Falkenberger, a young woman of some education and refinement.

Johannes does not seem to have occupied his portion of the land on the Delaware. In the year 1750 he was living in Readington Township, Hunterdon County, where he was interested in a tannery with Johann Jacob Klein (Jacob Kline), who had a few years before married his eldest daughter, Veronica Gerdrutta (Fanny). There is every reason to believe that at the time the homestead of Johannes was a farm of four hundred acres—two hundred of which were in black-oak timber—located adjoining the present line of the Central Railroad of New Jersey, midway between the White House and North Branch stations. Ultimately this property came into the sole possession of Jacob Kline, and on it he and his sons and grandsons carried on an extensive tannery business for over seventy-five years.

Johannes Moelich was an active member and officer of Zion Lutheran Church in Tewksbury (then Lebanon) Township in the same county. In 1749, Zion Corporation had been for some time in existence, and in that year a new church building "was solemnly dedicated to the service of God." An immense roof, converging to the center, capped the walls, in which small windows were set high from the ground. A huge sounding board surmounted the lofty pulpit, and in the center of the building, in the broad middle aisle, was a square pit in which burned in cold weather a bright charcoal fire. It has been suggested that this fire served not only for the comfort of the worshipers but as an illustration for the preacher, who pointed his finger at the glowing bed of coals when dwelling on the everlasting fire that awaited the ungodly.

As early as 1745 it appears that the Reverend Henry Melchior Mühlenberg occasionally supplied Zion pulpit, while at the same time having general charge of the affairs of the congregation. This divine—familiarly known as Father Mühlenberg—was born in Hanover in 1711; after graduating from the University of Göttingen, he settled at Halle. The early German emigrants to America were essentially a religious people, and to them no distress connected with exile was more grievous than the loss of the religious instruction they had known in the old country. During the first four decades of the century there was not in New York or New Jersey a properly accredited clergyman of the Luthern persuasion. The people of that faith repeatedly implored the home church to send them a minister. After much urging, Mr. Mühlenberg consented to accept charge of the American churches, and reached Philadelphia in 1742.

The labors, sufferings, and successes of this Lutheran patriarch are matters of ecclesiastical history. To the character of an humble and sincere Christian were joined natural qualifications and educational acquirements that peculiarly fitted him for the arduous and varied duties incidental to his position. He was a skillful surgeon as well as a ripe theologian, and could preach to his congregation with equal facility in English, German, and Low Dutch. Gentleness and firmness in him were singularly blended; his wise counsel and tender sympathies won such respect and devotion that throughout his life his influence among the Germans was unbounded. We are told that his eloquence was of an order that would equally move and melt the heart of the wildest frontiersman or rivet the attention of the most cultured and educated member of the synod.

In 1745 he removed from Philadelphia to the village of La Trappe—New Providence—in Montgomery County, Pennsylvania, which at that time contained the largest and most important German congregation in the country. From then until his death in 1787, he seems to have had a general oversight of, and to have exercised a sort of presiding eldership over, the churches of the Lutheran denomination. He was a wonderful organizer of congregations. Heat nor cold, storm nor wind, robbers nor Indians could daunt his energies or repress the enthusiasm of the missionary spirit which led him to travel thousands of miles through the middle and southern states at the call of his German brethren. The rare virtues and talents of this unusual man were, to a remarkable degree, transmitted to his posterity through successive generations. As clergymen, soldiers, statesmen, educators, authors, and poets, we find that his children, grandchildren, and great-grandchildren have taken rank with the most distinguished men of the country.

The first missionary of Zion Church was the Reverend Johannes Christophorus Hartwig (John Christopher Hartwick). He did not tarry long in Tewksbury as his usefulness was much impaired by an unfortunate repugnance he felt towards all womankind. Neighborhood gossip recites that he would cross the road, or even leap a fence, to avoid meeting one of the gentler sex. The story is told that when preaching in New York state, on awaking one morning at the home of a parishioner, he found that the good woman of the house had arisen in the night and silently spread a thick petticoat over the bed, lest he should suffer with the cold; so indignant was the clergyman that he made his way to the stable, saddled his horse, and rode off before breakfast.

The year 1751 approaches—one of the most important, perhaps, in the family annals, as it is the one in which Johannes finally decided where to plant the permanent homestead. Aaron, the oldest son—the great-grandfather of the writer—has grown to be a man of twenty-six years and is still unmarried. Veronica Gerdrutta, who is now twenty years old, has married her father's partner, Jacob Kline. Johannes' second son, Andrew, has reached majority, while his second daughter, Maria, is just budding into womanhood, being eighteen years old. Since reaching America two sons have been born—Philip on the ninth of October, 1736, and Peter on the fifth of December, 1739.

Since the arrival of Johannes in New Jersey he had been in search of a location that would meet all the requirements of a permanent home. His needs were not confined to good agricultural lands; a water power was also desired, advantageously situated for establishing a tannery. In 1751 Bedminster Township in Somerset County was decided upon as his future place of residence. On the first of November in that year he purchased of George Leslie of Perth Amboy three hundred and sixty-seven acres of wild or forest land, having a front of about three-quarters of a mile on the North Branch of the Raritan River.

The price paid for this property was "seven hundred and fifty-four pounds current money of the province, at eight shillings per ounce." This last clause of the consideration materially modifies the cost of the land. Money at eight shillings to the ounce meant a considerable depreciation from the standard values. In the seventeenth and eighteenth centuries English silver was coined on the basis of five shillings and two pence per ounce. The silver coin mostly in use in the American colonies was the Spanish milled dollar, or "piece of eight," which the English mint found to be worth four dollars and forty-four and four-ninths cents. This was established as the standard of relative value. But early in the eighteenth century the weight and quality of the Spanish milled dollar did not continue to realize this ratio, as the circulation of clipped and inferior coins depreciated all currency values. This rating consequently reduced the pound sterling to three dollars and fourteen and one-quarter cents. Thus we find that the actual consideration for the purchase of the Bedminster land was twenty-three hundred and sixty-nine dollars and forty-four cents, or about six dollars and forty-five cents an acre.

Previous to the Leslie conveyance the holders of the land had been but few. The Indians, of course, as far as Europeans know, were the first. The clan of the Delawares roaming the country north of the Raritan was the *Naraticongs*, though the whites gave them the name of the river along which they were located. Their dress was a blanket or skin thrown over the shoulders, deerskin fastened with thongs about the legs, and the feet covered with moccasins of the same material, so dressed as to be soft and pliable, being ornamented with quills and wampum beads. At the time of the settlement of Bedminster there were comparatively few natives in that part of the province; those remaining were of a friendly character and proved of great service to the settlers in supplying them with grain, skins, and furs.

That at one time the savages must have been in plenteous numbers in the Bedminster neighborhood is shown by the traces of them still to be found. The Old

43

Farm has produced a generous crop of stone implements and arrowheads planted by the aborigines in ante-European days. It is Hawthorne who writes of the "exquisite delight of picking up for one's self an arrowhead that was dropped centuries ago and has never been handled since, and which we thus receive directly from the hands of the red hunter. Such an incident builds up again the Indian village and the encircling forest, and recalls the painted chief, the squaws, and the children sporting among the wigwams, while the little wind-rocked papoose swings from the branch of a tree."

Of the extinguishment of the claims of the red men it is necessary to say but little. The modes of procedure in such cases were much the same in all portions of the colonies. Generally the usual number of blankets, jugs of rum, strings of wampum, guns, and handfuls of powder were exchanged for treaties and deeds which conveyed great areas of territory. In New Jersey the early settlers, before acquiring the legal title to their purchases, were obliged to satisfy the claims of the natives. The Indian title to the territory which embraced the Old Farm was conveyed to John Johnstone and George Willocks on the twenty-ninth of October, 1701, by *Tallquapie, Nicolas,* and *Elalie.*

The manner of the white man's acquiring possession of lands in New Jersey has been often and variously told; it is always an interesting story. All historians agree in naming Friday, the fourth of September, 1609, as being the day on which New Jersey soil was first pressed by the feet of Europeans. On the preceding day Henry Hudson, in his little Dutch *Vheboat,* the *Half Moon,* entered the Lower Bay, and the next day, dropping anchor in the Horse Shoe in four and a half fathoms of water and two cable lengths from the beach, sent some of his men on shore to discover what manner of men were the natives and whether they were kindly disposed. When the crew landed they saw "a great store of men, women and children who gave them some tobacco and some dried currants." The natives were dressed "some in mantles of feathers and some in skins of diverse sorts of good furres. They had red copper tobacco pipes, and other things of copper they did wear about their necks."

When the *Half Moon* again crossed the bar, her sails spreading for the homeward voyage, she left one of her company lying at the foot of a stunted cedar on Sandy Hook, filling the first white man's grave in New Jersey. John Coleman, with four shipmates, on the sixth of September explored the harbor in a small boat. Penetrating "two leagues to an open sea" (Newark Bay), he reported that the bordering lands "were as pleasant with Grasse and Flowers and goodly trees as any they had seene, and very sweet smells came from them." While returning, the fateful arrow of a treacherous red man ended Coleman's voyaging for this world. And now, after three centuries, the miniature waves of the Lower Bay are still sobbing on their yellow sands lullabies to the lonely sleeper of this pioneer grave, while on the outer beach the Atlantic rollers sound eternal requiems.

When Henry Hudson carried the news to Holland of the discoveries he had made in the new country, ships in numbers soon came sailing over the watery waste to visit this "goodly land." From then till now the ribs of many a stout craft have been battered to fragments on the bars and beaches of Sandy Hook. The first shipwreck known to have occurred at this point was as early as 1620, and connected with the stranding of the vessel there has come down to us an account of a most remarkable instance of the preservation of human life. On board was a young woman from Holland by the name of Penelope van Princis; at least such was her maiden name, that of her husband, who accompanied her, being unknown. Those of the ship's company who reached the shore in safety made their way on foot to New Amsterdam. Penelope's husband, being badly injured, was unable to undertake the journey; so she remained with him in the woods on Sandy Hook. Soon after the departure of their shipmates they were attacked by Indians, who left them for dead. The husband was indeed so, but the wife, though fearfully injured, revived. Her skull was fractured, and her left shoulder so cut and hacked that she never after had the use of that arm. Her abdomen had been laid open with a knife so that the bowels protruded and were only kept in place by her hands. Yet in this deplorable condition she lived for several days in a hollow tree, sustaining life by eating bark, leaves, and gum.

At the end of a week Penelope was discovered by two Indians, who were chasing a deer. One of them, an old man, moved by her condition and sex, conveyed her to his wigwam near the present site of Middletown, where he dressed her wounds and treated her with great kindness. Here she remained for some time, but eventually the Dutch of New Amsterdam, on learning that there was a white woman living with the natives in the woods beyond the great bay, came to her relief. Her preserver, who had cured her wounds and tenderly cared for her, interposed no objections to her rejoining her friends, by whom she was welcomed as one from the dead. Some time after, when in her twenty-second year, this young Dutch widow married a wealthy English bachelor of forty named Richard Stout. She survived her marriage eighty-eight years, attaining the extraordinary age of one hundred and ten, and leaving at her death five hundred and two living descendants.

By the year 1620, the Hollanders had made settlements in New Jersey at the mouth of the Hudson River and were soon in peaceful possession, and for forty-three years occupied what is now New York and New Jersey, under the title of New Netherland. After establishing New Amsterdam on Manhattan Island, the Dutch soon made their way westward.

In the year 1664 the English expelled the Dutch government from New Netherland. Having conquered the country, the King's claim now rested not only on discovery but by conquest as well. James, Duke of York, received from his royal brother, Charles II, a patent for an area of territory which included what is now New Jersey. The Duke of York not long after this conveyed that portion of the land included within the present boundaries of New Jersey to John, Lord Berkeley, and to Sir George Carteret. The nominal consideration was ten shillings, and an annual quit-rent of one peppercorn, to be paid on the day of the nativity of John the Baptist if legally demanded. The true incentive for the conveyance was the desire to reward the grantees for their distinguished loyalty during the civil war.

The recipients of this princely gift soon found that to give value to their estate it was necessary to secure inhabitants. In the autumn of 1665, through their representative, Philip Carteret, they wisely dispatched agents into New England, who published what was known as the "Concessions and Agreements of the Lords-Proprietors." These publications, by their liberal inducements such as property in estates and liberty in religion, resulted in quite a migration to New Jersey.

It was not until 1676 that a formal partition of New Jersey was made. Thenceforth Carteret's share of the province was what has since been known as East Jersey. In the year 1679 Sir George died. By his will he devised his East Jersey property to trustees, empowering them to sell the same for the payment of his debts. The trustees, in consideration of thirty-four hundred pounds, conveyed all of East Jersey to the "Twenty-four Proprietors of East New-Jersey," an association of landowners.

The new proprietors modified somewhat the "Concessions and Agreements" of their predecessors, though retaining many of their most important provisions. Very complete descriptions were published in Europe of the advantages that would accrue to adventurers who re-

47

moved to the province; the manner of the disposition of lands was explained, and a full account given of the physical condition of the country. In these published descriptions detailed statements were made as to the "goodness and richness of the soil"; that the country was "well stored with deer, conies, wild fowl," and other game; that the "sea-banks were well stored with a variety of fish such as whales, cod, cole, hake, etc. in great abundance, and easy to take." Much stress was laid on the fact of there being safe and convenient harbors, affording excellent opportunities for the export of the products of the province, among which were enumerated whale-fins, bone and oil, and beaver, mink, raccoon, and martin skins.

After dwelling on the salubrity of the climate, the good temper of the Indians, and the manner and costs of setting out from the old country, advertisements closed with the following excellent advice to the prospective emigrants:

All persons inclining unto those parts must know that in their settlement there they will find their exercises. They must have their winter as well as summer. They must labor before they reap; and, till their plantations be cleared (in summer time), they must expect (as in all those countries) the mosquitoes, flies, gnats and such like, may in hot and fair weather give them some disturbance where people provide not against them.

The mosquitoes seem to have been early recognized as among the most active of the inhabitants of the new country.

The distribution abroad of these plans and prospectuses induced a considerable emigration from Scotland, which country was undergoing great political convulsions. East Jersey greatly benefited by the Scotch blood that was then transfused into her veins. The unhappy scenes that just before and after the year 1700 were enacted in the Haymarket of the gray-castled city of Edinburgh, and the hunting of poor refugees through the mists of the bleak Highlands of that grim, sea-beaten land, resulted in the planting among the hills of Somerset of a sturdy stock.

In 1698 George Willocks from Kinny in Scotland acquired the tract of land in Somerset County known as the Peapack Patent, which included the area of the Old Farm. His title was formally legalized three years later by the purchase from the Indians, *Tallquapie, Nicolas,* and *Elalie.* The tract took its name from the "Peapack Path," a native thoroughfare which ran from east to west through northern New Jersey, frequently mentioned as the boundary of early land grants. George Willocks died in 1729. The bulk of his landed estate, which was very great, was devised to George Leslie and Ann Richie, his nephew and niece. George Leslie made no disposition of any portion of this property until the year 1751.

And so, we now find ourselves again at the conveyance of the Old Farm to Johannes Moelich. In returning to this deed it is interesting to notice that in phraseology and general form it does not materially differ from such instruments now in use. It was signed by George Leslie and his wife Elizabeth. Instead of the grantors having made acknowledgments as to their signatures, Samuel Nevill, one of the justices of the Supreme Court, certifies that the witnesses to the conveyance having been duly sworn made oath that they "saw the grantors seal, and, as their act and deed, deliver the same."

Judge Samuel Nevill ranked among the most important men of the province. He was a native of Stafford, England, and bred a lawyer in London, where for a time he edited a newspaper. Mr. Nevill crossed the ocean in 1736, settling permanently at Perth Amboy. His varied talents at once attracted attention and he soon rose to eminence. The then great dignity of being the mayor of this ancient capital was forced upon him; he became a member and speaker of the Provincial Assembly, judge of

49

the Court of Common Pleas, second judge of the Supreme Court, and in many other important ways served with honor the people and his King. Under the auspices of the Assembly, between the years 1732 and 1761 he published in two volumes an edition of the laws of the province. In 1758 he established and edited the first of New Jersey's periodicals and the second one on the continent. It was called the *New American Magazine* to distinguish it from its predecessor in Philadelphia, which relinquished publication upon the appearance of this competitor. It was printed at Woodbridge by James Parker, who, having served his time with the famous New York printer, William Bradford, had set up in 1751 the first printing press in New Jersey.

In studying the old records of Somerset one cannot fail to notice with interest how many prominent and leading men of the century have been directly or indirectly connected with the freeholds of the county. Gouverneur Morris may surely be classed among this number for, in reading the story of his life, discovery is soon made that he was a much greater man than the majority of his contemporaries. Had he been possessed of personal ambition his memory would occupy a more exalted place in history, as his present fame is far less than his abilities would have insured had he consented to place himself in the front of the many prominent movements with which he was connected. His eloquence in conversation was phenomenal; it is claimed that not only would intelligent listeners hang on his words in rapt admiration, but that servants, arrested by his table talk, stood open-mouthed, dishes in hand, to catch his glowing sentences. Put Morris where you would, he was always at home and always made an impression. So great was his equipoise, it was impossible to disturb the tranquillity of his mind and presence. When in France as United States minister, his marked individuality, eccentric and original manners, together with his undoubted intellect, made a strong impression on society in the French capital. Madame de Staël credited him with having *"l'air très imposant,"* and the King found in his features an extraordinary resemblance to those of the royal family. On one occasion, while attending an audience, the American statesman was approached by the monarch, who after looking fixedly for a moment exclaimed, "The likeness is, indeed, too wonderful to be accidental! Pray, Mr. Morris, was your mother ever in France?" Morris, with a respectable bow, quickly replied, "No, your Majesty, but my father was!"

As before recited, the consideration for the purchase of the three hundred and sixty-seven acres was seven hundred and fifty-four pounds. Of this amount Johannes paid three hundred and twenty-four pounds in cash, the balance by the execution and delivery of two bonds, payable in six months, for two hundred and two, and two hundred and twenty-eight pounds, respectively. These obligations were discharged on maturity, and, as Leslie had died soon after the sale was consummated, they bear the satisfaction receipt of his two children. Among my old papers relating to this property are these two satisfied bonds.

To the manuscript lover, much pleasure is derived from handling an old document that, having played its part in the work of the world, has in some mysterious way escaped the fate of like papers and is preserved to testify of circumstances and events of an age long past. How the world moves! Consider the changes that have come to people and countries since these old bonds were new. When these instruments—now in the sere and yellow, and valueless except as relics—were vested with the potentiality of enforcing the payment of a no inconsiderable sum, the land for which they had been given in part consideration was in truth as much of a howling wilderness as it had been for a thousand previous years. Lafayette, whose name was to be as familiar as household words in this hill country of New Jersey, was as yet unborn.

Washington, still unknown to fame, was a lad in his teens; and seventeen years must come and go before the Corsican babe would open his eyes on that Europe he was almost to master. Travelers still crossed the stormy Atlantic in frail pinks, ketches, snows, and bilenders. France was being pompadoured into a condition to make possible the fourteenth of July, 1789. And what of England, considered in the van of civilization? Its crown was worn by a Hanoverian dullard who hated "busic and boetry." In all the island there was not a macadamized road, and the royal mail was carried on "flying machines," protected from highway robbers even in the suburbs of London by guards armed with loaded blunderbusses. Parliament was a den of corruption, borough seats in the House of Commons being publicly advertised and openly sold. The British people knew but little of their lawmakers, as to publish the proceedings of their legislature was a misdemeanor carrying a heavy punishment. There were laws enough, however, and they were severe enough, for nearly two hundred crimes knew capital punishment as their penalty, and children of tender years were sentenced to death for pilfering. And yet we are constantly told that the world grows no better, that the movement and direction of mankind is not onward and upward.

3

The Old Stone House

BEHOLD JOHANNES—the proud possessor of three hundred and sixty-seven fertile Bedminster acres, land that has lain dormant for centuries, unconscious of its destiny but ever ready and eager to smile into fruitfulness upon the first advances of husbandmen. In fancy we can see him and his two stalwart sons betaking themselves to the hillside. Soon, crash after crash denotes the falling oaks that the sturdy strokes and keen axes of the Moelichs have marked as the most fitting contributors to the sills, walls, and gables of a new log house; for temporary shelter is necessary while the more permanent stone dwelling shall be rearing its massive walls.

Days are spent in the timber; tree after tree is attacked; they fall on every side! The undergrowth is cut down and heaped, and by and by the warm sunlight, for the first time perhaps in ages, breaks in upon a clearing of two acres, which from that time has been consecrated by the sorrows and gladnesses, rejoicings and repinings, and all the sympathetic experiences that rally around an enduring family farmstead. The location is well chosen. Now that the trees are prostrate, it shows an open cheery slope upon which the sun looks kindly down. The ascending uplands bar the chill north winds, and to the south and east the ground falls away gently to the meadows bordering the brook and river, which just here, with pleasant splash and babble, merge into one stream. Teams draw the big logs to the spot selected for placing the temporary dwelling. The ends of the logs are squared and so cut as to be let in or dovetailed together.

Now comes the memorable day of the "raising." Old neighbors from Hunterdon are invited and come in goodly numbers. They bring with them willing hearts and stout arms and plenty of provisions, for, as there are no dwellings near, the raising dinner must partake somewhat of the character of a picnic. Songs and merry stories go round as the walls and gables slowly rise from the ground. How easy to imagine the happiness of Johannes as he now aids in the work and now directs his friends and co-laborers! Mariah Katrina, too, is there, lending in the German fashion a strong and ready hand; and the boys occupy themselves in keeping up brisk fires with fragrant chips and crackling boughs and branches. Cannot you see the smiling, hear the laughing, and enjoy the joking, while they dine from off the logs and stumps, and drink to the future happiness of the new residents? The walls go up apace; by afternoon skids are necessary upon which to roll the heavy logs to their places; and when the western sky beyond the crest of the long hill is aflame with the rich colors of the afterglow, the rude house is raised, though still without roof, doors, or floor. When entirely completed it was nothing more than a square enclosure, with one story and a cockloft above, and a roof thatched with leaves or straw—a primitive cabin much like many others scattered along the narrow tracks and trails of this newly opened country.

As it was now late in the autumn, or early in the winter, nothing could be done in the actual erection of the stone house; but during the cold weather much was accomplished in the way of preparation. He who in building a house calls in the aid of architect and artisan, and himself supplies only money wherewith to pay for design and work, knows but little of the true sweetness of creating a homestead. Johannes must have felt to the full this supreme happiness, as with his boys he labored day after day in furthering the preparations for the building. Stones were hauled and dressed—a quarry having been opened in the extreme northwest corner of the property; materials were brought upon the ground, and round, straight trees were selected and rough-hewed to the line, converting them into the stanch, square floor timbers that today, exposed in the ceiling of the living room, show no signs of decay. With what interest must Johannes' wife and children have viewed the work, and how his heart must have leaped within him as they watched with delight the slow creating of the family nest. With the disappearance of frost the cellar under the western gable was excavated, and early in the spring the foundations were laid and the building was fairly under way.

To assist in the construction, the services were secured—so runs the story—of Caspar Berger, a German stonemason and a redemptioner. He had reached New York in 1744 and, being sold by the captain of his ship to repay the costs of passage, was purchased for a term of years by Cornelius Van Horne of White House in Hunterdon County.

The descendants of Caspar Berger claim that his emigration from the old country was involuntary, he with others having been enticed on board a ship by its captain, who then set sail for America. This is not improbable, as the masters of vessels were often guilty of cruel and unjust acts in this business of the importation of redemptioners. Isaac Weld, Jr., in his book of travels in America,[1] asserts that it was the custom of shipmasters at Rotterdam and the Hanse towns to inveigle the people into their

---

[1] Isaac Weld, Jr., *Travels Through the States of North America . . . 1795, 1796, and 1797 . . .* (London, 1799). There were a number of later editions.

vessels under promise of free passage to America. On reaching the colonies, announcement of the arrival of mechanics and laborers would be made, and persons in want of such would flock to the ships, and the poor Germans would be sold to the highest bidders, the captains pocketing the proceeds. Caspar Berger, after obtaining his freedom, by his frugality and industry prospered in the new country and soon waxed well-to-do.

Redemptioners, or term-slaves as they were sometimes called, constituted in the early part of the eighteenth century a peculiar feature of Colonial society. They were recruited from among all manner of people in the Old World, and through this channel Europe emptied upon America not only the virtuous poor and oppressed of her population, but the vagrants, felons, and the dregs of her communities. There was thus established among the first settlers a society that, in many places, was almost imbued with a moral pestilence. Among the redemptioners, however, were a fair portion of sturdy souls, strong in purpose and endeavor, who appreciated the great opportunity created for them by this complete change of life and country. At the expiration of their term of service, many by thrift and industry elevated themselves to a respectable position, and were absorbed into the middle class. Of necessity there were improvident and shiftless ones, who contributed to the vicious and ignorant element of the population.

There were two kinds of redemptioners: "indented servants," who had bound themselves to their masters for a term of years previous to their leaving the old country; and "free-willers," who, being without money and desirous of emigrating, agreed with the captains of ships to allow themselves and their families to be sold on arrival for the captain's advantage, and thus repay costs of passage and other expenses. The former—indented servants—were often trapped into their engagements by corrupt agents at home, who persuaded them to emigrate under false promises of tender and humane treatment and under assurances of remunerative employment at expiration of service.

The immigrants often discovered on arrival that the advantages represented to be obtained in America had been painted by the agents in much too alluring colors; frequently their masters forced them to most rigid labor and exercised an unnecessary severity. William Eddis,[2] a surveyor of customs in the province of Maryland, asserts that this class of servants often groaned beneath a worse than Egyptian bondage, as their masters, knowing that their servitude could last but for a few years, treated them with a rigor more severe than they extended to their Negro slaves, to whom, being actual property, they were more lenient.

The free-willers suffered even worse treatment at the hands of shipmasters and agents who had inveigled them into emigration by false and specious promises. They were led to believe that on arrival in America their services would be eagerly solicited by parties who would gladly pay the cost of their passages, which, being only nine pounds, the emigrants would soon be able to repay, and thus secure their liberty and all the enjoyments and prosperity that the new country offered to adventurers. Agreements were entered into whereby these deluded ones bound themselves that, if on arrival they did not succeed within a certain number of days in securing employment on their own conditions, they could be sold for a term of years to defray the charges for their passages. Alas! the "free-willers" with rare exceptions had a rude awakening on reaching the colonies. Under their agreements the captains had a legal lien on the persons of the immigrants until the ship charges were paid; consequently they were not allowed to go on shore, but were exposed to view on deck to the people who came on board in

---

[2] William Eddis, *Letters From America,* . . . *1769 to 1777* . . . (London, 1792).

search of servants. Except in cases of extraordinary qualifications very few of them were happy enough to make their own stipulations. The sanguine expectations of the redemptioners were doomed to disappointment, and they found themselves sold for several years of tedious labor and servitude.

Professor Kalm reached Philadelphia on the seventh of September, 1748, by the ship *Mary*, which had on board twenty-three Germans and their families. He narrates that when about to go on shore with his captain, the latter turned to the second mate and strictly charged him "to let no one of the German refugees out of the ship unless he paid his passage, or somebody paid for him, or bought him." Masters of vessels often acted with needless cruelty towards their bond-passengers. Published accounts of travel in America during the last century frequently tell sad stories of the enforced separation of husbands from wives, and parents from children. Doctor Ernest Otto Hopp, in a book on German slavery in North America,[3] tells of a ship captain by the name of Heerbrand who acquired a great reputation as a kidnapper of poor Germans for the American market. He had in his pay a number of men whose business it was to regularly steal beggars, vagabonds, and other people without connections, he paying the captors two florins a head for each victim delivered at his vessel. It is said that this man brought over six hundred such persons to America.

The terms and conditions of service differed in the different colonies. Among the archives of the Pennsylvania Historical Society are some original bonds or agreements between ship captains and redemptioners. From them we learn that the usual price paid in that colony for three years' service was twenty-one pounds, one shilling and six pence. When his time had expired, a man was entitled to receive two suits of clothes, a grubbing hoe, a weeding hoe, and a new ax. Children sold for from

---

[3] *Bundesstaht und Bundeskrieg in Nordamerika* . . . (Berlin, 1886).

eight to ten pounds, and their masters were required to see that they were taught to read and write, and had at least one quarter's schooling. In New Jersey—according to Leaming and Spicer [4]—no indented servant, if sold or bound after seventeen years of age, could serve above four years. If under that age, they were to be free on reaching their majority. At the expiration of service their masters were obliged to supply them with two good suits of clothing suitable for a servant, one good falling ax, one good hoe, and seven bushels of Indian corn. A servant was to be immediately freed in case of being so abused by master or mistress as to result in the loss of an eye or a tooth. The laws against aiding redemptioners to escape were very severe. A fine of five pounds was imposed for offering assistance in such cases, and the aider and abettor was obliged to make full satisfaction to master or mistress for all loss or damage sustained by the absence of or search for the runaway. Anyone who concealed or entertained an absconding redemptioner could be fined at the discretion of the court, and could be made to pay ten shillings to the owner for each day that he had harbored the servant.

It was not uncommon for thrifty Germans, who were possessed of enough money to pay their passages and defray the first cost of settling, to allow themselves to be advantageously, and on favorable terms, sold in order that during their servitude they might have an opportunity of learning the language and of growing familiar with the manners, customs, and institutions of the country. Advertisements announcing redemptioners for sale are frequently to be found in newspapers of the last century. One in the *Pennsylvania Messenger* of the fourth of April, 1776, offers for sale "a young girl and maid-

---

[4] Aaron Leaming and Jacob Spicer, Comps., *The Grants, Concessions, and Original Constitutions of the Province of New Jersey* . . . (Philadelphia, 1752). These were reprinted in Somerville in 1881.

servant, strong and healthy; no fault. She is qualified for the service now demanded. Five years to serve."

The same paper, on the eighteenth of January, 1774, contains the following notice: "Germans—we are now offering fifty Germans just arrived—to be seen at the Golden Swan, kept by the widow Kreider. The lot includes schoolmasters, artisans, peasants, boys and girls, of various ages, all to serve for the payment of passage." It seems rather odd that schoolmasters should be offered for sale in the market. You would think that they would have been eagerly sought for, but on the contrary they appear to have been a drug, as is shown by D. von Bülow.[5] He says:

It is easy to sell the farmers, but there are often men whom it is not so easy to dispose of, *e.g.*, officers and scholars. I have seen a Russian captain offered for sale eight days, and not one bid made. He had absolutely no market value. It was no use for his owner to put him up again and again, to offer to make fifty per cent discount. "He is good for nothing," was all the answer to the offer. The captain of the ship then had him walked about the town to show, but in vain. After waiting several weeks, he was finally sold at a ridiculously low price as a village schoolmaster.

In looking back on the many peculiarities, changes, and gradations of society in New Jersey's Colonial days, it is curious to note how the well-to-do immigrants, who brought with them or purchased after arrival redemption servants, often lost the prestige of their affluence, being unable in the new country to maintain their rank and influence. Their humble servitors, however, inured by hardship and labor to the stern necessities of Colonial existence, prospered and throve. The bondspeople, after serving their time, acquired lands and homes by diligence and saving; it was not uncommon in the second generation to find them taking in every way precedence over the

---

[5] Dietrich Heinrich, Freiher von Bülow, *Der Freistaat von Nordamerika in seinen neuesten zustand* . . . (Berlin, 1797).

children of the master who had owned their time during their first years in the country. The affluent immigrant, having been accustomed to ease, proved unequal to the struggle; and his children, through faulty and ignorant education, rapidly deteriorated.

Among the many odd tales of early days at the Old Stone House which have enlivened winter evenings around the great fireplace in the living room is the legend that at its building Johannes' wife, Mariah Katrina, carried mortar, balanced on her head, to the masons at work on the walls. Members of the family whose pride may rebel against belief in this story are at liberty to consider it fable; but the mortar, at least, must be accepted, for to this day it is as solid and impervious as the stones between which it lies. Builders of the present aver that its manufacture is a lost art, and that all of its component parts are not known. Visitors to this ancestral dwelling can attribute to this mortar the fact that it exists today. It has been the agent which has enabled these massive walls to withstand for nearly a century and a half of winters the wear and tear of time; and it still binds their stones together in one compact mass of masonry. Great-great-grandmother Moelich figures traditionally again at the building of the house. She is said to have vigorously protested against the introduction of so many windows—in reality they were ridiculously few and small. The good woman had probably not forgotten the window tax of the old country, and had in mind, perhaps, the possibility of such an impost being levied in New Jersey.

By early in the summer the house must have been completed. Very plain, both as to exterior and interior, with no fan-lighted doorheads or ambitious columns, pilasters, and carvings. Yet, as we view it today, its solid simplicity is truly architectural, for it bears on its every feature a dignified expression of truth—of being only what it claims to be, an humble farmhouse of simple utilitarian proportions and fashion, the general effect of whose eaves, rooftree, double Dutch doors, hall, and chambers but express the purposes of its construction. It is not altogether without picturesqueness. Bedded in the green of its surrounding elms, its wooden-seated porch, sloping roof, and rough stone gables coated with lime and pebbles present a homely picture of comfort and domesticity, in full accord with its setting. To one who appreciates in a structure the beauty of simplicity and appropriateness, the Old Stone House must ever be a delightful object. To those of us who claim kinship with its early builder, this ancestral home will always be a place of jealous regard; a spot where will linger reminiscences of former days and traditions of bygone generations, of men and women whose names have been associated with the sturdy walls and hospitable atmosphere of the brave old dwelling.

The huge German locks, with their exposed and complicated mechanism, were fastened to the doors; heavy pieces of furniture were placed in the rooms, one, at least, the stupendous Dutch cupboard, occupying today its original position; clean white sand from the brook was spread on the floors; and the great crane was hung in the deep-chested fireplace. Mariah Katrina, as priestess of the household, has put the first torch to the hickory boughs on the hearthstone; the crackling flames leap up the broad chimney, while wreaths of curling smoke soar heavenward, seemingly bearing in their pungent odors an incense of thanksgiving. The teakettle, suspended over the fire, sings its cheery note—the bubbling pot with savory breath joins in the chorus—the procession of generations of good cheer has commenced. Let us conceive the table spread in the living room, and the members of the family gathered about the board for their first meal in the Stone House. While regaling themselves with creature comforts from the good wife's newly stocked larder, if ever faces could be said to reflect content, so must have theirs as they congratulated each other on the comfort of their surroundings. Believing, as we do, in the deep religious feeling that controlled all the thoughts and actions of the sire, we do not doubt the erection of a family altar; nor that at the close of this all-important day, with a heart overflowing with thankfulness and a voice choked with emotion, Johannes' devout prayers of praise and dedication, borne on the wings of faith, ascended to the Most High.

4

Johannes Goes to the Post Office

JUST HERE it may be well to survey the appearance presented by Somerset County and East New Jersey at the time the Moelichs took possession of the Old Farm. In no better way can we do this than by—in fancy—accompanying Johannes to Perth Amboy, thirty miles away. He is going to see if John Fox, the postmaster, has a letter for him from the old country; for be it known that in the year of grace, 1752, the province boasted but three post offices—one at Amboy, one at Trenton, and one at Burlington. Letters were left at those places by the Philadelphia mail carrier, weekly in summer and once in two weeks during the winter; rather meager facilities for the people, but they had to be contented until 1754, when the service was considerably increased. In December, 1733, the following notice appeared in the Philadelphia *Weekly Mercury*: "There are a number of letters in the post office at Perth Amboy for persons living in Somerset, Monmouth and Essex counties."

To us of the present day, Johannes would have presented a striking appearance as, mounted on a stout cob, he clattered down the incline upon which he had built the new stone house and turned west up the long hill. He is now over fifty years of age, with a figure not tall but robust, having a high color, blue eyes, and, had the fashion of the day allowed, the whole would have been supplemented by an abundant reddish-brown beard. His German origin is still readily recognized, though many of his foreign characteristics have been lost. He speaks English, but not with the facility of his mother tongue, and his dress is that of a well-to-do Colonial yeoman. A coarse gray coat with generous skirts cut square, buttons across his brawny chest, not hiding an ample leather waistcoat. His breeches, also of leather, meet at the knee stout blue yarn stockings, drawn over a pair of sturdy calves, which are further protected by deerskin leggings extending over his buckled shoes. A short gray wig and a three-cornered hat complete his decently picturesque appearance, while his further belongings comprise a fresh cut whip of sapling and a pair of saddlebags suspended on either side of the horse.

As he climbs the hill and overlooks his broad acres, he turns in the saddle for a good-bye glance at the new house resting so cosily against its sunny bank. What wonder that as he rides through the fresh dewy morning air his face glows with satisfaction! We can well imagine it because of his thoughts dwelling on the pleasant surroundings of his newly established home, and on the peaceful promise it seems to give for the future as compared with the unhappy uncertainties of the German life he had known on the banks of the far distant Rhine. Johannes' first thirteen years in America have been preparatory, and to an extent migratory; but now he feels about him the atmosphere of an abiding home. He recognizes and appreciates that he is no longer a pioneer but a permanent member of a community, where each individual has an interest in the commonwealth and in the continued growth and improvement of the neighborhood. Here he expects to end his days—here be buried; and here he hopes his children will live and their generations prosper.

The road Johannes traveled was but little more than a broad path cut through the woods; the trees pressed close on either side of the ruts and wheel tracks, often the bark of the flanking oaks and hickories showing the marks made by the hubs of passing vehicles. It must have been pleasant, riding along for miles under the arching branches, the air surcharged with the balsam of the aromatic breath of thousands of acres of giant trees: monarchs of the forest that for centuries had towered over the hills and dales, enriching the ground with their yearly falling leaves till the soil, rank with vitality, only needed the warm sun and man's command to blossom into fields of abundance. Occasionally, on the roads emerging from its long green arcade, our traveler came upon isolated dwellings seated amid little clearings, from which in many instances the stumps had not yet disappeared. The smoke that gently curled heavenward from the chimneys of these dwellings perfumed the morning air with the odors of burning fresh-cut wood—such smoke as can only come from fires fed by glowing oaken back-logs and crackling hickory boughs, over which the good wife has swung the great black kettle. These rude homes of new settlers were few, however; population had been very slow in penetrating this portion of Somerset. The country lay in a broad and almost unbroken extent of fertile waste, with but infrequent traces of human habitations discernible. As the grass covers a rolling meadow, mantling it in continuous green, so the forest buried the Bedminster and Bridgewater hills and valleys in vast undulations of leafy verdure. From the Morris County line on the north to the Raritan River on the south, from Bernards on the east to Hunterdon on the west, the whole area was a broad expanse of woodland wilderness, the continuity of green being interrupted here and there by a few houses clustering as an embryo village, while an occasional interval, open to the sun, marked the germ of a future farm.

At Pluckamin the nucleus of a society was forming; and at Lamington—a corruption of the more majestic

Indian name *Allametunk*—the Presbyterians had erected a church edifice in 1740, though services had been held in a barn for several preceding years. At this time the church building had just been enlarged, and the pastor of the congregation was the Reverend James McCrea, he having accepted a call from the congregation known as that of "Lametunk, Lebanon, Peapack, Readington and Bethlehem." He was the father of that Jennie McCrea whose tragic death on the upper Hudson by the tomahawks of Burgoyne's treacherous Indians allies was to send a thrill of horror throughout the country.

Though much of Bedminster remained in a state of nature, beyond its borders in adjacent townships communities had been planted and many acres of farming lands were cleared. On the north the settlement of Morristown by people from Newark and New England dated from early in the century, and its Presbyterian church had been established since 1738, the year of the organization of the county. Until about that time the neighborhood had been known as West Hanover.

By the year 1713 squatters' cabins existed at Roxiticus, now Mendham. Its Presbyterian congregation is first mentioned in 1738. In this year, 1752, the congregation possessed a small frame church building which together with its site, was conveyed by deed of Edward Burnet. He may have been a good man, but he surely was an evil speller. He describes himself in the conveyance, "Edmon Burnnant of Rocksiticus in yere County of Summerset in east nu Jareses in Amaracah." The description of the premises conveyed begins, "Scairteen pees of parsel of land on which the meeting hows Now Standeth."

Basking Ridge, in Bernards Township, already possessed a flourishing community with a well-established Presbyterian church under the charge of a Scotch worthy, the Reverend Samuel Kennedy. He was in 1751 ordained pastor of this congregation, which he faithfully served for thirty-six years at a salary of one hundred and ten pounds. In addition to his ministerial duties he practiced medicine, and established and took charge of a classical school which attained to great celebrity.

New Germantown was thriving in the west, and toward the south in the direction of White House were comfortable homesteads and cultivated lands. But as Johannes rode toward the Raritan he traversed almost a wooded solitude. The road from Bernardsville to Lamington had been marked out since 1741, but was a mere trail and but little traveled. South of this road the forest continued with hardly a break to Pluckamin.

At this time there was no bridge where the Pluckamin Road crosses the North Branch of the Raritan. The river was often too high to be forded. At such times travelers southward were obliged to cross the river near Mine Brook, or often as far north as Peapack Brook, and thus make their way through Bernards Township. On reaching Pluckamin Johannes found there about a dozen small houses and a tavern. This inn was the first place of entertainment established in the township; it was built in 1750 by Jacob Eoff, who was one of the pioneers of the village. His tavern remained standing for sixty-four years. During the Revolution it was the meeting place for the Committee of Safety, and when Washington's army was quartered in this and adjoining counties its boniface dispensed hospitality to many of the leading men of the country. After Jacob's death the tavern was kept by his maiden sister Sarah, who in turn was succeeded by Jacob's son, Christian; he abandoned the old structure to his brother Cornelius, who occupied it as a residence. Christian built on the opposite corner a long, low building called the "Barracks." Here he waxed famous as a popular host. With the best society of New York and Philadelphia this landlord's name became synonymous with good living; and summer visitors to Schooley's Mountain—a watering-place then in its glory—always arranged that the night necessarily spent on the journey should be passed at Christian Eoff's tavern. Aristocratic coaches with the family arms emblazoned on their panels, and drawn by four and six horses, were not uncommon in those good old days in this quaint village of Pluckamin.

It is fair to presume that Johannes dismounted at Eoff's tavern to wish "*Guten Morgen*," and discuss with him the quality of some of his best Jamaica. It is to be regretted that Johannes, in this and other visits to the village, did not ascertain and transmit to posterity the origin of its name. It has long been a vexed question, and has served as a subject for many arguments and communications. A popular belief among the villagers is that this strange cognomen was occasioned by the assiduously acquisitive habits of an early innkeeper, who, in his eagerness to serve customers, would "Pluck-'em-in." This ancient tavern-porch tale is an antiquated joke, and without doubt dates back to the founding of the village. The same mythical tavernkeeper has been found at Mendham (I'll-mend-'em), New Jersey, and in Tarrytown, New York. No one, however, has ever known his name or in what year he flourished.

The road upon which our rider pursued his way ran along the edge of the mountains to Middlebrook, or Bound Brook. Below Pluckamin was a tract of four hundred and seventy acres belonging to William McDonald, who had recently built on the ravine of Chambers Brook a mill that ground the grists of Bedminster people until after the Revolution. Upon crossing this tract the road plunged directly into the forest, and from there on was but little more than a bare wagon track.

Let us imagine Johannes traversing this shady way. As he puffs his pipe and rides musingly along, he gives rein to his steed and abandons himself to agreeable reflection. While his mind dwells on the future grainfields, barns, mills, and improvements in contemplation for the Bedminster hillside, he turns his horse on the soft green moss that carpets either side of the trail, and as he slowly moves

69

on between the stately trees, breathes with delight the cool sweet breath of grass and leaves and forest. Now he threads a little bridle path or cutoff, which leaving the highway runs under a mass of foliage through which wild honeysuckles and blossoming grapevines clamber from bush to tree, filling the air with their fragrance. On every side the shadowy dells and bosky bowers are vocal with the chirping, twittering, and singing of early summer birds. On the branches overhead saucy gray squirrels, with a whisk of their spasmodic tails, scurry up the tree trunks to safer altitudes, from where they peer down on the horseman below through a curtain of trembling leaves. Perhaps a bear with its awkward cubs shuffles across the trail before him, or a startled deer bounds away through the glades of the forest, disappearing in its somber distances. There were other beasts and game at this time frequenting the quietudes of these Pluckamin hills, for we know that in 1730 a law was passed in the province offering a bounty of twenty shillings for full-grown wolves, five shillings for whelps not able to prey, and fifteen shillings for panthers. Notwithstanding this inducement for the extirpation of wolves, they seem to have grown more numerous, as in 1751 an act was passed increasing the bounty to sixty shillings and to ten shillings for whelps.

And now the thicket and undergrowth recede; the ground falls away, and the trail descending to the broad level of the Raritan loses itself in the "Great Raritan Road," which had been a thoroughfare of early Colonial travel since the year 1700. It commenced at a point on the north bank of the river opposite New Brunswick, and following the stream to its branches extended west to the Delaware. Here Johannes finds the already old village of Bound Brook (Middlebrook), its location then as now being one of much natural beauty. Seated on the grassy banks of the Raritan, it overlooks that stream just where with a graceful bend it sweeps to the south, and so makes

70

its deepening way through a fertile valley to the sea.

To one fond of the beautiful in nature this valley of the Raritan abounds in rural loveliness. It is but its superficial charm. He who has an appetite for the quaint and old, and is eager to discover localities around which memories of the past cluster thickly, finds much along this river upon which to feed his antiquarian tastes. Its associations are among the oldest in New Jersey—none more so, save those of the Hudson and the Delaware. After the establishment of the capital of the province at Perth Amboy in 1682, the Scotch and English soon made their way northerly as far as the forks of the Raritan. Long before this time the Dutch had been quick to discover the agricultural promises of this favored region. These pioneers, toiling in the vanguard of settlement, while making their way through the thick gloom of the woods bordering the river were attracted by the intervals of broad meadow spaces, horizoned by zones of forest and rich in abundant grasses. Under the shadow of their bordering trees often stood Indian cabins, for the red men had used these savannas for raising corn, beans, and pumpkins. The Hollanders had good cause for rejoicing at finding in the dense woods lands destitute of trees and ready at once for the plow.

Bound Brook has the honor of being Somerset's oldest settlement, the land on which the village stands having been purchased in the year 1681 by Governor Philip Carteret and others from two Raritan Indians. The Scotch and English multiplied in this vicinity, and by the year 1700 they were in sufficient numbers to warrant forming the "Presbyterian Congregation of Bound Brook," which before long became one of the most flourishing and important religious organizations in the colony. We have no record of where the first services were held—probably in one of the log dwellings that were distributed along the willow-fringed banks of the river. It was not until 1725 that the congregation erected its first edifice, a low one-story house. A second and more pretentious building was completed about the year 1760, the funds having been obtained from the proceeds of a public lottery. When Johannes visited Bound Brook, John Wacker taught the village children in a low one-story building within the present church grounds. Doubtless the Colonial lads found that pedagogue's name to be appropriate to his calling, for schoolmasters of the olden time considered that mental perceptions were precipitated by knuckles and palms being well ridged by hard rulers.

Among the citizens of this ancient burgh was Tobias Van Norden, who built a store in 1749. It was a long building of but one story, with two dormer windows in its sloping gambril roof. Van Norden continued as Bound Brook's storekeeper until after the Revolution, and we can imagine Johannes dismounting, either going or coming, in order to fill some little commissions from home, as at this time it was the nearest shop to the Old Farm. A grandson of Van Norden says that for some twenty-five years previous to 1765 his grandfather was extensively engaged in baking ship bread, which he exported direct to the West Indies, carting it in wagons to New Brunswick where it was transferred to vessels.

Speaking of a lottery as a means of raising money for completing the church brings to mind the prevalence of lotteries in Colonial times. It was the financial fashion of the age and considered quite legitimate. The following curious extract from the diary of the Reverend Samuel Seabury, father of Bishop Seabury, shows the peculiar views prevailing as to the propriety and morality of lotteries and gambling: "The ticket No. 5,886, in the Lighthouse and Public Lottery of New York, drew in my favor, by the blessing of Almighty God, 500 pounds sterling, of which I received 425 pounds, there being a deduction of fifteen per cent; for which I now record to my posterity my thanks to Almighty God, the giver of all good gifts."

Judging from the advertisements appearing in the middle of the last century in the New York papers, there was hardly a settlement in the province that had not on foot some plan for a lottery. The beneficiaries of those extraordinary monetary schemes were most varied in character, and they were often for the aid of private as well as public enterprises. One set up in New Brunswick was for the relief of an insolvent debtor. Peter Bodine advertised another having one hundred and ninety-five prizes, "many of them being lots in the heart of that growing place, Raritan Landing, which is a market for the most plentiful wheat country of its bigness in America." It would seem that speculative real estate bubbles were early afloat in the New Jersey air. The Landing must have stopped growing very suddenly, and one would need to search diligently now to find that number of lots in this then-called market. Within a few years of that time the Presbyterian "meetinghouses" at Amwell and Bound Brook, the English church at New Brunswick, St. John's Church at Elizabethtown, and Trinity Church at Newark were all completed with the assistance afforded by lotteries. In Philadelphia in 1749 one was established to raise fifteen hundred pounds for the benefit of Nassau (Princeton). In 1773 that institution, in conjunction with the Presbyterian Church at Princeton, secured by the same means fifty-six hundred and twenty-six pounds. Toward the end of the century lotteries had grown in bad repute and were generally prohibited; but immediately after the Revolution the legislature of New Jersey granted the borough of Elizabethtown the privilege of holding one "to raise a sum of money for building a court-house and jail, and finishing the academy, which during the late war was burned by the enemy."

5

Indian Path to King's Highway

As JOHANNES LEFT Bound Brook and rode southerly down the valley of the Raritan, the country quite lost that impress of solitude it had borne during the earlier stages of his journey. The heavy timber was now left behind, the trees grew more sparsely, for he had reached a region where settlers under the first proprietors earliest penetrated and established their plantations. He was now in Middlesex County, and the township he traversed had for fifty years been occupied by the husbandman. Generous orchards and abundant fields had long before taken the place of tangled mazes and impenetrable thickets, and much of the bottom and bench lands had been wrested by the hand of cultivation from the grasp of nature.

No longer were the rude structures of logs that had housed the families of pioneers the sole architectural features of the landscape; in many instances they had made way for more pretentious farmhouses, the homes of permanent, well-established residents; and ample barns bore testimony to the fertility and productiveness of the surrounding acres. The board houses were of one story, with long sloping roofs extending over a porch in front and descending nearly to the ground in the rear. Here the overhanging eaves sheltered the big Dutch oven, and a broad space where russet-gowned maids sang at their spinning wheels and where busy housewives did the family weaving at their clumsy looms. These frame houses

74

were generally unpainted and rapidly grew venerably dark in color. Their interiors were divided into but few rooms; one or two sufficed for the needs of the family, while others harbored pumpkins, carrots, and potatoes, with dried apples and peaches hanging in festoons from the ceiling. The humble log hut, which had originally done residential duty, stood like a poor relation at a respectful distance, often degraded to the menial service of sheltering pigs and kine. Sometimes it was converted into a rude brewhouse, for the Raritan settlers manufactured and drank great quantities of malt liquors.

On reaching Raritan Landing, two miles above New Brunswick, Johannes found it, for those days, a place of considerable prominence, its marked growth of a few previous years having given rise to expectations of ultimate commercial greatness that the future was not to realize. Its prosperity was gained mainly from the fertile valley bordering on the Raritan and the rich fields of wheat and corn that were rapidly multiplying between that river and the Delaware. This, together with the fact that the Landing was on tidewater and at the head of sloop navigation, gave it an importance second only to that of New Brunswick, and by many it was thought to be a serious business rival to that city. In addition to its shipping interests this point had active manufacturing industries. The Raritan was here dammed, and mills were in successful operation, both for grinding the grain of the back country and for manufacturing flour and meal for shipment to New York and more eastern ports. Ralph Voorhees, in one of his sketches of the early settlers, tells us that the water power at the Landing was destroyed about the time of the Revolution by the people along the upper Raritan, who were exasperated because it prevented shad from ascending the stream.[1]

---

[1] Ralph Voorhees, "The Raritan and Its Early Holland Settlers," *Our Home*, I (Somerville, New Jersey, 1873). Only one volume was published.

When Johannes reached the Landing he was much interested in viewing what was then considered, and properly so, a very grand mansion. It was surpassed by few, if any, residences of the province. Nearly fifty feet square, it elevated a dormer-windowed hipped roof above two stone stories, presenting a strong contrast to the ordinary wooden buildings of the surrounding country. Johannes crossed the river on the riffle below the dam, and making his way down the opposite shore he was soon in New Brunswick, where he dismounted in front of a tavern on Water Street, the city's main thoroughfare. After his long ride we can imagine him quite ready for what someone has called the hope of the hungry, the rest of the weary, the consolation of the miserable—dinner.

The antiquated college town of New Brunswick, which the traveler Philadelphia-ward finds perched on the high rolling banks of the Raritan, is located on the most ancient highway in New Jersey; a road that, before the foot of the first white man had trod the American continent, was centuries older than were its flanking oaks, chestnuts, and hickories. In those remote days a faint path could be traced on nature's carpet of fallen leaves and twigs, running east and west through the thickets and undergrowth of the vast and somber forest. It was the soft impress of the moccasined feet of the *Lenni-Lenape*, made while on their frequent way to the *Lenni-Wihittuck*, or Delaware River. This Indian path started at what is now Elizabethport and plunging into the solitudes of the wilderness extended almost in a direct line to a point on the Raritan opposite where Albany Street in New Brunswick now terminates. Here the red men at low water forded the river or at higher tides paddled across in their birch canoes. Passing up the present line of Albany Street, the footpath traversed the hoary woods with but little deviation till it reached the Delaware, just above where the capital of the state is now located.

This was the Indians' thoroughfare—their main artery

76

of travel. It was intersected by others, the most important being the one by which the Monseys and more northern tribes found their way to the sea. Commencing on the Delaware in what is now Sussex County, near where three states converge, this trail, known as the Minisink Path, ran southeasterly to within five miles of Elizabethtown. Turning to the right, it stretched across the country to the Raritan three miles above its mouth. Following the south bank of the river and the shore of the Lower Bay, the footpath continued through what is now the village of Middletown, and so onward over the pleasant rises and gentle declivities of Monmouth till it penetrated the hemlock heights of the Highlands, and descending on their ocean side reached the river which the red man had named *Nauvessing*. When the Dutch first landed on the shores of this part of Monmouth, they wrote down the Indian name for the place as it sounded to them, thus *Nauves-sing*. The English converted the word into *Navesink*, from which *Neversink* is, perhaps, a natural result. Another Indian trail branched from the first one at the Raritan ford, and following the river bank extended north and west by the way of the site of Bound Brook to the forks of the stream, where it divided. It was over this trail that settlers first made their way up into Bedminster.

Early in the seventeenth century other than Indian forms were to be seen passing along our ancient highway. Over this path which had never been pressed by human feet save by those of the soft-stepping, stealthy savage strode burly Dutchmen wearing hats of generous brim, broad belts, and stout leather jerkins, the smoke from their pipes, fragrant with the odors of the best Virginia, mingling with the breath of the woods and exuberant herbage. The Hollanders had settled New Amsterdam; sailing in their high-pooped shallops through the *Kill von Koll*—"the Creek of the Bay"—they landed on the west shores of the *Achter Koll*—"the Back Bay"—and found this Indian trail a most convenient route to their settlement

77

on the Delaware. Later on, when the English had captured New Amsterdam, they too discovered that the natives had marked out an excellent line for a road across the Jerseys—and a road it has been from that day to this.

A mutual good will soon existed between the Dutch and English and the dusky occupants of the little wigwam villages that were planted in cool and shady glens or by the side of sparkling rills. The white man had not long used this forest trail before signs of human thrift began to break in upon the wildness of nature. He traveled not only with matchlock and hanger, but with mattock and ax as well. The wild grapevines and stunted bushes that encumbered the path were cleared away; the decaying tree trunks, giants that had fallen from mere weight of years, no longer impeded the passer-by. Footlogs crossed the little streams, and soon the glittering ax hewed out a clearing here and there on the side of the path from which rose little log cabins, premonitory symptoms and prophecies of populous hamlets and villages soon to follow.

Early in 1681 John Inian located for himself on the west bank of the river twelve hundred acres, embracing the present site of New Brunswick. A charter for a ferry was granted him in 1697 for the term of his or his wife's life at the yearly rental of five shillings. Soon quite a settlement grew up about Inian's Ferry, and travelers by the old Indian path began to be frequent. This lost its early appellation and became known as the Dutch Trail; indeed, for many years later it was little better than a trail through the woods, and was used only by pedestrians and horsemen. In 1716, nearly twenty years after the establishment of the ferry, the tariff named only "horse and man" and "single person." Within a few years this old Dutch Trail began to present some of the characteristics of a road, and we find imposed upon the innkeepers of Elizabethtown, Woodbridge, and Piscataway a total annual tax of ten pounds for keeping the highway free from fallen timber. This impost was laid for the preservation of the "lower road," which, following a branch Indian path, diverged from the main trail a few miles beyond the Raritan, its trend being southwesterly, by the way of Cranbury to Burlington. This tax was necessary, as the act declares, because of the unsettled condition of the country which the road traversed, whereby it was in danger of falling into "decay to the great inconvenience of travelers who may pass and repass that way unless care be taken to maintain the same until such time as it may be maintained by those who inherit it."

The town grew apace, and before 1717 there were people enough to necessitate the building of a church. From this time the tide of settlers rose, and rolled steadily on toward and beyond the Raritan. In 1730 the population of New Brunswick was augmented by the arrival of a number of Dutch families from the upper Hudson, who planted themselves on either side of the road leading up from the ferry. Not only the town by the river benefited by this influx of newcomers; the back country of Middlesex lost its aspect of a solitude. The old Dutch Trail was rapidly being transformed into the King's Highway; clearings multiplied, and what had been clearings were now converted into arable fields and well-tilled farms. Immigrants from Germany landing in New York traversed this road, seeking that Mecca of all pilgrims from the Rhine, the province of Pennsylvania. Finding their route bordered by goodly lands, many of them abandoned their proposed goal, and turning aside made their homes among the Dutch and English settlers.

The country in the vicinity of this highway, when much of New Jersey was still a wilderness, had the appearance of being comparatively well cultivated and long occupied. James Alexander, the father of Lord Stirling, in a letter written in 1730 says that "In the year 1715 there were but four or five houses between Inian's Ferry and the Delaware River, but now the country is settled very thick; as they go chiefly on raising of wheat and the making of flour, and as New Brunswick is the nearest landing, it necessarily makes that the store-house for all the produce that they send to market; which has drawn a considerable number of people to settle there, insomuch that a lot of ground in New Brunswick is grown to be near so great a price as so much ground in the heart of New York."

Professor Kalm, when journeying in 1748 from Philadelphia to New York, expressed the greatest surprise at finding so cultivated a region, and declared that in all his travels in America he saw no part of the open country so well peopled. At Trenton, which he reached by sloop, his landlord told him that twenty-two years before, when he first settled there, there were hardly any houses, but the increase since that time had been so great that there were now nearly one hundred. Along the road to the Raritan there were great distances of forests, but yet on much of the way he found extensive fields of grain, and almost every farm had abundant orchards. He especially noticed the great Jersey barns, which in many instances he thought to be as big as small churches, so large in fact that—which to the foreigner seemed most extraordinary —they housed horses, cattle, grain, mows, and threshing floors. Their great double doors enabled farmers to drive loaded teams "in one side and out the other." The Professor attributed this generous farm architecture to the Germans and Dutch, whom he reports as occupying most of the country.

On the thirtieth day of December, 1730, two weeks before New York was incorporated as a city, King George II bestowed on New Brunswick, under the great seal of the Crown, its first charter. The inhabitants agreed in consideration of the privileges granted by this precious document to pay annually to the Kingdom of Great Britain one sheaf of wheat.

The citizens of New Jersey in the olden time had great confidence in the future prosperity of the province. In laying out their towns and cities they established corporate limits great enough for that extensive population, the coming of which they so surely anticipated. Thus Perth Amboy—already for twelve years a chartered city—included several thousand acres east of the Raritan, while on the opposite side of the river its northerly line extended from the mouth of South River westerly nearly to Hightstown, and its southerly parallel line ran fully as far into Monmouth County from the mouth of Cheesequake Creek. New Brunswick, equally ambitious, extended its boundary on the one side to the Amboy line, and on the other almost to Princeton. And so the two great cities of Middlesex adjoined each other.

It is quite time that we return to Johannes; we may reasonably suppose that he has finished his dinner, and before again taking to the saddle is looking about New Brunswick, which he is visiting for the first time. He finds it rather an attractive little town, lying mostly under the hill, on the river bank. At that time it had but two prominent streets, and the houses were generally constructed of plank, though the Dutch of Albany Street occupied two-story brick dwellings, they having brought bricks and building materials with them when they migrated. These latter houses presented their peaked gables to the street, and were approached through little wooden-seated porches on which the stout burghers and their families would gather in the cool of summer evenings. Kalm writes that the Dutch of the city were an exclusive set, keeping much within themselves and quite looking down on their poorer neighbors. We can accept this statement *cum grano salis*, as in more than one place in his book of travels we find the Swede especially severe on America's Holland citizens.

New Brunswick, in addition to its milling and shipping interests, rejoiced in a copper mine that at this time gave promise of developing into an important industry. In the year 1748 virgin ore was plowed up in a field about three hundred yards back from the river and just north of the houses of the town. A company was formed, a shaft was sunk sixty feet, and a large body of ore found. For a number of years many tons of pure copper were annually shipped to England, and the stockholders antici-pated much prosperity for their enterprise. But eventually, the ore vein being exhausted, New Brunswick awoke from its dream of becoming a great mining town and settled back to the prosaic glories of its mills and the much vaunted honor of being at the head of sloop naviga-tion.

We have loitered long enough in this Middlesex city. So has Johannes. And now we find him mounting his waiting horse ready to proceed on his journey. He crosses by the ferry scow and his route lies in a southeasterly direction along the King's Highway; a ride of less than two miles brings our traveler on the main street of the old village of Piscataway, flanked by lofty trees. Those of us who are familiar with the time-stained houses, old-fashioned gardens, and aged churchyards of this early settlement know it to be now a far less important place than when in the heyday of youth, a half century and more before the date of Johannes' visit. In those good old colony times its men still loved the King, and met at Hull's Tavern to drink his health in long draughts of fiery Madeira or in modicums of more potent West India rum. His Most Gracious Majesty's Governor, Council, and Assembly have more than once met in this ancient burgh. On such occasions these roadways, which now seem sunk in the torpor of ages of sleep, were enlivened by very important gentlemen wearing gold-laced, cocked hats and full-bottomed wigs, and arrayed in broad-skirted scarlet coats, satin short-clothes, silk hose, and burnished knee and shoe buckles; who, while exchanging greetings and pinches of snuff, discussed the best interests of the colony.

The first congregation of Seventh-Day Baptists in New Jersey had its origin in this township. In the year 1700 Edmund Dunham, a Baptist exhorter and the owner of one hundred and ten acres of the town lands, felt called upon to admonish Hezekiah Bonham for working on Sunday; whereupon Bonham defied him to prove divine authority for keeping holy the first day of the week. Dunham, after investigation, failed to do so to his own satisfaction, consequently he himself renounced the observance of the first day. In the year 1705 he formed a congregation of Seventh-Day Baptists and was appointed its pastor. This was the second church of that denomination in America, the first having been established at Newport, Rhode Island.

Enough of Piscataway! Our cavalier rides on over the high levels of Middlesex. The trend of our "solitary horseman" is now more easterly, and facing the salt water, he canters over a pleasant country of low hills, gently subsiding into shallow valleys, diversified with woods and patches of cultivated lands ornamented with homesteads. It was yet early in the afternoon when he came in sight of Perth Amboy—its unrivaled location presenting a charming shore panorama of grove-crowned knolls, meadows of waving grass, bay, rivers, and varied beaches.

6

Colonial Capital

To one possessed of antiquarian tastes there is a singular pleasure in looking back through the long vista of years and picturing in the mind the appearance that a familiar place must have presented in those remote and seemingly almost poetic days known as Colonial times. A professor of comparative anatomy is enabled by securing a few fossil remains to reconstruct a species of animal long since extinct. So the delver in days of yore, by the proper placing of his few historical facts, illumined by a well-controlled imagination and a fancy verging perhaps on the romantic and picturesque, essays to again bring to life a past social condition and create appearances and fashions long out of date.

Thus would we fain endeavor to rehabilitate in its antique dress the city of Perth Amboy that has dozed for two centuries amid its groves of sycamores and oaks. When in the full tide of its lusty youth, this town had virile ambitions and aspired to be the metropolis of a new world. But those days, now long past, are almost forgotten, and for many decades this borough quietly slept on its pleasant banks by the wide-spreading waters, apparently well content to sit apart from the cares and vanities of its more successful rivals in trade and population. An endeavor will be made to unfold such a scene as met Johannes' eyes when in this spring of 1752 he rode over the high rolling lands bordering the Raritan and entered ancient Amboy—for it is ancient, having enjoyed the proud distinction of a city charter and all the honors of a mayor and corporation since 1718.

The dignity and importance of the borough at that time were by no means confined to the fact of its possessing municipal rights. From its natal day it had been the seat of government, and royal governors had frequently made it their place of residence. The first chief magistrate under the Crown was Lord Cornbury, who also ruled New York, as did several succeeding governors. He was a cousin of the Queen; there his nobility ended, for in personal habits and character he was of a low order. He persecuted Presbyterians and other dissenters, and violated the agreement entered into between the English and Dutch at the time of the capture of New Netherlands, whereby the latter were guaranteed religious liberty. Lewis Morris, in a severe letter to the Secretary of State, charged him with all manner of malfeasance in his high office, and closed his communication in the following words: "He dresses publicly in women's clothes every day, and puts a stop to all public business while he is pleasing himself with that peculiar but detestable magot." On attaining to the earldom of Clarendon in 1708, this noble Englishman fairly fled from the colonies to avoid paying his creditors, many of whom were poor tradesmen.

Lord Lovelace, his successor, arrived in December of the same year, but his government had but well commenced when he died. Then came Robert Hunter. This popular governor resigned in 1720 in favor of Robert Burnet, the son of the famous bishop, and godson of the King of England—William of Orange having stood as his sponsor and given him his name. He ruled until 1727, when he was removed to Massachusetts and was succeeded by John Montgomerie. Both Governors Hunter and Burnet passed much time in their comfortable Amboy homes on the banks of the Raritan, and added greatly to the importance and pleasure of the society of East Jersey. The latter governor is described as having been a man of gay and condescending disposition, the delight of men of sense and learning and the admired friend of the ladies, to whom he was much devoted. He visited every family of reputation in the province, and letters to his predecessor, Hunter, say that their writers do not know how the fathers and husbands may like the new ruler, but they are sure the wives and daughters do so sufficiently.

John Montgomerie was a well-known courtier who had been a colonel in the household troops and groom of the bedchamber of the Prince of Wales, afterward George II. There has been preserved some account of the personal effects and equipage of this royal governor; we are thus enabled to gain an inkling of the state in which a colonial magistrate lived. His many articles of furniture included an eight-day clock valued at forty dollars in our money, and a "fine yellow camlet bed" estimated at seventy-five dollars. There was silverware in profusion, and the wines and liquors were set down as twenty-five hundred dollars; a barge with its accoutrements, one hundred and twenty-five dollars; books, one thousand dollars; and eight slaves, one of them a Negro musician, over one thousand dollars. In his stables were one saddle horse, eight coach horses, two common horses, two breeding mares, two colts, and a natural pacing mare; a coach and a four-wheeled chaise; a fine suite of embroidered horse furniture, a servant's saddle, and two sets of coach harness, brass mounted; a postillion's coat and cape, together with saddles, holsters, and housings.

The governor in office at the time of the visit of Johannes to Amboy was Jonathan Belcher. On the eighth of August, 1747, while the early morning mists still hung over the broad expanse of the Lower Bay, all the people of the town had assembled on its banks to welcome that dignitary, who disembarked from a barge of the man-of-war *Scarborough*, on which he had crossed the Atlantic. He was escorted to the Town Hall amid the acclamations of the multitude, where he presented his commission—a portentous document of parchment of three sheets about two feet square, plentifully besprinkled with Latin and weighted by a heavy pendant disc of stiff brown wax bearing the royal arms of England. In a gracious reply to the loyal addresses of the Council and citizens, he congratulated the people on the beautiful location and thriving appearance of their town. Notwithstanding his fair words, the Governor, after making the customary tour of the province, established his home in Elizabethtown, where he died in 1757. In the following year Amboy had restored to her the glories of being the home of the King's representative.

The last Colonial governor, William, the son of Benjamin Franklin, received the appointment without solicitation on the part of his father and when only thirty years of age. He reached Amboy on the twenty-fifth of February, 1763—an intensely cold day—escorted by the Middlesex troop of horse and numbers of the gentry in sleighs. The New York *Gazette* chronicles that he took possession of the government in the usual form, the ceremonies being conducted "with as much decency and good decorum as the severity of the season could possibly admit of." The young Governor is said to have hired one of the best houses in the town at an annual rental of sixty pounds—equaling one hundred and forty-four dollars. His salary was twelve hundred pounds—or about three thousand dollars. In good time we shall have more to say of this royal governor. Meanwhile, we must return to Johannes, whom we left entering the city.

The proprietors, in their published description, asserted that "Amboy Point is a sweet, wholesome and delightful place"; and it was further described as being "covered with grass growing luxuriantly, the forest trees, as distributed by groups, diversifying the landscape with

87

light and shade, and all nature wearing the fresh aspect of a new creation." These characteristics at the time of our visitor's arrival had not disappeared. Great trees that cast a vast area of shade were still a distinguishing feature of the ancient capital, and its most popular pleasure-ground was a fine bit of locust timber on the banks of the Raritan, just west of High Street. It rejoiced in the suggestively tender appellation of "Love Grove." Under its cool shadows the townspeople gathered on summer afternoons to enjoy ocean breezes that came freighted with the balsamic odors of forest-clad Monmouth. Here in the long twilights Colonial youths and maidens met to enjoy the agreeable prospect of each other's society and in this sylvan retreat many a youthful troth was plighted to the pleasant musical accompaniments of the river's murmuring waves.

Another favorite resort of the citizens was the elevation overlooking the Raritan near Sandy Point, devoted to the fairs and races. All ancient chronicles of the colony refer to the old English custom of "Fair Days." This custom prevailed till the time of the Revolution. These were days of great revelry and mirth. Horse racing and all manner of games were permitted—any description of goods and merchandise could be sold without license, and on this breezy pleasure-ground at such times were to be seen all the peddling, hawking, thimble-rigging, cudgel-playing, bustle, and prevailing confusion that characterized such festivals in the old country. It was a time of general license, and under the law no one could be arrested during the continuance of the fair except for offenses against the Crown and for crimes committed on fair day.

To the east of "Love Grove," at the foot of High Street, was the "Long Ferry." Here too was the famous Long Ferry Tavern, a quaint structure of stone with an odd sloping roof, dormer windows, and high Dutch stoop. Built in 1684, it not only offered rest and refreshment for waiting passengers, but served as a rallying point for the gossip-loving citizens. In warm weather it must have been an inviting inn in which to take one's ease; in the winter we can well imagine that "mine host" Carnes—a giant in stature—kept thrust in the open fire a loggerhead (a red-hot poker), ready on the arrival of guests to be plunged into cups of flip—a mixture of rum, pumpkin beer, and brown sugar. It was a favorite hot drink in the colonies and it is said was far from being an unpleasant cold-weather tipple.

While at the time of which we write the location of the streets was much as now, the aspect they presented differed materially from the appearance of the thorough-fares of the prosaic Amboy of today. From a tall pole in the center of the town green, which interrupts High and Market Streets, floated the royal cross of St. George; while in one corner of the square stood what would now happily be unfamiliar objects, the stocks, pillory, and whipping post—dread menaces to the evildoers of that rude and turbulent period.

Why is it that the founders of towns and villages of this country so rarely established public greens—those sunny opens that are such pleasant features of English boroughs and hamlets, and which must of necessity strengthen the local attachments of a neighborhood? The playground of childhood—the rendezvous of youth—the verdant mead on which maturity and age assemble. There is something in the beauty and appropriateness of such a common bit of ground, in which all have equal rights, that reaches much beyond the gratification of the eye. It suggests a community of interests, where man is bound to man by affections that have been engendered by this little bit of sward—a sentiment that seems quite opposed to the selfishness that necessarily attaches to individual holdings. The instinctive fondness for such a spot by its joint owners must grow into an enlarged feeling, and expand into that expression of patriotism which can only be known by men when united in numbers and interests. It is a nursery of virtue and unselfishness. With rare judgment the successors and descendants of the early proprietors have preserved their town green—this attractive relic of a bygone age and of the wisdom of their predecessors. For over two hundred years it may be said to have been the theater of all the events connected with the life of this community, and to learn all that has transpired upon its emerald floor would be to turn over every page of Amboy's history.

The county courthouse and jail, occupying one building, our traveler found a prominent feature of this public square. It stood on the northeast corner of High Street, and from 1718 to 1765, when it was destroyed by fire, it continued to be the focus of all the important events of the colony and of much of its pomp, parade, and ceremony. Here not only the courts were held, but the bewigged and beruffled members of the General Assembly sat in solemn conclave and enacted those severe laws that were then considered necessary to preserve the peace of the province and the honor of the king. Permit me to quote one deemed meet for the times by those ancient legislators: "That all women of whatever age, rank, profession, or degree, whether virgins, maids, or widows, who shall after this act impose upon, seduce, and betray into matrimony any of his Majesty's subjects by virtue of scents, cosmetics, washes, paints, artificial teeth, false hair, or high-heeled shoes, shall incur the penalty of the law now in force against witchcraft and like misdemeanors."

To this Jersey *Hôtel de Ville* and the one that succeeded it, came with successive processions and cavalcades all the representatives of the English ministry from the days of the virtuous Queen Anne to those of the third Hanoverian king, each telling the same story of the love borne by the Crown for its faithful American subjects. Such stories were always received with loud shouts of fealty from the loyal throats of the populace massed on the square. The time arrived, however, when different messages came from the monarch beyond the sea, and public tranquillity was disturbed by the growls and threats of the British lion. Even then, though the spirit of liberty hovered around the ancient capital and the Jersey people in general were electric with patriotic impulse and endeavor, many of Amboy's citizens refused to abandon their allegiance. A large element of its population, especially among the richer class, were dominated in their sympathies by the many years' influence of royal power. At the close of the war but a very small proportion of those who had formed the Colonial aristocracy remained residents of Amboy.

The houses of the Colonial gentry were generally sprinkled along the bluff, where the most favored locations were early sought and secured. In most instances they were simple in construction and unambitious in character, but here and there was one of architectural merit, showing on the part of its builder an appreciation of a design where outline and surroundings should bear some relation to each other. These dwellings of the quality-folk were Amboy's architectural exceptions—not typical examples. Its houses, of which at that time there were about one hundred and fifty, were as a rule poor enough; a visitor of a few years later, while recognizing the beauty of the location, writes that "notwithstanding being the capital of the province, Perth Amboy has only the appearance of a mean village."

So with our traveler; as he made his way through the streets, he found many of their flanking buildings slovenly in appearance, showing them to have been hastily put together. Their rough-hewn flat-boarded frames lacked the dignity of the log dwellings seen in the clearings during the morning journey; these latter, with their feet buried in herbage, seemed less incongruous and more in harmony with surrounding nature. Many of these Amboy houses

91

were unpainted and already showed signs of the rustiness of age, but, bleached and patched by sun and shower, their crazy, weather-stained sides were less crude and staring than were the variegated colors of some of the newer houses, whose fronting gables and thick board shutters were painted white, while their remaining sides were covered with a dingy red. Architectural taste was, of course, entirely wanting, and in most instances a single story sufficed for the needs of the occupants.

Of churches there were two. The Reverend John Cross of Basking Ridge is said to have first supplied the Presbyterian pulpit, and among that denomination's historical flotsam rescued from the ocean of time is the fact that in 1735 Gilbert Tennant preached at Amboy on the comforting and encouraging topic of the "Necessity of Religious Violence to Durable Happiness." A text of severe sentiment, you will say!—but at this time the spiritual shepherds were wont to feed their flocks with food abounding in strength rather than sweetness. The angel of mercy hovered aloft, while the avenging one stood in the dwelling, at the roadside, in the pew, ever ready under the tutelage of the pastors to wield the flaming sword of justice. The stern Calvinistic tenet that election and perdition were predestined by the divine plan irrespective of human merit was taught and believed, and the believing lacerated many a tender heart.

The religious atmosphere of the middle of the last century was dark with the heavy clouds of doctrine and theology. Polemical controversy was rife in the churches. Foreordination, predestination, election, and eternal damnation went hand in hand with free agency; the effort to reconcile these conflicting and apparently opposing dogmas provoked labored sermons from the pulpit, and prolonged arguments and discussions in farmhouse, field, and shop. Ministers waxed severely eloquent in their terrible warnings to the unregenerate; while with equally solemn earnestness from such texts as "I could wish myself accursed from Christ for my brethren, my kinsmen," they preached to the pious and devoted ones of their congregations "the doctrine of disinterested benevolence," a doctrine that proclaimed the necessity of entire self-abnegation and a willingness to accept for one's self eternal condemnation, if such could redound to the greatest good to the greatest number and God's ends be better accomplished.

The interpreters of the Scriptures held before their people as tests of abiding faith the necessity of eliminating from their religion every element of selfishness, in order that they might have minds and affections so disposed as to be able to accept with complacency the possibility that it might be God's sovereign pleasure to damn them eternally. Such views of life and the future state evolved a gloomy piety. Agonies of doubt beset the most faithful when intent on severe internal examination in the endeavor to discover evidences that they were not under the ban of God's wrath. Such earnest souls, after lives of the most conscientious well-doing, often died still uncertain of the attainment of eternal happiness. Jonathan Edwards, who died in Princeton in 1758, was capable in his sermons of producing so great pain to the quick sensibilities of his hearers that during his discourses the house would be filled with weeping and wailing auditors; on one occasion another minister present is said to have cried in his agony, "Oh! Mr. Edwards! Is God not a God of mercy?"

This celebrated preacher succeeded the elder Burr, who died in September, 1757, in the presidency of Princeton College, but he did not take his seat until in February of the following year. Mr. Edwards held the position scarcely a month, dying while undergoing inoculation for the smallpox. He has been called the turning point in the spiritual existence of the congregations of the last century. It is asserted that New England and New Jersey in the age following him, under the guidance of such disciples as his son, Dwight, Bellamy, Hopkins, Brainerd, and Tennant, gave more thought to religious philosophy and systematic theology than the same amount of population in any other part of the world.

7

The King's Councillor

THERE WAS MUCH of interest to Johannes in this provincial capital besides the churches, and the public and private buildings. The bustle, animation, and variety of its thoroughfares presented picturesqueness in Colonial times that must have added much to the light and shade and general effect of ordinary scenes. In those early days population occupied only the fringe or border of the great wastes and solitudes; we have seen that New Jersey's cultivated lands were largely confined to a narrow strip extending from the Hudson to the Delaware. Belts of wilderness stretched across New York and into New England; indeed, the whole country east of the Mississippi was covered with vast forests, with but occasional signs of civilization and cultivation along the borders of the sea and in the valleys of the larger rivers. At the centers of population—one of which Amboy at that time fairly could claim to be—the people, congregating as they did from many quarters of the globe, formed to each other strong contrasts, and the local color of civilization must to the chance visitor have made an interesting picture.

The Indians were still in goodly numbers about New Jersey towns, and they appeared much more like the children of the forest of our imagination than do those now to be seen on the reservations of the Far West. They

came into the town with skins, and also supplied the
people with baskets and wooden dishes and spoons. The
redemptioners must have heightened the general effect;
and the trappers and hunters, fresh from the woods with
their rifles, powder horns, moccasins, and linsey shirts
fringed with deer skin, contributed their bit of color and
form to the kaleidoscopic appearance of the streets.
Among the expatriated Irish, Dutch, Germans, and English inhabiting the vicinity there must have been many
curious and picturesque specimens of the genus *homo*.
Necessarily many of these latter were worthless characters, and the pillory, stocks, and whipping post on the
public square doubtless had a marked influence in preserving the peace and proprieties of this rough age.
Opposed to this type was the less conspicuous but more
useful element of society, the sturdy yeomanry—the
stout-hearted middle class; men who themselves, or whose
fathers before them, often had left the old country for
political and religious motives rather than a mere desire
for adventure and trade. "God sifted a whole nation,"
said stern old Governor Stoughton[1] of New England,
"that he might send choice grain over in this wilderness."

The published account of travels in America in the
last century all corroborate each other's assertions in
speaking of the German portion of this latter class—the
bone and sinew of the provinces. They bear universal
testimony that population in the Middle Colonies was
powerfully promoted by its German element; a people
who in their own country had been disciplined in habits
of industry, sobriety, frugality, and patience, and were
consequently peculiarly fitted for the many laborious
occupations of a new land. Among the yeomen, husbandmen, and mechanics they were regarded as the most
economical as well as the most industrious of the population, and the least attached to the use of rum and malt

---

[1] William Stoughton (1631–1701), Connecticut.

liquor. They were slow in contracting debts and were always endeavoring to augment their means of subsistence.

But it was the gentry, richly dressed in all the magnificence of the times, that presented in customs, manners, and apparel the strongest contrast to the other actors on this stage. In Colonial times there were in the provinces society distinctions now unknown. Both in town and country the gentry were as distinctive from the people at large as were the upper classes in England. Extensive landowners, persons with important connections abroad, members of the King's Council and the General Assembly, and those near the government were held in high consideration and rank as the great men of their respective counties. Their personal dignity was sustained by their dress, manners, modes of life, and the civil and military offices distributed among them. Amboy, being at this time the capital, was eminently aristocratic, and presented social aspects and phases that would now be considered both brilliant and picturesque.

New England is peculiarly rich in descriptive Colonial literature; perhaps it would be difficult to add to its fund of information on this subject. Our poverty in this regard, however, offers a field full of local color for the historian of old New Jersey society. Early church and county records, the archives of the historical societies and of the Board of Proprietors of East New Jersey, and the family manuscripts distributed throughout the state are mines from which many rich historic social nuggets could be unearthed by the patient delver, and a most interesting work compiled. In the absence of such a volume, that we may learn something more of the Amboy of the middle of the last century let us summon a member of his Majesty's Council from his bed of mold in St. Peter's Churchyard. Perhaps he may be able to tell us of social events and observances in old colony days.

Here he comes, making his stately old-fashioned way along Smith Street. He cuts a strange figure in this workaday world of ours, with his broad-skirted scarlet coat—white silk waistcoat embroidered with flowers—black satin breeches, and paste knee and shoe buckles. As he tickles his nose with snuff from a gold box, his bewigged head shakes despondingly—he is disappointed! When this King's Councillor stepped out of his grave, he expected to find Perth Amboy a great city. To him and his fellows of the olden time it had seemed designed by nature for an important commercial metropolis. Hopes had been entertained that, owing to its nearness to the sea and its unrivaled harbor, commerce would center here, and that for all time New Jersey's capital would be of great political and commercial consequence.

The Councillor in all his magnificence seems oddly out of place among the ugly, modern brick shops of this business street. We will seat him in a high-backed chair in a broad hallway of one of the old houses of his own time—now he appears in a more appropriate setting. You need not offer him a glass of whiskey! He is not acquainted with the beverage. Rum punch? Yes! he will take that; I doubt not but that he and his co-councillors have swallowed many a jorum of such toddy while wrestling with knotty questions affecting the good of the province. Now that our Colonial friend has washed the dust from his ancient throat, let us hear what he has to say. Evidently, when in the pristine glory of existence he was a gallant man, for his first topic is the ladies; how they appeared—like birds of paradise, if he is to be believed, with stuffed satin petticoats, taffetas and brocades, tall hats, lofty coiffures, long feathers, powder, and patches. Their gowns were buoyed out one or two feet on either side of the hips, but not in front or behind, consequently—as he tells us with a chuckle—a lady of fashion when in full dress, in order to gain admittance to her own door, was forced to present her flanks and thus sidle in like a crab.

Our resurrected one describes the flutter in Amboy society caused by the arrival of the first theater company to the colonies and its presenting plays in the town hall on the public green; he says that the ladies in order to secure seats were obliged to send their black servants early in the afternoon to occupy them until the time of the performance. This theatrical company was under the management of the Hallams, who first opened with it in America in 1752. Dunlap, who was born in Amboy, asserts that he has heard old ladies speak in raptures of the beauty and grace of Mrs. Douglas—the leading lady of the company—and the pathos of her impersonation of the character of Jane Shore.[2] Our New Jersey ancestors took more kindly to the stage than did their brethren in Massachusetts. The Assembly of that province in 1750 prohibited theatrical presentations because—as the bill recited —"they tend greatly to increase immorality, impiety, and a contempt for religion."

A graphic portrayal is given by the Councillor of the appearance of the gentlemen and ladies on Sunday mornings as they assembled on the bluff to worship at St. Peter's: the dignified walk of the men, with crimson and gilt garments, silk stockings, cocked hats, and tall gold-headed canes; and the young lads—in dress, brilliant but ludicrous reproductions of their elders. The *grandes dames* with high heels and stiff stays came ballooning along, their voluminous skirts swaying and fluttering in the fresh sea breeze. With what ceremony did they greet each other! As the men raised high in air their gold-laced hats and bowed low their curled heads, the ladies, stopping short in their promenade, placed one foot twelve inches behind the other and dropped a formal, stately, and prolonged curtsey.

It is very agreeable listening to his tales of the ostenta-

---

[2] William Dunlap, *A History of the Rise and Progress of the Arts of Design in the United States* . . . (New York, 1834).

tion and parade at New Jersey's capital in the heyday of its youth: how one "Moneybaird" conveyed to Lord Neil Campbell's son John all his Amboy interests in consideration of Campbell's sending a footman to hold his stirrup and wait on him during the meetings of the Assembly; how the Mayor, while acting officially, had a mace-bearer who carried before him this ancient insigne of corporation rank; how the judges, while sitting on the bench, wore judicial wigs and resplendent robes of office; and how it was obligatory for counsellors-at-law, when pleading before the bar of the Supreme Court, to be arrayed in gowns and bands as worn by barristers in England. He has much to say of the flourish and ceremonies attendant upon court days; of the judges on circuit being met outside of the town by the sheriff, justices of the peace, and other gentlemen on horseback, who escorted them in honor to their lodgings. At the opening and closing of court, in going to and from the courthouse, the judges were preceded by the sheriff and the constables carrying their staves of office, and all evildoers trembled in the presence of the august procession.

And now he entertains us with descriptions of the grand balls given at the town hall in honor of royal governors; where the dancing was not confined to the youthful belles and beaux, but all ages of the gentlefolk participated; stepping the decorous minuet or going down the middle in the but-little-dignified contre-dance. Altogether, in the last century this home of our narrator must have been a gala Amboy. He could give us more interesting information, if he would, as to its historic charms and associations, and the manners and customs of its people. But the old gentleman is running down; his voice is beginning to cackle. We will relegate him to that mysterious shade from whence he came. Exit, the King's Councillor!

There was a dark side to this old-time picture—the Negroes. The evil of slavery took deep root in Colonial New Jersey. The reason is readily understood when we remember that in the early days of the province the slave trade was encouraged by the English people, fostered by the home government, and enforced by the action of the British ministry. In 1702 Queen Anne instructed the governor of New York and New Jersey "to give due encouragement to merchants, and in particular to the Royal African Company." Up to the time of the Revolution, Great Britain directed her colonial governors to combat the attempts made by the colonists to limit the slave trade, and under pain of removal to decline assent to any restrictive laws. Only one year before the American Congress—in 1776—prohibited the slave trade, the Earl of Dartmouth addressed the following words to a colonial agent: "We cannot allow the colonies to check or discourage, in any degree, a traffic so beneficial to the nation."

During a debate in the House of Commons on the question of the suppression of this trade, a wise legislator produced a labored argument against its abolition on the ground of injuries that would result to the market for the refuse fish of the English fisheries, which were purchased in large quantities by West India planters for their slaves. This astute debater was Brook Watson, who was called an American adventurer and who not only became a member of Parliament but afterwards Lord Mayor of London. We are able to relate one incident in the life of Watson where he was of advantage to the world at large. It was to all our good fortunes that when a small boy he fell overboard in the harbor of Havana and just escaped being devoured by a shark. This gave to the brush of the great American artist, Copley, the subject for his well-known painting, "The Rescue of a Boy From the Jaws of a Shark."

The extent of the importation of slaves in the province of New Jersey is unknown, but it is estimated that before the Revolution between three and four hundred thousand Negroes were introduced into the American colonies. The Abbe Raynal[3] supposes that the number of blacks taken from Africa by Europeans before 1776 to have equaled nine millions. Mr. Bancroft[4] affirms the English importations in all the continental colonies and in the Spanish, French, and English West Indies to have been nearly three million souls, to say nothing of the hundred and fifty thousand thrown into the sea. He estimates that the profits of English merchants in this traffic previous to 1776 were not far from four hundred million dollars.

This historian draws in strong outline a sad picture of the miseries endured by the blacks while on the voyage from Africa. Small ships that could penetrate the shallow rivers and bayous of the coast were used, and often five hundred Negroes were stowed in vessels of not over two hundred tons burden. They were generally chained in pairs by the ankles; and below decks, when sleeping, each was allowed a space of but six feet by sixteen inches. For exercise they were made to dance and caper on deck to the tune of a whip. The Africans were chiefly gathered from various points in the far interior of the Dark Continent, in order that the freight of a single ship might be composed of people of different languages and nations. When they reached the seacoast at unfavorable seasons of the year, diseases were engendered which culminated on the voyage; this, together with the narrow space afforded their manacled bodies, the bad air, foul stenches, and limited food and water, caused a death rate often equaling fifty and never falling below twelve per cent of the shipment. Sailing masters on approaching a slaver at sea made it the rule, when possible, to keep to the wind-

---

[3] Guillaume Thomas François Raynal, *A Philosophical and Political History of the Settlement and Trade of the Europeans in the East and West Indies . . . newly Translated from the French* (London, 1783). 10 vol. There were other editions, including a pirated one in this country.

[4] George Bancroft, *History of the United States*. There were numerous editions.

ward in order to avoid the horrible odors that belched from the open ports and hatches of ships laden with human cargoes.

Strange as it may seem, the men who sailed these ships appeared to be ignorant of the fact that they were doing the devil's work. Neither the captains of slavers nor the persons comprising the companies who employed them seemed to have considered that they were practicing on their fellow men revolting cruelty and hideous wrong. This was so, at least, in the earlier days of the traffic. Sir John Hawkins commanded the first English expedition to Africa for slaves. His squadron comprised four vessels, and to their captains he issued the following sailing orders: "Serve God daily; love one another; preserve your victuals; beware of fire; and keep good company." So successful was he in this and subsequent voyages that Queen Elizabeth rewarded him by granting him permission to wear on his crest "a demi Moor, bound and captive."

In contemplating the slave trade as connected with our own country, we must not fall into the error of thinking that the infamy of the traffic attached only to the people of the South, where the greater number of slaves were marketed. It was the well-to-do deacons and church members of New England who controlled the business: men who deemed it a sin to pick flowers on the Sabbath; who thought it wrong to stroll along the banks of a stream, or wander in the woods on that day; men who would dispatch the tithing man to arrest the stranger who was hurrying through the town on Sunday on an errand of mercy. The history of that time reveals Peter Faneuil on the one hand piling up profits from his immense slave trade, while on the other occupied in private and public charities, and in the erection of the cradle of liberty in Boston.

In the eighteenth century the coasts of Mozambique and Guinea were white with the sails of Massachusetts and Rhode Island slavers. These vessels on the outward voyage were loaded with New England rum, which was traded to African chiefs for prisoners taken in their tribal wars. The blacks, together with such others as the ship captains had been able to steal, were then carried to one of the West India islands or to a southern American port, and there exchanged for molasses. This cargo was brought to New England and converted into rum for a further shipment to Africa; thus a three-fold profit was secured on each voyage. In the year 1750 Newport carried on a most extensive business of this character; three hundred distilleries were in operation, and the tonnage of the vessels lying at the town's wharves exceeded that of the city of New York.

As at the time of Johannes' visit Perth Amboy was New Jersey's chief port of entry, the blacks were to be seen there in goodly numbers; many of them were freshly imported, bearing their tribal marks and exhibiting their native characteristics as if still inhabiting the wilds of Guinea. It was thought desirable, when possible, to have the slaves brought into the colonies from the West Indies rather than direct from Africa, as after remaining for a time at Barbados or one of the other islands they were much better able to endure the severities of the American climate. In 1757 the British West Indies contained a total population of a little less than three hundred and thirty thousand souls, of which two hundred and thirty thousand were slaves.

Negroes on landing in the province were eagerly sought for by the settlers and were in the service of all families able to pay from forty to one hundred pounds for a man or a woman according to age. A child of two or three years sold for from eight to fourteen pounds. As showing the value of slaves in the last century, Mr. Snell [5] publishes an inventory of the personal effects of Theunis

---

[5] J. P. Snell, comp., *History of Hunterdon and Somerset Counties, New Jersey* (Philadelphia, 1881).

Post, one of the "helpers" of the North Branch Reformed Church. The following chattels are mentioned: "One negro named Ham, valued at £70; one negro named Isaac, valued at £30; one negro named Sam, valued at £70; one negro girl named Betty, valued at £10; one negro named Jane, valued at £60; one negro wench named Sawr, valued at £30." The last name is short for *Saertje*, the Dutch diminutive for Sarah.

As the character of these imported or, more properly speaking, stolen Negroes was necessarily savage and but little understood by the Jersey people, they were naturally much feared, and the most severe laws were enacted by the colony to insure their control and subjection. One of the official acts that constables were the most often called upon to perform was that of whipping slaves for minor offences. Any Negro found five miles from home it was the duty of these officers to arrest, and to flog with a whip, into the thongs of which fine wire was plaited that the severity of the punishment might be increased. For this service the owners of the derelict blacks were obliged to pay the constables five shillings, which materially augmented the income of those officials and added largely to the value and importance of the position.

The blacks on arrival were physically powerful and good workers, but without much power of reasoning or of controlling their undisciplined imaginations. Though barbarians, their affections were strong, and the marked progress made by Negroes in America may be said to be largely due to that fact. They soon outgrew their savagery and, affiliating in their sympathies with their work and the lives of their masters, in a very few years became an attached portion of the domestic life of the Jersey people. In Somerset County especially, the slaves soon fell under the sway of kindly influences, and became almost portions of their owners' families. They were comfortably clad, and when sick, well cared for.

But before the whites had in part advanced and civi-

lized the blacks and learned from experience the weakness
and strength of their bondsmen's characters, much cruelty
was inflicted through fears of risings and rebellions. The
New York *Gazette* of the twenty-fifth of March, 1734,
gives an account of a threatened rising early in that year
in the vicinity of what is now Somerville, in consequence
of which several Negroes, two at least, were hanged.
Punishments were extremely severe; murder and assault
often insured the culprits' being buried alive, and for even
petty thefts and misdemeanors they were hanged with
short shrift. On the twenty-third of September, 1694,
John Johnstone—he of the Peapack Patent—while sitting
as presiding justice of the Monmouth Court of Sessions,
sentenced a Negro convicted of murder in the following
language:

Caesar, thou art found guilty by the country of those
horrid crimes that are laid to thy charge; therefore, the court
doth judge that thou, the said Caesar, shall return to the place
from whence thou camest, and from thence to the place of
execution, when thy right hand shall be cut off and burned
before thine eyes. Then thou shalt be hanged up by the neck
till thou art dead, dead, dead; then thy body shall be cut
down and burned to ashes in a fire, and so the Lord have
mercy on thy soul, Caesar.

In those days of severe punishments the penalty followed closely after conviction. On the tenth of January,
1729, a slave named Prince was tried at Perth Amboy for
murdering one William Cook, and being found guilty
was sentenced to be burned alive "on ye twelfth of this
Inst." On the fifth of July, 1750, in a ravine just north of
Perth Amboy, two Negroes were burned alive at the
stake, one for murdering his mistress, who had mildly
censured him for misconduct, and the other for being
accessory to the fact. In these more lenient days the accessory would have escaped with a lighter punishment;
he was a mere lad and, as was shown at the trial, had been
coerced by fear into aiding the elder and more vicious
Negro. At the execution all the slaves of the neighborhood

were obliged to be present, that the scene might serve as an exemplary warning and a terrible example.

In 1791 burning seems to have been abandoned as a punishment for Negroes, one being hanged for murder in that year in front of the old courthouse at Newark. As was the custom the condemned was taken to the First Presbyterian Church, where his funeral sermon was preached by Doctor Uzal Ogden. Whitehead [6] narrates that the church was crowded and that the good dominie, in alluding to the reputation of the Negro, thoughtlessly finished his discourse by expressing a hope that the latter end of his numerous hearers might be like the criminal's.

In the province of New Jersey slavery especially flourished because of its large Dutch and German population; and the greatest number of slaves were to be found in the counties where those races predominated.

At Amboy Johannes had the choice of two leading taverns; one of them kept by John Gluck, the other by Obadiah Ayres. There was no choice as to expense, as the justices of the peace at the October quarter sessions of 1748 had established the following uniform and moderate rate of charges for all the taverns of the county: "Hot meal of meat, etc., 10*d.*; Cold meal *do* [ditto], 7*d.*; Lodging per night 4*d.*; Rum by the quartern 4*d.*; Brandy *do*, 6*d.*; Wine by the quartern 2*s.*, 8*d.*; Strong beer *do*, 5*d.*; Cyder *do*, 4*d.*; Metheglin *do*, 1*s.*, 6*d.*; Lunch *do*, 1*s.*, 2*d.* Provision for Horses: Oats by the quart 1½*d.*; English hay per night 8*d.*; *ditto* for 24 hours 1*s.*, 6*d.*; Salt or fresh hay per night 8*d.*; *ditto* for 24 hours 1*s.* 0*d.*"

These inns were rival hostelries, each being the headquarters of opposition lines of boats and stages to New York and Philadelphia. Daniel O'Brien in October, 1750, had established the first line by this route. His sloop left New York every Wednesday; the passengers were supposed to spend Thursday night at John Gluck's in Amboy, a stage wagon leaving on Friday morning for Bor-

[6] William A. Whitehead, *East Jersey under the Proprietory Governments* . . . (Newark, 1846).

dentown, where another sloop proceeded to Philadelphia. His advertisement promised to carry passengers through in forty-eight hours less time than did the stage which traveled the old road from New Brunswick to Trenton. The time actually consumed was from five to eight days. O'Brien could be "spoke with at the house of Scotch Johnny in New York on Mondays." The success of the above line was so great as to induce some Philadelphians in 1751 to establish an opposition. Their sloop started from the Quaker City at the Crooked Billet Wharf every week for Burlington, "from where"—as their advertisement reads—"at the sign of the Blue Anchor, a stage wagon with a good awning will run to the house of Obadiah Ayres at Perth Amboy, where good entertainment is to be had for man and beast." This advertisement goes on to lay much stress on the fact that the sloop of this line, sailing between Amboy and New York, had a fine cabin fitted up with a tea table.

The stage route referred to as passing over the old road had been established in 1742 by William Atlee and Joseph Yeats. They sold out in 1744 to one Wilson, who ran his stage wagon twice weekly. Professor Kalm attributed the great prosperity of Trenton to the number of travelers that journeyed that way from Philadelphia. He remarked on the many stage and freight wagons starting from Trenton, and wrote that its inhabitants largely subsisted by the carriage of people and all sorts of goods across to New Brunswick.

Wilson's charge for carrying a single passenger in his stage wagon from the Delaware to the Raritan was two shillings and six pence, with an extra payment for luggage. The fare by sloop from Philadelphia to Trenton was one shilling and six pence, in addition each passenger being obliged to pay extra for luggage and to provide for himself food and drink. This last was important, as, though the distance was not great, adverse winds often prolonged the voyage into many tedious hours. From New Brunswick passengers had a choice of three routes to New York: by sloop; by way of stage wagon to Elizabethtown Point, thence by sloop; and by way of stage wagon to Amboy, crossing by Willock's Ferry to Staten Island, crossing to Long Island at the Narrows, and thence to Flatbush and the Brooklyn Ferry. The inhabitants of the Raritan Valley and of the vicinity of Flatbush were at this time in close alliance. Late in the seventeenth and early in the eighteenth centuries the Dutch had taken up all of the agricultural lands on the west end of Long Island; consequently many of the second generation of this Holland stock were forced to seek tillable acres in East Jersey.

Picture to yourself a traveler of 1752 occupying six days—one hundred and forty-four hours—in traversing the distance between New York and Philadelphia. Imagine for a moment the discomforts and actual pains of such a journey during the winter months. Huddled on a crowded sloop for from twelve to forty-eight hours, fighting icy head tides, beating against winds, chill, drear, and contrary, eating cold snacks supplied by yourself— even "a fine cabin fitted up with a tea table" could hardly have palliated the miseries of such a voyage. In October, 1723, Benjamin Franklin, when making his first visit to Philadelphia, was thirty hours on his passage from New York to Amboy. His sloop was nearly lost in a squall, and one of the passengers falling overboard narrowly escaped being drowned. Over fifty years later a traveler tells of being twenty hours sailing sixteen miles on the Delaware in a sloop while on a journey from New York to Philadelphia. The same traveler was nearly shipwrecked in New York Bay, and lost some of his baggage at Amboy.

On reaching Amboy passengers were lodged in uncomfortable taverns; they slept on straw-filled ticks, usually with two or three bedfellows, and had but little choice as to company. The passage overland to the Delaware was none the less disagreeable. The stages were ordinary Jersey wagons without springs, with white canvas covers stretched over hoops, those at the front and rear being very high, which gave somewhat of a picturesque appearance to the rude vehicle. The wheels revolved on primitive boxes, kept greased by a frequent application of tar that was carried in a bucket suspended under the wagon body. Clumsy linchpins were supposed to secure the wheels, but they had a habit, with but slight provocation, of hopping out and letting the axle down with a thud in the mud, sending the passengers sprawling on the straw-covered floor of the stage.

The roads were in a wretched condition with alternating stumps and holes. The rivers and streams had to be forded, and after heavy rains long delays were incurred while awaiting the subsiding of the waters. The men travelers were expected to partly work their passages by walking up the steep rises, and by putting their shoulders to the wheel when the steaming horses were stalled in a slough. But this outside work was not much worse than being jolted on the hard seats within, while the lumbering vehicle lurched and strained over the uneven roads or staggered across corduroyed swamps, giving the passengers very much the feeling of having had their backbones driven up into their skulls. It was many years before there were any decent roads in New Jersey. Between 1765 and 1768 numerous unsuccessful efforts were made to float a lottery for raising money to improve the highways across the province. Governor Franklin, in an address to the Assembly in 1768, thus refers to their condition: "Even those which lie between the two principal trading cities in North America are seldom passable without danger or difficulty."

As Johannes smoked his pipe in the taproom of Ayres' tavern on the evening of his arrival at Amboy and listened to travelers' tales of hardships by land and water, how incredulous he would have been had he been told that his posterity would travel between New York and Philadelphia in a less number of minutes than it took hours for Ayres' customers to traverse that distance; that America would be bound and interlaced with iron and steel roads on which carriages would roll without visible means of locomotion. Still more absurd would he have considered the statement that in place of the clumsy sloops and springless wagons there would be luxurious coaches and mammoth steamboats; that passengers, instead of suffering extraordinary fatigues, would stroll about elegantly appointed saloons, recline on softly cushioned chairs, or sleep on comfortable couches while being whirled over thousands of miles of thickly populated country.

8

Life on the Old Farm

INTELLIGENT INDUSTRY will overcome many difficulties. The Germans in the province, generally being a quiet industrious folk, made themselves most valuable citizens. They were plodding, intent on their own business, attentive to the duties of religion, but were interested, perhaps, too little in politics. McMaster[1] writes that wherever a German farmer lived were to be found industry, order, and thrift. Their buildings, fences, thoroughly tilled fields, and nurtured orchards were in marked contrast to the lands and improvements of their more careless English and Scotch neighbors. Other writers on the condition of the American colonies in the last century speak of the simple and primitive manners and frugal, industrious habits of the Germans, which, together with their contented spirits and honest dealings, made them valued acquisitions to the communities and most suitable infusions among the inhabitants of the provinces.

Well! Johannes and his sons are now fairly at work on the Old Farm, and we must proceed with the telling of its story. He, like other early settlers, is occupied in making history; not in the sense of the brilliant achievements of heroes; his a more humble mission—to subdue a wilderness and civilize a community, to make smooth the way

---

[1] John Bach McMaster.

of future generations and to secure for his posterity a comfortable and complete homestead. It took time to transform his heavily wooded lands into arable fields; meanwhile many privations had to be endured, and that labor which conquers all things had to be vigorously and assiduously expended.

In clearing New Jersey lands in Colonial times the settler began by felling the smaller trees and cutting off the stronger branches of the greater ones. Next, the oaks, hickories, and other large trees were attacked. Well girdled by the ax, these were left to stand until the following year, by which time, having been robbed of their sap, they were dead and ready for the burning. Encircling fires at the base of their trunks were ignited; the trees fell and by midsummer the sun began to operate on land that, being formed almost entirely of rotten vegetation, was rank with productiveness. Instead of rooting up the trees, many of the farmers after burning the stumps let them stand and decay. It gave the newly cleared land a very ugly appearance, but in four or five years the stumps would have so rotted that they could be beaten to pieces and plowed under. By July of the second year the ground was ready for a crop, which was generally buckwheat. After harvest in the autumn, the land was plowed and sown with rye. Often, owing to the richness of the soil from the long drinking of the juices of decaying vegetation, the first year's crop all grew to straw, and it was not uncommon for several seasons to go by before the ground had been sufficiently toned by cultivation to produce good yields of wheat.[2]

Agriculture was but imperfectly understood by the new settlers, and no knowledge seems to have been had of the value of the rotation of crops. Instances are given where new lands produced rye for ten years, and then for ten successive harvests yielded wheat. The virgin soil,

---

[2] Corn was often planted on new land during this interim period, as it was more likely to produce a good yield.

having been fertilized by nature for centuries, was for several decades prolific, but in time it became exhausted and the crops correspondingly poor. Farmers who had wasted the early strength of their fields were slow in appreciating the value of a plentiful use of lime and manure, and it was not until after the Revolution that impoverished lands began to be properly nourished and crops again to be abundant.

It is said that the first Somerset farmer who gave heart to exhausted land by the use of lime as a fertilizer was Doctor John Reeve, who sent all the way to a quarry on the Delaware for the stone. In addition to profitably working a large farm near Rocky Hill, he was a physician in good practice. Old residents of the county remember him as a tall man of a majestic presence, and as a graceful and fearless rider. His professional journeys were always made in the saddle, and as nearly as possible in an air line; scorning such ordinary means of communication as highways and byways, he rode bravely across the country, taking fences as if following a pack of hounds in full cry. Although Bedminster Township had abundant limestone within its borders, none was burned until 1794, and it was 1830 before Peapack lime came into general use. In the eighteenth century natural meadows supplied all the grass and hay for livestock; it was in the year 1800 that Jacques Voorhees introduced clover seed into Somerset County; the growing of grass on uplands inaugurated a new era in farming and great benefits resulted to husbandmen and the country.

To one accustomed to the improved appliances that aid and abet the agriculturist of this age, the tools and implements that Johannes had at his command would seem illy contrived for tilling the soil. The plows throughout the country at this time were rude and ineffective and mostly homemade. They were clumsily constructed of wood, the moldboard being fashioned from a block which had a winding grain approximating the curve required.

Thomas Jefferson is said to have first suggested the proper shape and proportion of this part of a plow. It was 1776 before a wrought-iron plowshare, some bolts, and a clevis were introduced, and the moldboards after that time were often plated with strips of iron made from hammered horseshoes. Our state has the honor of being the first to have used cast-iron plows, they being the invention of a New Jersey farmer. Their introduction was not general until the year 1797, the people being prejudiced against their use, and it is said that they claimed that the cast-iron poisoned the soil and ruined the crop. Our forefather sowed his seed by hand, and when harvest time came no cradler with glittering knife swung his graceful way through the golden grain, marking the field with lines of even swath. Rye, wheat, and buckwheat were cut with a sickle, but oats, like grass, fell under the scythe. The sickles used were long and narrow, their sharp edges having close teeth on the inner side. This manner of harvesting continued until after the Revolution, when farmers were delighted by the appearance of the cradle.[3]

During the first years of life on the farm there was much to do besides clearing and tillage. Gun and worm fences were built—the great barns and mows were erected, and their long, sloping roofs thatched with the big rye straw grown on strong new ground; orchards were set out, and below the hill the water power was improved, and the meadow facing Peapack Brook pierced for tan vats. A little above, the mill was planted; on its oaken floor a huge wooden-cogged wheel slowly revolved, crushing the black and red oak bark. An early undertaking was that of making the garden to the east of the house a combined kitchen and flower garden, as was the fashion of the time, in which was planted the

---

[3] Probate records of New Jersey farmers show that some farmers used the cradle, doubtless imported from England at first, before 1740. *See* Hubert G. Schmidt, *Rural Hunterdon* (New Brunswick, New Jersey, 1946), pp. xi, 98.

still blooming bed of German lilies. Horticulture was then in its infancy, or more properly speaking unknown as the word is now used. Old-fashioned gardens contained in the way of flowers but little else than hollyhocks, snowballs, roses, lilacs, pinks, tulips, sunflowers, morning glories, and a few more primitive blossoms. As for fruit, no grapes were to be had excepting the poor native fox variety; and the improved kinds of peaches, pears, plums, and melons had not yet been introduced. Of pears as well as of apples there were plenty, but no knowledge being had of nursing and grafting, they did not attain anything approaching their present perfection and deliciousness. So with the small berries, they were in great abundance, though uncultivated, growing wild in the fields and woods.

The vegetables of that period were few in variety and poor in quality. Potatoes were a staple, as were in their season cabbages, beans, and Indian corn; but tomatoes, cauliflower, Mercer potatoes, okra, lettuce, eggplant, and rhubarb had not yet been heard of. It will thus be seen that "living" at the Old Stone House in the olden days was much simpler than those of us found it who were so fortunate as to gather about its well-spread board in the generation just passed. Johannes' table was well supplied with ham, bacon, and smoked meats. Traditions smack their lips over the deliciousness of the tender juicy hams that hung in rows from the ceiling timbers in the cool cellar. Their rich and nutty flavor was gained from being cured in the fragrant smoke of burning hickory and oak, together with the fact of their having been carved from young pigs that had roamed in the forest, fattening on acorns, hickory nuts, and aromatic herbage. Occasionally fresh meat was had, as it was the custom of farmers when they slaughtered a "critter" to distribute joints and pieces among their neighbors for miles around, relying for pay upon a return courtesy. The family had not yet outgrown its love for sauerkraut, as is shown by the writer's having the antique mortar—cut out of a solid block of wood— and pestle which were used in the preparation of this compound, so dear to the German palate. A dish that garnished every meal was *kohl-salat,* or cabbage salad. The Dutch called it *kohl-slaa,* and from these two old country terms has come the degenerate word "cold-slaw."

Our yeoman's table, while ignorant of modern pre-pared dishes disguised by strange sauces, was abundantly beset with solid substantial food: poultry, eggs, cheese, and such farm diet there was, of course; hot breads were in vogue; shortcakes, made with buttermilk and baked on a griddle, were in daily demand, and pies, doughnuts, and *olekokes* were features even of the morning meal. *Soupaan*—well-salted Indian mush eaten with milk and molasses—was the standard Sunday supper, though oc-casionally a raised biscuit called *zweibak,* or "twice-baked," took the place of mush; this biscuit was made in large quantities, bushels at a time, and then dried in the oven until as hard as a rock; in a bowl of rich milk it made a toothsome dish—to the truth of which more than one of Mariah Katrina's descendants can bear witness.

As for beverages, a great favorite was madeira, though except on festive occasions it was rarely found save on the tables of the rich. Farmers were content with hard cider, beer, and Jamaica rum. A hot drink common at that time was soured beer simmered over the fire with crusts of brown bread and sweetened with molasses. Another de-coction or concoction of which the Germans of New Jersey were fond was the extraordinary combination of chocolate and links of sausages, boiled in a kettle, served in a bowl, and eaten together with a spoon; a feast of which I am sure but few of my readers would care to partake. It is said that when tea was first introduced in New Jersey its manner of use was for some time unknown. The people in their ignorance boiled it well, throwing away the liquor; the herb was then dished, buttered, and eaten as greens.

For sweetening purposes molasses and maple sugar were commonly used, as at that time brown or "store sugar" was yet considered a luxury. The story is current that the introduction of white sugar in the Moelich family was by Johannes' daughter, Veronica Gerdrutta, some years later on the occasion of a social tea-drinking. It was then both a curiosity and a treat among farmers, and especially to the Germans, who were a very economical folk. Fanny's husband, old Jacob Kline, not having been informed of the surprise in store for the guests, on sitting down at the table used the sugar as salt, supposing it to be such. This so annoyed his wife that she cried out somewhat angrily in German, "O you dumb Irishman, you never will know anything!"

In calling her husband an Irishman the good wife poured upon his head the full vials of her contemptuous vocabulary. Among the colonists of Pennsylvania and New Jersey there were representatives of many nationalities with widely dissimilar natures, but fortunately the unifying conditions were sufficient to ultimately blend their discordant elements. Yet, for a number of years the Irish and Germans were mutually repugnant, and each held the other in very low estimation; consequently "Irish" and "Dutch" were bandied between the thrifty Germans and the sons of the Emerald Isle as epithets of contempt. In a letter from the elder Mühlenberg to the fathers of Zion Church in 1772, the Patriarch complains that his conduct in a certain transaction had been misconstrued, and goes on to say: "You must have peculiar thoughts of me, as if I tried to cheat you out of something or desired to play Irish tricks on you."

Building barns, making gardens, and raising crops are fair-weather work. There was much that could be done on the Old Farm in tempest as well as in sunshine. On stormy days and during the long winter evenings Johannes and his sons were occupied with labor that would now be done at wheelwrights' shops, factories, and forges; but shops of all kinds were then few and at remote distances. Our forefathers cobbled their own shoes, repaired their own harness, and at extemporized carpenter and blacksmith shops made much of the household furniture and many of the farm and kitchen utensils. The Baroness Riedesal, the companion in misfortune of her husband, the Hessian General who was captured with Burgoyne, made and published many notes [4] on the American army; among them, one as follows: "Their generals who accompanied us were some of them shoemakers, and on the days we halted made boots for our officers or even mended the shoes of our men." The Baroness was in error: they were not shoemakers, but the custom of Colonial times was for the men to know all about the working of leather —they being able to make their own harness, saddles, and shoes—just as it was for the women to spin and weave. Doubtless these American officers in sore need of money were glad to exchange this knowledge and service for German or English coin.

There were few or no luxuries in the olden time that would be recognized as such now; the industries of the families were of the most complete character, as within each homestead was produced to a large extent the necessities of its members. In farming communities, upon the women of the household devolved not only the duties of cooking, washing, milking, and dairy work as at present; in addition, they made their own yarn, wove the family linen and woolen goods, smoked and cured meats, dipped tallow candles, brewed beer, and made soap. Their pleasures were limited, being confined principally to quilting frolics, apple-paring bees, and husking and "killing"

---

[4] Friederika Charlotte Luise Riedesel, *Letters and Journals Relating to the War of the American Revolution, . . . Translated from the Original German . . .* (Albany, 1867). There were other editions.

frolics. The latter took place when the men met at each other's houses to do the autumn hog-killing, the women coming in the late afternoon to join them at supper and have a dance in the evening. The "wood frolic" was also an institution which brought together most of the people of the congregation annually at the parsonages. While the men occupied themselves during the day hauling the minister's yearly supply of wood, the wives and daughters came in the late afternoon and prepared a bountiful supper, to which the tired wood haulers doubtless brought excellent appetites. The spinning-visit and the donation-visit were both occasions for festivities. At the former it was the women who spent the day in work, the men coming at suppertime to contribute to the pleasures of the evening.

Fielding writes that "bare walls make gadding housewives." Could he have visited the living room of the Old Stone House he would not have expressed this sentiment without noting an exception. It had bare walls, it is true, but Mariah Katrina was no gadding housewife:

> *She was a woman of a stirring life,*
> *Whose heart was in her house; two wheels she had,*
> *Of antique form—this large for spinning wool,—*
> *That small for flax; and if one wheel had rest,*
> *It was because the other was at work.*

In many of the customs and courtesies of life she was doubtless rude and unpolished. A helpmate to her husband, she did not disdain to aid him in the field. While occupied with household duties her dress, and that of her daughters, was coarse homespun; and often in the summer, to make her many busy stops in the farm kitchen the lighter, she discarded shoes. But for all that, her posterity have no cause for being ashamed of this industrious German matron; she was the mother of vigorous children who developed into men and women useful and beloved.

They in turn transmitted to their descendants capacities for leading worthy and profitable lives.

The farm kitchen was Mariah Katrina's kingdom, as it has been for all the housewives of the Old Stone House from that time down. It served for many purposes, and it was there that all the home life centered. With the exception of what was baked in the Dutch oven in the outer kitchen, the cooking was done before or in the cavernous fireplace, around which were hung warming pans, flat-irons, skillets, teapots, and other necessaries, while from the "chimbley's" capacious throat depended cranes, hooks, pots, trammels, and smokejacks. This was even before the time, in farmers' families, of tin roasting jacks; turkeys used to be suspended by twine before the fire and kept revolving, while the basting gravy dripped to a pan below. The domestic conveniences of that age did not include closets; household articles were distributed about the walls of this farm kitchen, hung on cop-stocks—wooden pegs driven into the beams of the low-studded ceiling. On the dresser were rows of polished pewter platters and vessels standing cheek by jowl with well-scoured wooden trenchers, while laid away on the shelves of the great walnut press were piles of the family's coarse linen. In the corner stood two small wooden mortars, in which were pounded and powdered the mustard and coffee; and on a convenient shelf were placed the lights for this world and the next—a round iron tinderbox with its attendant flint and steel, and the huge family Bible, its pages black with quaint German characters. Pewter and copper were the materials from which many of the drinking vessels and utensils were made, china and glass being in but little use. The precious metals were not common except among the very rich, although all well-to-do farmers carried a silver watch and snuffbox, the latter being in frequent requisition. Tobacco was smoked in pipes, of which Johannes had brought a good supply from the old country; cigars were unknown in the Old

Stone House; indeed, throughout the colonies in that century they were rarely seen outside of the large cities.

Much of the space of the chambers in this Bedminster dwelling was occupied by mammoth "four-posters," stuffed with thick feather beds that were covered by many-colored quilts and counterpanes of calico, durant, and calamanco—whatever the last two may have been. Testers of cloth and curtains of chintz hung from above, while valances of dimity reached to the floor. Much of the bedroom furniture was heavy, cumbersome, and homemade, red cedar being the favorite wood, as it was considered vermin-proof and indestructible. The upper rooms like the one below, then as now, were destitute of closets. People are not apt to feel the need of what they have never possessed; otherwise we might suppose that Mariah Katrina and her daughters were much inconvenienced for the want of closet room.

If you are curious to know in what kind of garments they were accustomed to array themselves, we may, in fancy, mount the oaken staircase to the garret and there behold the treasures of clothing, of which the women in the olden time had a great profusion. Hanging on pegs driven in the wall and depending from lines stretched from the eaves were shortgowns, overgowns, outer garments, and petticoats. The number of the last would now seem excessive, but Colonial women thought at least fifteen necessary, while the Germans and Dutch often had twice that number. They were generally of tow, flannel, and linsey-woolsey, and the young women of the household spent much of their girlhood in laying in a stock of petticoats for matronly uses. The shortgowns were of kersey, calamanco, and homespun, but the frocks and outer garments were made of gay fabrics, the names of some of which are now obsolete; beside satins, silks, and velvets, there were in use taffety, beaver, French tabby, millinet, moreen, groset, Holland linen, bombazine, and "boughten calico."

The men of that time, even in farming communities, were not insensible to the picturesqueness of variety and color in their garb. For daily wear buckskin, leather, homespun, and worsted fabrics were common, but on Sundays and on gala occasions prosperous yeomen were often clad in white, blue, and crimson broadcloth coats, with shortclothes of plush, stockinet, yellow nankin, and even velvet.

In the farm kitchen the meals were eaten, friends were entertained, and the spinning done; while just beyond the door, in the cellar on the same level, stood the clumsy loom upon which the women banged away at odd times in making linen cloths and woolen goods for the family clothing. Flax was to Johannes a most important crop; its treatment was largely within the province of the women of his household, from the pulling in the fields to the making, dressing, hatcheling, and spinning. This was before the days of cotton, and flax had many uses; in addition to being prepared for the loom, mats and cushions were made from the coarse "hock-tow," and the rope, or finer tow, was twisted by the hands into long strands of yarn, from which were manufactured the farm cords and ropes.

Delicate girls would seem to have had no place in the social economy of Colonial farm families. They must needs have had strong arms and stout hips to have been able to lug the big iron kettles or to have hung them on the great swinging crane of the yawning fireplace. Strength was also necessary to handle the large sticks of hickory that kept the pot a-boiling, or the vast oven heated to just the point necessary for properly browning the batches of rye and wheaten loaves, the big pan of beans, and the cakes, puddings, and thick pies. Washing-day must have been a sore affliction to the womenfolk of the Old Farm. When Monday came a roaring fire was built alongside the wash-house—on the side of the brook—over which was suspended an iron pot in which the clothes were boiled.

Washing machines and wringers were not known—and even their predecessors, the corrugated washboard and washtub, were unknown. The stream furnished a generous tub, and stout arms did the wringing. When the dirt and grime had been loosened by boiling, the coarse clothing was put in the pounding barrel and well thumped with a wooden pounder until the dirt was supposed to be eliminated. A rude washing machine—but it is said to have done effective service, though the fine fabrics of our day would find such rough handling rather severe; not only the dirt, but the texture would be eliminated.

The years roll on! All this time the three hundred and sixty-seven acres of wild lands are gradually developing into a fine farm. Changes, too, are taking place in the family in which we are so much interested. Aaron, the first born, has brought home a wife—Charlotte Miller. Their first child, John, was born on the thirty-first of July, 1758. To man Heaven gives its best gift in a good wife; and so was Aaron blessed in Charlotte. Though we are ignorant of her parentage, she was evidently the daughter of a good mother, for of such are the best wives made. For over forty years she added to the comfort and happiness of her husband and children, and lived in the Old Stone House the life of Solomon's virtuous woman, for "the heart of her husband safely trusted in her, and she did him good, and not evil, all her days."

There has not been preserved to us an account of Aaron's marriage. It is to be regretted, as in the olden time there were many quaint customs and observances attendant upon weddings. They were not confined to the ceremony; the occasion of bringing the wife home—called the infare—was one of great festivity, often prolonged for several days, the kinsfolk and neighbors being bidden from far and near. The laws regarding marriages were then exceedingly strict. It was necessary for the contracting parties to have the bans published three times, or else procure from the governor of the province a license, which would not be granted unless the bridegroom appeared in person before the chief magistrate accompanied by two prominent citizens. These latter were obliged to testify that they knew of no lawful obstacles to the marriage; and to give a bond that they would be answerable for any damages that might arise because of any previous promise of marriage having been made, or for any complaints against the contracting parties by their relatives, guardians, or masters. All of the above preliminaries having been complied with, the governor delivered the license upon the receipt of twenty-five shillings currency, which fees materially added to the amount of his annual income.

There were other peculiar marriage laws in the province. One relating to widows was particularly diverting. This was before the day of acts protecting the rights of a married woman. She could hold no property individually, and on the death of her husband had not legal ownership of her own wearing apparel unless bequeathed to her; otherwise the clothes on her back belonged to the estate of her husband. If that estate proved insolvent and the widow remarried, care had to be taken that the perplexities of her first husband's affairs did not attach to those of the second. To do this it was necessary for her to be married in nothing but her shift, the giving up of her clothes to the creditors of her deceased husband releasing her from further claims. After the ceremony she was at once arrayed in clothing presented by her new husband.

The procession of the generations has commenced. The Old Stone House is now a home in the truest sense, for its rooms have echoed to the cry of a baby; within its walls for the first time a mother has looked with eyes of love into those of her infant—the sweetest, tenderest, happiest look that can come from a woman. Johannes and Mariah now mount to a higher plane in the family circle.

Clothed in the honor and dignity of their advancing years, they sit on either side of the fireplace with their grandchildren at their knees. For the first little one did not remain king; others followed to claim their share of the household affections—Catherine, born the fifteenth of July, 1761, and Daniel, the writer's grandfather, born on the twenty-eighth of October, 1763. The house can now be said to be furnished; for it is Southey, I think, who declares that none can be called completely so until there is a kitten on the hearth and a child of at least three years playing about its chambers.

It is now many years since Johannes, his wife, and their little flock passed through the *Bach*-gate of the ancient town of Bendorf and turned their steps westward. He was still a young man then, but now his hair and that of his dame is thin and rapidly frosting. As he looks back there can be no call for regret at his having come to America. Surveying his comfortable homestead and contented household, he must appreciate how signally he has prospered. Successful in his pursuits, honored by his brethren of the church, and loved by his children, for what more could he have asked? Death has not crossed his threshold; his family is intact though not all together. Aaron, his prop and his stay, is to succeed him on the farm and in the tannery; Fanny is already the mother of several children. Another of the brood being old enough to fly, has taken wing and left the family nest, for Andrew, the second son, having found a wife, has made his way into what is now Warren County. The two other boys and the daughter Maria, though men and women grown, are still at home, contributing their share to the family toil and joy.

9

The Sober Evening of Life

AND NOW JOHANNES' days are on the wane. Their meridian has long since passed, and the short afternoon having merged into the sober evening of life, he is reaping the comforts and consolations resulting from the active and useful employments of youth and middle age. Like a traveler who at the close of day has reached a high hill whose summit is bathed in the hues of the setting sun, he is able to look back with satisfaction over the pleasant country that has been traversed. Our pilgrim has attained that quiet dreamy hour of life "between the lights" when his ripened years bring the tranquil enjoyments of repose and retrospection. He is relieved from labor by the children who have learned habits of industry by his example and who now repay him for many days of anxious and devoted care.

Sooner or later all things must pass away. The undaunted one—the messenger of death—inevitably draws near. Johannes must leave his lands, his well-built house, his orchards and his woods, and take up his abode beyond that mysterious shade—that dim spectral mist which curtains time from eternity. There came a day, when the year 1763 was hastening to its close, on which Johannes' hour was come. The mellow October weeks had gone—the Indian summer had passed—the goldenrod still stood thickly along the fences, but the many-colored asters

127

which alone remained in the old garden were sprinkling their petals over its lonely beds. It was on the sixteenth day of that gloomiest month of all the year, when the chill November rains were robbing the earth of its fruits and verdure and beating from the branches of the trees their russet leaves, that our German ancestor folded his hands and was laid at rest. Calm was his exit, for his end was peace. He was mourned in the Old Stone House, but he found a companion awaiting him, for his faithful old wife Mariah had died on the seventeenth of October— old no longer, for we may believe with Mohamet that old women never reach heaven—they all grow young on the journey.

Let us preserve the memory of these honest German people. In their dreamless sleep they have lain side by side under the long grass of the Lutheran burying ground at Pluckamin. Generations that followed in their footsteps have like them disappeared from the earth. But we, who yet linger amid scenes that were familiar to their eyes, may consider with gratitude and affection our indebtedness to these simple Rhine folk and their fellow pioneers. Their hands grew hard in making smooth paths on which we now walk with ease. Let their names be revered by their kindred and their honest hard-working lives noted and recorded. "They rest from their labors, and their works follow them." These simple-minded men and women—the forefathers and foremothers of Bedminster—found this township a wilderness. By their virtue and their intelligent industry they left it planted with churches, schools, and homesteads, and guarded by laws, social and legal, in which were laid the foundations of the happiness of future generations. Johannes is dead, and his first-born reigns in his stead. The father left behind him the name of a good man. He also left to succeed him a good son, well able to take up his work where it had been laid down, and quite equal to perform all the duties of life with the same honesty of purpose and simple earnestness of endeavor. With the progression of the story of the Old Farm there will be much to tell of the busy and useful life passed by Aaron on these ancestral acres and in the community before he ceased to labor, and at the rounded age of eighty-one made way in his turn for the worthy son who succeeded him.

Seedtime and harvest come and go! Springtime and autumn slip by! Meanwhile the country roundabout has undergone great changes. Latent forces that have been lying buried for aeons of time in these Bedminster hills and valleys, ready to respond to man's endeavor and desire, are now in active operation. The warm, palpitating sunlight heretofore arrested one hundred feet from the ground by the foliage of the rounded treetops now bathes with its genial heat broad open spaces here and there throughout the township, where children play in gardens and orchards, and the lusty corn tosses its yellow tresses over well-tilled fields. The rude dwellings of the early inhabitants have undergone prosperous transformations, and during the eleven years that the Old Stone House has been standing many industries have sprung into active existence. Across the brook a gristmill and sawmill are in operation, and homesteads begin to mosaic the hills that roll away toward Peapack. In the direction of Lamington, farms are multiplying; and on the Axtell tract human thrift has been busy, until patches of open and woodland alternate, and sunlight and shadow checker all that portion of the township.

Immediately adjoining the Old Farm on the south, Jacobus Van Doren purchased two hundred and eighty-three acres of land and erected a house. Jacobus was the eldest of seventeen children of Christian Van Doren and Alche Schenck, who settled on the Amwell Road in Middlebush about 1723. Christian was an elder in the First Dutch Reformed Church at New Brunswick, and Ralph Voorhees tells us in *Our Home* that it was his custom on Sunday mornings to ride to church, accompanied by his wife and ten children, all well mounted on separate horses. Methinks this cavalcade would serve a painter as an excellent subject for a Colonial picture; and that this peaceful Sabbath-day march for good-man Van Doren, with his household troop, would present a scene quite equaling in interest those of the cavalry that often seem just ready to step out of a canvas of De Taille or De Neuville.

The memory of Mrs. Christian (Alche) Van Doren is revered as that of one of Somerset's mothers in Israel. She was a constant attendant at church until her ninety-fifth year. When this remarkable old lady died she left three hundred and fifty-two living descendants, among whom were two hundred great-grandchildren and six great-great-grandchildren. The size of families in those early days would seem to have been commensurate with the needs of population. Of her children, all but one lived to an old age and raised families; and one of her grandchildren, following her grandparent's example, had seventeen children. The most of her twelve boys were called after the patriarchs, prophets, and apostles, nor would she ever permit their names to be shortened; there were no Jakes, Abes, Ikes, Petes, or Jacks in her household.

Previous to the year 1763, without doubt the most important addition to this Bedminster neighborhood was the organization of the congregation of the Dutch Reformed Church and the erection of its first church building. If not a majority, certainly a great number of the settlers of the township were of this religious persuasion and were connected with one of the Dutch congregations of the Raritan Valley. When the Presbyterians had erected their house of worship at Lamington, and the Lutherans had organized Zion and St. Paul's churches at New Germantown and Pluckamin, many as a matter of convenience joined those congregations, but most of the people still made their way southward each Sunday. The nearest houses of worship were the "Raritan Church" at

Van Veghten's Bridge and the "Church of North Branch" at the village of Readington. These two churches in the beginning of the century were "collegiate" along with the one at Three Mile Run, which before 1717 divided and erected churches at Six Mile Run and at New Brunswick.

These four congregations were without regular preaching; occasionally they would be visited by some missionary, when communion, baptism, and other religious rites would be administered. It is fair to presume that services of some kind alternated in the different churches conducted by the congregation's lay preachers or "fore-readers."

The four congregations, about the year 1717, joined in applying to the home church in Holland for a permanent pastor. Two years later Theodorus Jacobus Frelinghuysen was sent out to them. He did a great work in thoroughly establishing the Dutch church in Somerset. He is said to have been a ripe scholar in Latin, Greek, and his own language, and some students rank him among the Blairs, Tennents, Mathers, and other eminent clergymen of his age. Whitefield, Jonathan Edwards, and Gilbert Tennent have left on record their appreciation of the labors and unceasing diligence of this Dutch Calvinistic minister, whereby the "wilderness was converted into the garden of the Lord." Domine Frelinghuysen lived at Three Mile Run, just west of New Brunswick, on a farm of two hundred acres. Before his death his duties, which extended over three hundred square miles of territory, had been increased by the organization in 1727 of the congregation "op de Millstone." After Mr. Frelinghuysen's death, the congregations of New Brunswick and Six Mile Run withdrew from the others of the Raritan Valley. The remaining churches invited Mr. Frelinghuysen's second son, John, to become their pastor. He preached his first sermon in the Raritan Church in the summer of 1750 from the text, "Instead of thy fathers shall be thy children." He had just returned from Holland, where he had been to obtain from the classis of Amsterdam license to preach. He brought with him from the old country a wife, Dinah Van Bergh. During her long life of fifty-six years in Somerset it is said few ministers exercised more influence for good in that community than did—as she was afterwards known—the *"Jufvrouw* Hardenbergh."

A copy of John Frelinghuysen's call from three consistories is preserved among the archives of the Somerville Church; after stipulating that he should preach the word of God in the Dutch language, faithfully exercise discipline upon offending church members, and generally perform the duties of a servant of Christ, it goes on to say:

Now in order to be a little more definite, Your Reverence will be required to preach, alternating, in each of the aforementioned churches, and, when in health, twice on each Lord's Day, except in winter, and then only once, as the custom here is, and also upon the so-called Feast Days, as is customary in the Reformed Low Dutch Churches. Also, your Reverence will be required to take charge of the catechizing of the youth, of the visitations of families and of the sick, as time and opportunity permit.

To assure your Reverence that this is our sincere desire, we promise you, in the name of Your churches, besides all love and esteem which belongs to a faithful servant of Christ, to provide, first, for a yearly salary of one hundred and twenty-five pounds, current money at eight shillings an ounce. The half of which collected by the elders and the deacons, shall be paid each half year; and a suitable dwelling, with thirty acres of land.

The house referred to in the call was erected in 1721 and was constructed of bricks brought from Holland.

John Frelinghuysen's pastorate lasted but three years. While visiting relatives on Long Island he was taken alarmingly ill, and there died in September, 1754. Mrs. Frelinghuysen, who had accompanied him, returned home with the body of her husband in a boat so contracted and inconvenient that, as her biographer recounts, she was compelled, with a very great shock to her sensibilities, to step upon the coffin in passing to shore. The children of this marriage were a son and a daughter. The former—Frederick—grew up to be eloquent at the bar, wise in the councils of the nation, and valiant in Revolutionary fields. Of all the five sons of Theodorus Jacobus, John was the only one who left descendants.

At the time of this minister's death he had with him in his house of Holland bricks three young men as students. Among them was Jacob Rutsen Hardenbergh, then but sixteen years old, who was preparing for the ministry. Young Hardenbergh must early have evinced much talent and ability, as we find that John Frelinghuysen's congregations decided that as soon as ordained he should be their new minister. In the meantime Mr. Frelinghuysen's widow was determined, after her short residence in America, to return with her two children to her parents in Holland. Within a few months preparations for the journey were completed, and the day fixed for leaving for New York where she would embark.

Meanwhile, propinquity, that godfather of so many marriages, had been doing its work on the susceptible heart of the young divinity student. Alarmed at the prospect of the near departure of the object of his affections, he suddenly surprised the widow of less than a year with an offer of marriage. In her astonishment she is said to have cried out: "My child, what are you thinking about!" Although not immediately, the young lover ultimately had no difficulty in convincing her of just what he was thinking. The good Dutch lady could not withstand the temptation of a young and ardent husband, so her effects were unpacked and the voyage to the old country abandoned. They were married, and she retired to the manorial homestead of her new husband's father near Kingston, New York, where she awaited his majority and the completion of his studies. Hardenbergh was at this time not yet seventeen, while his wife was approaching thirty.

In May, 1758, Mr. and Mrs. Hardenbergh were again occupying John Frelinghuysen's brick house in Somerville, or as that whole section was then known, Raritan, and the young man of barely twenty-one had been installed as the pastor of the four united congregations of Raritan, North Branch, Millstone, and Neshanic. The ecclesiastical history of Somerset County will never be completely written without devoting many pages to the character and attainments of *Jufvrouw* Hardenbergh.

Her father was an Amsterdam merchant and a man of wealth and fashion. She was educated in a superior manner, and her tastes were cultivated to a high degree; but to her parent's great disappointment, at the early age of fourteen her religious impressions became so fixed as to cause her to find no pleasure in the allurements and amusements of the society of the metropolis. It is said that on one occasion, when forced by her father to attend a dancing school, she to his great anger hid behind the seats and resolutely refused to participate in what she considered a frivolous amusement. At another time— while she was yet a child—her parents were entertaining some friends, and the guests were amusing themselves by playing cards for money. She did not hesitate to walk into the drawing room and in severe tones solemnly warn her father and his friends against the danger of so vain and sinful a pleasure.

Every incident in the daily life of this remarkable woman produced a religious influence, and it would seem that no experience could be hers without resulting in an individual blessing. Throughout her life she had implicit confidence in special providences, and many instances are related in which she claimed to have experienced undoubted proofs of direct answer to prayer. It was her constant habit to make affairs of either great or minor importance a matter of personal appeal to the Almighty.

Once, when she was still living in Amsterdam, she was stricken with a fever in a friend's house and her life was despaired of. But on praying for recovery she informs us in her journal that an intimation was given her that on a certain date—the sixteenth of September—convalescence would begin. She told her friend, and awaited with confidence the day. It came, and though previously helpless, she arose and walked several times across the floor, and recovery was assured from that hour. The attendant physician, who was an unbeliever, had considered her death imminent; he was so affected by this sudden restoration to health that it resulted in his conversion. The good woman always insisted that this visit to her friend was heaven-directed in order that her miraculous healing might be the means of awakening the soul of this skeptical doctor.

Her coming to America and both of her marriages were due, as she believed, to a special providence. When young John Frelinghuysen was in Holland seeking ordination, he pleaded in vain for Dinah Van Bergh to return with him as his wife. Soon after setting out on his home voyage, his vessel was disabled in a violent storm and forced to return to port. The young minister renewed his suit, urging that the Ruler of Storms clearly indicated by the disaster and his consequent return that the Divine pleasure was for her to yield to his desires. This time Dinah received intimations, and overcoming her scruples against leaving kindred and native land, she braved the opposition of her parents and embarked for a wilderness beyond the seas as Mrs. Frelinghuysen.

The story is told that during the passage the ship sprung a leak. After days of arduous labor at the pumps the captain abandoned all hopes of saving the vessel, and so informed passengers and crew. Dinah apparently had no fears of a watery grave. She retired to her cabin and submitted the case to her Heavenly Father. Having full confidence in the efficacy of her prayers, she then sat down and awaited with composure the result. Nor did she wait long—for almost immediately the waters ceased rushing into the hold—the pumps again did their work—the ship was saved. Upon examination being made, it was found that a swordfish had miraculously become wedged in the open seam of the bottom of the vessel and thus effectually closed the leak. So it was in the affairs of her life.

The closing years of Mr. Hardenburgh's life were passed in the pastorate of the Dutch church at New Brunswick and in the presidency of Queen's, now Rutgers, College. At his death it was greatly desired that he should be succeeded by Doctor John L. Livingston of New York, who, however, declined at that time to change his field of labor. There has been preserved a letter written to him by *Jufvrouw* Hardenbergh, urging that he alter his decision and remove to New Jersey. This communication is a curious and interesting exhibit of the freedom and authority with which she addressed the eminent clergyman, for although she used the most elevated and respectful language, no bishop in admonishing and warning a recalcitrant priest could have been more authoritative in counsel and advice.

This excellent woman survived her second husband seventeen years, dying in 1807 at the ripe age of eighty-one. She was the first to occupy in the Dutch Reformed congregation of Bedminster the important position of minister's wife. About the time that young Domine Hardenbergh assumed charge of the united congregations many of his flock who lived north of Pluckamin, feeling in need of a church nearer home, urged the organization of a new congregation. The most prominent families in this movement were those of Jacobus Van der Veer and Guisbert Sutphen. When it was decided to build Bedminster Church, two acres of land were donated by Jacobus Van der Veer, who also furnished fifty pounds sterling and one-third of the oak timber. The same amount of money, together with one-half of the oak necessary for the frame, was the gift of Guisbert Sutphen. Not then, as now, were architects, contractors, carpenters, and masons called together to contribute their brains and labor toward the erection of the edifice. The members of the congregation assembled with ox teams, axes, and strong arms. By them were the oaks felled, the timbers squared and drawn to the spot selected; perhaps the services of some good mason was secured for laying the foundations, but without doubt much of the work was contributed by those most interested.

And we can well imagine with what interest these simple countryfolk watched the growth and assisted in the completion of their new house of worship. The church meant more to the early settlers than now—in those days religion was not a matter for Sunday's consideration alone—it stood first in everyone's estimation, taking precedence of all matters secular. Philosophy had not yet opened the eyes or befogged the minds of the honest Jersey people, and for one of their number to have been a doubter or in any way unorthodox would have insured not only the passive but active condemnation of every able-bodied man in the neighborhood. Nor was there at that time the carelessness and callousness as to spiritual things which the distresses and demoralization of Revolutionary years subsequently engendered. To a community, therefore, whose chief interests and hopes of life circulated about the church, we can readily appreciate that to have been without a house of God would seemingly have endangered not only its peace in the next world but the possibility of success in this. So it is easy to picture the rejoicing and prayers of thanksgiving when the last nail was driven and the finishing touches given to the new building.

When completed, a more bare or a more unimaginative structure could hardly have been conceived. Prosaic to a degree and entirely wanting in decorative details, it was wholly without architectural results save that it enclosed space and shut off the weather; in other words, it was a meetinghouse, nothing more. It was nearly square, being a little greater in breadth than in length. A peaked roof without cupola or belfry capped low walls, the side ones being each pierced with two square windows. The roof and exterior walls were similar in appearance, both being covered with shingles rounded at the ends that had been riven and shaved by members of the congregation. In fact all of this prim and precise building was "homemade," excepting the window glass and nails. The latter were probably wrought at Mendham. The Dodds and Axtells of that place used to manufacture iron in a primitive fashion from ore that was packed over from Dover in sacks on the backs of horses.

In the broad front gable of the new church was the entrance, the door of which opened directly on the ground without any porch or protecting portico. A single aisle extended to the steep staircase which led up into a lofty, round, box-like pulpit, perched on a tall pillar or column. The interior was not plastered, the walls and ceiling being lined with cedar, and a short gallery stretched across the south end of the auditorium. There were no stoves or any means of warming the building; old ladies during the winter months, in order to keep their feet warm, brought "to-meetin'" perforated wooden boxes containing an inner casing of iron filled with live coals. It was not until after the erection of the second church in 1818 that, in the face of much opposition, wood-burning stoves were introduced. Many of the good people thought that as God's grace had warmed both souls and bodies from the beginning it should do so till the end.

To the worshippers this plain, gaunt structure, destitute of paint outside or in and without comeliness of symmetry, appeared as a commodious temple. It is to be regretted that no record has been preserved of the first services held in this primitive church. We can without

138

difficulty, however, see in imagination the rude and naked interior peopled by a homely but happy congregation. We know that high up in the tall, undraped pulpit under a broad sounding board stood the young minister, while below him was the precentor, or lining-deacon, who lined out the good old Psalm tunes to the members of the flock, who were seated in great square pews, the middle-aged and old people with their faces toward the domine, the children opposite; while to the right and left sat the stalwart youths and modest maidens, who lent their ears to the sermon but like the lads and lasses of today's congregations, I doubt not, gave their glances to "eyes which spake again."

The Folly

THE PROCESSION of the seasons continues, and life on the Old Farm goes bravely on. No sooner has the ermine mantle of winter disappeared under the kindly influences of the soft south winds of spring before the crocuses cleave the still half-frozen earth. The pond and river, swelling in volume, burst their icy bounds, and the drear days brought by overcast heavens give place to sunnier skies and longer hours. The woods that have so long exposed their anatomy to the keen wintry blasts again show signs of awakening life; green can be discovered among the sassafras branches and yellow among the willows, while the maple buds redden sufficiently to give a warm hue to the entire tree. Leaf and blossom again take possession of the earth, clothing it with glory.

Soon the hillsides are marked by plow and harrow, and the seed falls in generous showers. The crocuses have long since had their day, and June roses illumine the newly planted dooryard. And now the haymakers have come and gone in the meadows, reapers are on the upland fields, and pyramids of golden sheaves adorn the landscape. Bees hum in the clover, the breath of all nature is sweet and redolent with wild thyme, mint, and fragrant aromatic herbage, while harvest apples in heaps of red and yellow lie under the trees in the orchard. Summer drifts into autumn. Pumpkins show their golden sides under the corn shocks, and the noise of the flail is abroad in the land. The world begins to glow in color as the October sun paints in deepening crimson and ocher leaf and herb and lichen. The distant hilltops now blend with the heavens, and a golden shade diffuses itself over the face of the country. In the mornings amber-colored mists hang lightly over the lowland pastures, and the landscape is veiled in the vague, yellow indistinctness of Indian summer days. The brown acorns drop from their browner cups; the walnuts and chestnuts rattle through the branches upon the heads of expectant urchins who welcome below the toothsome hail. Again the paths through the woods are deep in the dry mummies of summer's luxuriance; the gusty winds blow over fields that, having lost their bloom, lie brown and dusky on the long hill that stretches westward toward the gray horizon. Once more the feathery flakes descend, covering the ground with whiteness and silence.

Not only were the lands improved, the outbuildings increased in number, and fences made more substantial, but under Aaron's care the tannery below the hill developed into one of the most important industries of that character in the province. A large frame structure was erected adjoining the house, in which the leather was curried, both Negroes and whites aiding in the work and that of grinding the bark. The number of vats below the dam was increased to eighteen and the water power much improved. This latter was done in connection with the joint owners of the water rights on the opposite side of Peapack Brook, who utilized their portion in grinding grist and sawing lumber. The exact date of establishing a flouring-mill at this point has not been ascertained, but it is well known to have been the first mill in the township.

The owners had not been milling many years before they discovered that Peapack Brook did not at all times contain sufficient water to supply the races that turned three mill wheels. They consequently conceived the idea of increasing the volume by diverting water from the North Branch of the Raritan. For the benefit of those unfamiliar with the locality, it would be well to explain that Peapack Brook, about a quarter of a mile above its mouth, runs for a considerable way parallel with and some three hundred feet distant from the Branch. These streams are separated by a long narrow hill known as the "Hogback." The highway climbed this ridge and ran along its spine. At this point a dam was built which, checking the flow of the Branch, created a reservoir. The hill was then tunnelled, forming an aqueduct six feet high and three feet broad; it being constructed on an incline, a considerable quantity of additional water was led through it into the smaller stream, thus greatly augmenting the powers of the latter stream in serving the mills near its mouth. With the strange fatality that often attaches to local nomenclature in rural communities this undertaking has always been known as the "Folly." It may have been that the results were not considered commensurate with the outlay. At any rate, before completion of the work the owners of the mill became financially embarrassed and were forced to sell their property in 1766.

This watery basin and its mysterious outlet have always possessed peculiar fascinations for Bedminster boys. It was their rendezvous in my early days for miles around. In January its flanking hill shut off the north winds, securing a sheltered skating pond of smooth firm ice. Travelers by the old highway over the "Hogback" on winter Saturdays were sure to hear the ring of the skaters' steel, and to be greeted by their joyous shouts as they "ground the bar," cut the intricate "pigeon wing," or mastered the "outside edge"—feats of no little difficulty on the old-fashioned, clumsy, gutter-runnered skates. In August the same hill guarded a cool, shady pool, which fairly invited a plunge into its pellucid depths. At no place along the Branch did catfish, dace, or shiners congregate in greater numbers, or appear more willing to be enticed to the surface by the rude tackle of the country lads. And then there was the "Folly"! Was there ever a more weird or forbidding spot upon which the imagination of a stripling could feed? What horrors might not lurk within its grim and silent portals? To explore its interior and brave its ambushed uncertainties was the one supreme test of youthful valor.

Where is the small boy that could ever withstand being "double-dared"? Not the writer, at least, in his callow years. It was this goad that incited him one summer's day of long ago to penetrate the "Hogback" through the dread "Folly." Certain it is that Dante could not have felt more dismayed on reading "All hope abandon, ye who enter in" than did he when girt for the journey. With him there was no encouraging Virgil, as pushing aside the vines that partially hid the low entrance to the tunnel, he boldly groped his way into the very bowels of the earth. Altogether it was a solemn place for a small boy to find himself in. The walls were moist and slimy, and as the waters flowed in a swift current about his naked ankles, imagination peopled them with eels, snakes, and all manner of creeping things; with every step on the rocky bed, squirming creatures seemed to escape from beneath halting feet. On nearing the center of the dark and gloomy conduit daylight gradually disappeared, and courage began to ooze away. Suddenly a jagged dripping wall opposed further advance. The aqueduct having apparently come to a sudden end, for a moment terror paralyzed all efforts at progress, but discovery was soon made that it turned sharply to the left. Its construction had been simultaneously undertaken from both sides of the hill; through miscalculation the workmen had failed to meet in the center, rendering a double elbow in the tunnel necessary. Feeling his way around these corners, the urchin could discern the glimmer of sunlight from the

143

farther end, lightening his heart as well as lighting the ghostly recesses of the archway. Pressing on with increasing confidence and more hurried steps, he soon made egress into daylight on the Peapack Brook side of the hill, where his companions received him with open arms and great honor. For many days thereafter your narrator was the hero of the small-boy society of that neighborhood.

But let us return to the mills, a direction in which your scribe's steps have always turned with eager anticipation. Even now, when the halfway house of the ordinary span of life has been passed, he never approaches this sequestered vale and feels the warm breath of summer, cooled by the balm that rises from its rapid streams, without his heart pounding with delight. Descartes writes that a person should not seek to gratify his desires so much as to endeavor to restrain them; notwithstanding such excellent advice, and though remembering that what may give pleasure in the writing may not prove equally agreeable in the reading, I cannot refrain from further youthful reminiscence. I must tell of these mills and of their attractive surroundings.

Is there any picture more completely to a boy's fancy than an old mill with its alluring adjuncts of pond and dam and rock-paved stream? Or for that matter, to a man's fancy, if, as I suspect is the case with many of us, a good boy has been spoiled in the man's making? Just such a picture can be seen in the entourage of what is now known as Schomp's Mills, which are seated in the deep valley where the descending acres of the Old Farm end. In attempting the description of simple scenes made beautiful by early associations, one finds it difficult to convey impressions, the birth of which is largely due to the deep sympathies of well-remembered youthful pleasures. Were my pen unchecked it would run riot with adjective and exclamation; while this might be sufficient for the needs of my expression, it would not go far toward conveying to others an idea of this old water power and its pleasant surroundings. Let us suppose then that all effort at description is abandoned, and leaving the old homestead, together we will visit the mill below the hill. You can see for yourself what it is like—but remember! I shall look at it with boyish eyes—be sure that you do the same.

Passing through a decrepit wicket at the lower end of the garden, a little path, worn smooth by over a century of footfalls and winding down the side of the hill, leads to the brook below the pond. Time was when its bordering strip of meadow was pierced with vats. Memories shoulder each other just here, and the ground seems to exhale ancient odors which, borne over the years of time, fashion in the mind a picture that includes an antique bark mill with its complaining wheel, great heaps of tan, long lines of drying hides, and piles of sacks of freshly ground oak bark. Recollection paints, too, a scene in which your guide figures in the foreground as a truant toddler, staggering with the delight of forbidden joys among the tan vats, while in the middle distance is the view of a nursery maid, with fluttering skirts and a nimbus of dishevelled hair, flying down the hill with warning cries to rescue the youngster from a possible immersion in the acid baths.

But enough of youthful remembrances. Here, facing us, is the Peapack Brook. Is it not an inviting waterway? Interspersed with grassy islands and arched by venerable trees, it is fed by the curving waters falling in rhythmic melody from the dam, and on the hottest of summer days the air is fresh and cool with the fragrant breath of the descending flood. Crossing the stream by springing from mossy stone to slippery boulder—you must not mind wetting your feet—we are soon in front of the mill. It is much like many others planted along the numerous watercourses that swell the flood of the Raritan River. A succession of lofty doors rise one above the other to the apex of the gable, in one of which generally stands the

145

dusty miller, drawing in fat bags of grist from the overhanging tackle or guiding descending sacks of flour to the
farmers' teams below. The great water-soaked overshot
wheel, which in my boyish days creaked and groaned on
its ponderous dripping revolutions, is no longer here. Its
work is now less picturesquely but more powerfully and
silently done by two insignificant turbines, sunk deep in
the rapid current of the race.

On entering, our nostrils are tickled by the floating
particles of the floury atmosphere, and the building trem-
bles with the rumbling of turning shafts and swiftly moving gear. Passing between bins of grain and barrels tiered
ceiling high, we ascend to the grinding floor, which is
almost on a level with the pond. The interior of the building is yellow with the deposits of years of gently descending mealy showers that have long since hidden the
original color of its beams and joists, while the burring
sound of the grinding stones falling upon the ear is one
of the pleasantest of all the busy hums of human industry.
The western gable—resting on piles—rises directly from
the pond; its image reflected in the tranquil water has
much of the completeness of the mill itself. Often on a
summer's afternoon have I from its rear door cast the
baited hook, and, if not rewarded by a nibble, have been
more than content in idly watching the sleepy bosom of
the pond mirror the fleecy clouds floating in the blue
expanse above. On such occasions the rural sights and
sounds seen and heard on every side were always a
source of delight. Stretched on a soft pile of bags, dream-
ing away a few summer hours in lazily watching the
floating cork swirl in the eddies and in drinking in the
moisture-laden atmosphere of the watery landscape
seemed ever a happy occupation and never a loss of time.

On the right are rich fields of grass and grain, and
between them and the water on the gently ascending
incline of the bank rests a group of farm buildings. They
almost surround an ample barnyard, from which come

the pleasant country sounds of lowing cattle and bleating sheep, while awkward ducklings noisily quack as they waddle down to their convenient element. To the left is a little sawmill—not much more than a timbered skeleton —through whose ribs you see flashing the upright saw, jagging with hoarse cry its hungry teeth into the slowly approaching logs. Beyond is the great floodgate, with little gurgling rills percolating through its seams and fissures; it is framed with massive, slimy beams, from which the frequent small boy of the neighborhood spends many a happy hour in endeavoring to beguile the wary catfish from the cool depths. The stone dam with its liquid curtain extends from the gate to the farther shore which, with a graceful curve, lies in the deep shadows of a steep bank of bordering trees, whose drooping branches pressing outward overhang the peaceful pool—Narcissus-like, in rapt admiration of their own mirrored beauty. At the head of the pond the waters shallow, and from their meager depths rise bullrushes and reedy weeds, which finally overgrow the surface and harden into low banks of bog and sedge through which the supplying brook slowly makes its way.

Thinking over the long ago, arresting memory brings to mind many interesting spots in the vicinity of this old mill that are associated with youthful experiences. I have one now in my thoughts—a famous swimming place called the "Jinny Hole." It is not far from the head of the pond; the brook suddenly deepens, and its almost perpendicular sides admit of one's diving in safety from the sedgy banks. It must be confessed that ambitious plungers, who in the heyday of my remembrance sank too deep beneath the wave, found plenty of soft mud lying in wait at the bottom; and clambering out on the low banks was always a miry business. But there were compensations, not the least being the interest that attached to the tales that were apt to be told while dressing of the individual from whom the hole derived its name

—Miss Jane Bailey, a simple maiden of complex attainments, who, like Betty Flanigan, could recollect her "frinds for a month" and her "inimies for a year." Jinny has since gone over to the "silent majority," which has also absorbed most of her "frinds" and "inimies," but fifty years ago she was a noted character along the Peapack Brook.

James Bailey and his wife Peggy were Irish Presbyterians, who came to this country about 1790 and settled on forty acres of land adjoining the Old Farm at the head of the millpond. They both died before 1810, leaving two daughters, Jinny and Peggy, who continued living on the property. Jinny did all the farm work, plowing, planting, sowing, and reaping, without calling in the aid of any of the neighbors. Peggy died in 1831, after which Jinny lived alone until her death in 1836. She is remembered as a short spare woman, bent nearly double with rheumatism; her face, the color of parchment, was furrowed and wrinkled by age, while coarse, white, uncombed hair covered her head and hung down to her shoulder. Her dress was always the same, a blue, linsey, home-woven short-gown and petticoat, with a tow string tied around her waist and a man's straw hat on her head; she always walked with a cane much taller than herself.

Jinny's appearance was in accord with her character; she believed in witches, ghosts, dreams, signs, and sounds, and among the ignorant people of the vicinity had a most uncanny reputation. She was Irish to her crooked backbone, but though superstitious, was always ready to fight the Church of Rome from the lowest-down Catholic up to the Pope. As a red rag is to an infuriated bull, so was the mention of the "Scarlet Woman" within Jinny's hearing. It was only necessary for predatory bands of boy-tormenters to hint that all Irish men and women were papists to cause her tawny face to flame with passion and to call out her richest vocabulary of vituperation. At such times she looked a veritable Witch of Endor. Waving

148

her shrivelled arms and shaking her hoary locks in anger, she shrieked contumely upon the heads of her tormentors and upon those of every Catholic that ever lived, while her haggard eyes flashed with all the rage and hate of a Meg Merrilles when cursing the enemies of the heir of Ellangowan. I am afraid that these pages are Jinny's only monumental stone; there is none to mark the grave in Lamington churchyard where she lies buried. Her only relics are among my papers. One is the inventory made after her death of her personal effects, which consisted mainly of spinning-wheels, thatching forks, a hatchel, a flax breaker, a calabash, and a few farming implements. Another is Jinny's note of hand given in 1812 to Daniel Melick for two dollars, which notwithstanding her anti-Catholicism, she signed with a cross large enough to suggest the possibility of its having been made with the end of her long staff.

There is another spot about this old mill that has an especial charm of its own. It is reached by following the stream a short distance to where the highway crosses by a dusty wooden bridge, the center abutments of which rest upon an elongated island that splits the rapid current of the brook. Dropping from the bridge you may make your way down this green island to where the divided waters join. Seat yourself, now, on this mossy bank under the shadowy concealments of these low-spreading branches; you will find that you have penetrated deep into the heart of rural loveliness. Do you not think it a cozy nook? Although the clear waters of the rapidly flowing stream babble at your feet, the green canopy above is astir with twittering birds, and the soft wind comes laden with the faint cadences of the splash of the dam's cascade, yet such an air of repose broods over the spot that you feel the environment of an atmosphere of intense quiet until you imagine yourself secluded from the world, as if you had found your way to a place of rare beauty hitherto undiscovered. What a bower in which to drowse away an afternoon with Thoreau or John Burroughs! Or, should you have no book, just to lie supinely in the long grass, inhaling the woodsy-watery odors—the subtle emanations of earth, trees, and stream —till your entire being seems permeated with the very essence of the hidden secrets of nature.

After all, the picture we have attempted to draw is not wholly true. It is of the aspect of the brook in the past rather than of the present. What a disappointment on revisiting familiar boyish scenes to find that they differ from the picture one's memory has carried through the years! That hills grow smaller may be charged to the lengthened leverage of adult legs, but the decrease in the volume of the waterways can be more directly explained. As we meet the streams of our childhood, ranging through wood and meadow, they bear an altered face. Like us they have changed with the years. While it is to be hoped that we with advancing age have grown deeper and broader—not so with the rivers. The vandal hands that robbed the timbered hillsides that guarded their sources were at the same time shallowing their pools and bringing the impeding stones of their beds much nearer the surface. Now, in foamy agitation, they protest with loud voice against the loss of their former torrents.

The procession of the seasons continues, and life on the Old Farm goes bravely on! As the years have rolled away, many changes are to be noted among the occupants of the Old Stone House. Three more children have come to Aaron and his wife: Elizabeth, born on the eighth of November, 1765; Margaret, on the twenty-second of December, 1767; and Maria, on the twenty-fourth of March, 1771. Not only new lives entered into the family, a little grave is to be seen by the side of those of the grandparents in the Lutheran burying-ground at Pluckamin, for death for the third time has knocked at the door and claimed his own. Elizabeth, one unhappy

May morning before she was three years old, while playing about the bark mill fell under its great revolving wheel and was so crushed that within eight days, on the fourteenth of May, 1768, she died. Aaron and his family, together with his dependents, are now (1775) the sole occupants of the Old Stone House, his brothers and sisters having married and made their homes elsewhere.

Mutterings of the Coming Storm

IT REQUIRES no special sagacity to discover that the embarrassments peculiar to a work of this character are many. The writer often finds himself encompassed by a mass of material from which to choose subjects for his pages, ranging from the merest social and personal trifles up to those important political events that now begin to crowd the stage upon which his actors are distributed. The difficulties of selection are great, and he is forced to contend against the temptation of choosing those pleasing trifles that will embellish the pages, rather than to dwell on more momentous affairs which would give added weight and value to the narration.

Yet, who shall say what is important—which of the trifles or traditions have value or should be preserved. The warp and woof of local history are often made up of little motes that the sunbeams of research discover floating in the dusty and indistinct atmosphere of antiquity. Placed on the loom by the weaver of history, they soon fashion themselves into an interesting web, and in conjunction with other facts and theories gradually form a fabric that bears on its texture in the vivid colors of the present a picture of circumstances and events that fitly and beautifully illustrate a past age. But just here there is no need of hesitating as to the choice of trifles.

Important events elbow themselves forward and assert recognition.

We have now reached a time when the mutterings of the coming storm could plainly be heard as an angry hum of distrust and resentment. The colonists were rapidly losing their loyalty to and affection for the mother country. The people of the different provinces seemed of one mind; without concerted action and almost without correspondence they held informal meetings, and formed self-constituted committees for the purpose of obtaining intelligence and of advising with the inhabitants of other colonies as to what means should be employed to prevent further encroachments on the vested rights and liberties of the King's subjects in America.

In New Jersey a general Committee of Correspondence had been appointed by the Provincial Assembly in February, 1774, composed of nine members. Their duties at first seem to have been confined to corresponding and consulting with prominent citizens of the different counties in order to insure a unanimity of sentiment and action when the time should come for the people to assert their individual and collective rights. The committee met on the first of June in New Brunswick, when by letter to the people in Massachusetts they pledged the citizens of New Jersey to act in concert with the other colonies in whatever steps should be generally agreed upon. They also called upon Governor William Franklin to convene the Provincial Assembly before the first of August. This the executive declined to do, giving as a reason, "There is no public business of the province which can make such a meeting necessary."

During the months of June and July a series of meetings were held in the several counties of New Jersey for the purpose of organizing for defence, and for choosing deputies to represent the province in a Continental Congress, which had been called to meet in the following

153

September. The resolutions passed at the different meetings were much of the same character. They bound the citizens to act in conjunction with those of other counties in any measures that might be decided upon insuring the happiness and safety of the people. They were unanimous in expressing the sentiment that the sufferings and injustice visited upon the people of Boston by Great Britain should be a common cause of grievance for the inhabitants of the entire continent, and that the rights and privileges of America should be protected, even though necessitating the adoption of the most severe and extreme measures. Permanent Committees of Correspondence were appointed.

At two o'clock on the morning of the twenty-fourth of April, 1775, the Middlesex Committee of Correspondence received at New Brunswick a dispatch from the New York Committee announcing that the Battle of Lexington had occurred on the nineteenth. The committee endorsed this message, and the express-rider flew on to Princeton, thence to Trenton, and on to Philadelphia, reaching there at nine A.M. on the twenty-fifth, having been one hour less than six days in coming from Watertown, Massachusetts, including stops at all the principal places on the way. The country was, of course, in a blaze of excitement. It was now no longer the mutterings but the storm itself that the people of New Jersey were forced to face. For months the black clouds of strife and dissension had been slowly and surely rolling on, enshrouding the land in gloom and apprehension; now the citizens awoke to the realization that civil war with its attendant horrors was to be the heritage of their generation. The general Committee of Correspondence was at once convened. It directed the chairman to call a Provincial Congress which met at Trenton on the twenty-third of May.

This Congress, recognizing the impending conflict, proceeded to put the colony on a war footing by passing

a militia bill which boldly declared it to be "highly necessary that the inhabitants of the Province be forthwith
properly armed and disciplined for defending the cause
of American Freedom." An ordinance was also passed
laying a war tax of ten thousand pounds, proclamation
money, of which Somerset's proportion was about nine
hundred pounds. Other provinces, and the Second Continental Congress then in session, were notified of the
steps taken in New Jersey.

While the people in all parts of New Jersey were
quick to respond to the recommendations of Congress
that they should arm and discipline themselves for defense, it would seem that Somerset County took the lead
in putting muskets in the hands of its citizens. The
Pennsylvania Packet of the twelfth of June states:

The martial spirit which prevails among the inhabitants
of Somerset County, in New Jersey, truly merits the attention
of the public. We have certain intelligence that they are
forming themselves into companies, and daily exercising, to
become complete masters of the military discipline; and particularly, that the township of Bridgewater, in said county,
met at Raritan, the sixth instant, and chose Mr. Abraham
Ten Eyck, captain, under whose command eighty-five volunteers immediately enlisted, to be in readiness at an hour's
warning, to march for the assistance of any neighboring colony, on any emergency. Their pay and other necessaries are
provided by said township. The other counties and townships, it is hoped, will follow their example, as it may be
necessary to repel force by force, in order to secure our
national rights and privileges.

Bedminster did not need the example of Bridgewater
to fan the flame of patriotism, for its men had already
taken the initiative and were arming for the fray. They
had even anticipated the action of the Provincial Congress
of the twenty-third of May, as is shown by the following
minute made at a meeting of its Committee of Observation and Inspection held on the eighteenth of May: "Bor-
rowed from John Wortman in cash £2.0s.0d. to Gow

to new york to Buy arms [three words blurred] Stephen Hunt chosen to go to new york to Buy the arms." At another meeting, "when the Committee met to Rase men," the minutes show that it was agreed "that the Captain shall have one Dollar per Day to treat his men when he trains his men that once a wick."

Among the many duties of the Committee of Observation and Inspection, not the least arduous one was that of securing guns, powder, and ball. As early as in October, 1774, the British ministry instructed all the royal governors to seize whatever arms and ammunition might be imported into their provinces. Munitions of war were consequently scarce; after the supplies of the cities of New York and Philadelphia were exhausted, it became necessary for the members of the Committee to ransack the country and purchase of farmers, mechanics, and others old muskets, shotguns, and firelocks of every description. Those out of order were sent to be made serviceable to the gunsmiths. The raw material for bullets was more easily obtained, although the people were forced to make many personal sacrifices in order to comply with the requirements of the hour. The Provincial Congress had directed the township Committees "to collect all the leaden weights from windows and clocks; all leaden weights of shops, stores, and mills, of one pound weight and upwards; also all the lead in and about houses and other places." Commissioners were appointed to receive the same from the committees, paying therefor sixpence per pound proclamation money together with expenses. Bedminster was soon denuded of what had suddenly grown to be considered a precious metal, many of the families even cheerfully sacrificing their pewter dishes and platters, which were much valued by Colonial housewives.

The most important of New Jersey's Provincial Congresses, and the final one for the year 1775, opened on the third of October and continued for twenty-two days.

Its members had been elected by the people, the previous bodies having been provisional in character, the delegates emanating from the choice of informal county meetings or conventions. The amount of business transacted at this session was very great. The whole colony was in a state of intense agitation, and excitement ruled the hour. It was a time of civil discord, when neighbor feared neighbor and friend suspected friend. Disputes and difficulties between the people were rife, culminating in all manner of charges and complaints which were poured in upon Congress in the shape of accusations, petitions, and appeals. Communications from township and county committees had to be received and deliberated upon, charges against Loyalists investigated, and many complaints of personal grievances considered.

All this time the Second Continental Congress was in session and in constant communication with the Congresses and Committees of the several provinces. The second of July was the day on which was broken the last political link binding the colonies and the mother country. A committee was at once appointed to draft a declaration of reasons justifying this all-important step taken by the delegates. Two days later, on the morning of the fourth, Thomas Jefferson as chairman of the committee presented to the Continental Congress the Declaration of Independence. Among the illustrious men who listened to the reading of this document there is one figure that stands sharply defined on the canvas which portrays the scene of the crowning act of this historic body. It is that of John Witherspoon, a distinguished representative from New Jersey, whose patriotism and foresight at a crucial moment is believed to have powerfully promoted the prompt acceptance of the Declaration of Independence.

After Jefferson had finished the reading of this paper, the members of Congress were appalled by the solemnity of the occasion and by the apparent realization for the first time of the portent of the document. The knowledge seemed suddenly forced upon them of what its adoption must entail upon the country. It meant a continuation of the war and all the miseries that would necessarily follow a prolonged civil conflict. Should the American arms not prevail, complete subjection of the entire people must follow, and for the signers and promulgators of this incendiary and rebellious instrument naught could be expected but an ignominious death. Through the halls of Congress an intense silence prevailed. It was a critical moment. When the painful hush should be broken the temper of the first speaker might decide the weal or woe of the people. As has been said by a witness: "The very destiny of the country seemed to be suspended upon the action of a moment."

Suddenly a stalwart form arose—that of a man full of years, his hair whitened by the snows of many winters. "There is," said he, "a tide in the affairs of man, a nick of time; we perceive it now before us. The noble instrument upon your table, which insures immortality to its author, should be subscribed this very morning by every pen in the house. He who will not respond to its accents, and strain every nerve to carry into effect its provisions, is unworthy the name of a freeman. Although these gray hairs must descend into the sepulchre, I would infinitely rather they should descend thither by the hand of the public executioner than desert, at this time, the sacred cause of my country." The speaker sat down, and a great sigh of relief and murmur of approval went up from his listeners. In the debates which followed, the speeches of the members displayed much of the spirit of firmness that had characterized the timely appeal of this excellent man, resulting finally in the adoption of the document which secured the independence of the thirteen states.

John Witherspoon was a Scotch divine who in 1768 had been called to the presidency of the College of New Jersey and to the pastorate of the Presbyterian Church in

Princeton. This was not his first appearance in the arena of rebellion. When the Highlanders flocked to the royal standard unfurled by the young Pretender in the north of Scotland, Witherspoon, though the pastor of a parish, raised a corps of militia and marched to his support. The young parson-soldier's enthusiasm carried him into the battle of Falkirk, where he was taken prisoner; he lay captive in the castle of Donne until after Culloden. In America he proved a patriot of great influence in the councils of the nation and served the state in Congress with honor and ability.

It must be remembered that until early in 1776 the semblance of royal government continued to exist in New Jersey. Up to the fourth of July all official documents and proclamations ended with the phrase, "God save the King." All this time, with the exception of that grand old "Rebel Governor," Jonathan Trumbull of Connecticut, there was not in all the thirteen colonies a chief magistrate but that was strongly prejudiced in favor of British interests and zealous to check the uprising of the people. Governor William Franklin occupied the proprietors' house at Perth Amboy. His duties mainly consisted in keeping his government advised as to the treasonable acts of the citizens.

On Monday, the tenth of June, the most important of all New Jersey's Provincial Congresses met at Burlington. This Congress enacted all laws for a time in the name of the colony, but, having on the second of July adopted a state constitution, on the eighteenth of the same month it assumed the title of the "Convention of the State of New Jersey," thus giving birth to a free and independent commonwealth. Another act of this body distinguishing it above all preceding Congresses was the deposition of the Royal Governor.

There is no doubt that the greater part of Governor Franklin's administration was much to the advantage of the colony, as he fostered and encouraged many enterprises that promoted its prosperity. Could the people of New Jersey forget his subsequent conduct as a vindictive Loyalist, they would be better able to look back upon his government with respect, and appreciate that for much of the time during his long administration he displayed a commendable desire for the welfare of the province. Such without doubt is his record, and we may even accord him sincerity of opinion and purpose in identifying himself with those who were endeavoring to sacrifice the liberties of the country. But with the dissensions that arose between the executive and the citizens he is said to have become petulant and unwise. As the people grew to be alert in regard to every question touching their rights, his arrogance increased, and he rapidly became destitute of prudence and self-control.

As has been said, the Governor was a son of Benjamin Franklin—a natural son, whose mother is not known. He was taken home by Benjamin Franklin and reared and educated as though born in wedlock. The New Jersey people, who well knew of this bar sinister on the Franklin escutcheon, were much chagrined on learning in 1762 who was to be their new Governor. William Franklin, just after being appointed Governor of New Jersey, was married in St. George's Church, Hanover Square, London. Strange as the coincidence may be, he too had an illegitimate son, born two years before. As his father had done, so did he; naming the child William Temple Franklin, he took him home to his bride, and the boy was reared with as much solicitude as if the offspring of marriage.

Benjamin Franklin grieved much over the failure of his son to espouse the cause of the colonists. He wrote "that nothing had ever affected him with such keen sensitiveness as to find himself deserted in his old age by his only son; and not only deserted, but to find him taking up arms against him in a cause wherein his good fame, fortune, and life were at stake." The grandson was a warm adherent of the Americans, and, deserting his father, allied his fortunes to those of his grandfather, with whom he remained associated until his death.

The prestige and patriotism of the Governor's father caused the people to judge leniently of the attitude the son assumed toward the cause so dear to the popular heart; this, too, at a time when Loyalists were looked upon with extreme disfavor. But, as the months rolled on, his pronounced acts in support of the British ministry were too great for the forbearance of the people in their newly born sovereign capacity. An intercepted dispatch in January, 1776, had led to Lord Stirling's placing him under arrest and on parole. For some months he continued to occupy the gubernatorial residence at Perth Amboy and to nominally direct the affairs of the province; but when he called upon the old Assembly to meet on the twentieth of June, the Provincial Congress declared this to be in direct contempt of the orders of the Continental Congress. On the fifteenth of June, William Livingston, John Witherspoon, William Paterson, and John Mehelm were appointed a committee to cause the arrest of the Governor and to depose him from office.

The Governor was brought before the Provincial Congress under guard. He treated that body with great indignity, did not hesitate to charge its members with being low-bred men who deserved to be hanged as rebels, and declared them to be without sufficient education for the devising or carrying out of plans for the public weal. When he had finished his violent tirade, Doctor Witherspoon sprang to his feet and fixing his keen eyes upon the King's representative poured on him a copious stream of irony, delivering a "rebuke so withering as to cause the boldest to hold his breath with astonishment." In concluding, after referring to Franklin's illegitimacy, he said: "On the whole, Mr. President, I think that the governor has made us a speech every way worthy of his exalted birth and refined education."

Acting under the advice of Washington it was decided

by Congress to transfer the deposed executive to the keeping of Governor Trumbull of Connecticut, whereupon Franklin was confined in a house in East Windsor. Here he remained a prisoner for two years; upon being exchanged, he established himself in New York, which continued to be his home until 1782, when he returned to England. To cover his losses the British government allowed him the sum of eighteen hundred pounds and an annual pension of eight hundred pounds. William Livingston was appointed governor in his stead, a position which he ably filled.

William Paterson, who was New Jersey's second governor, has always been considered one of the great men of that time. He, too, displayed the most intelligent devotion to many public trusts in state and country; he represented New Jersey in the Senate of the nation, and died in 1806 as judge of the Supreme Court of the United States. His residence was an antiquated stone mansion on a plantation known as the Paterson Farm, lying two miles south of Somerville on the Raritan River. Here, as the guest of Judge Paterson, Aaron Burr spent much of his time while an undergraduate at Princeton, and here he prepared for admission to the bar. As to William Livingston, his sound judgment in counsel and his coolness and courage in action and execution brought inestimable benefits upon the country, and his services in the cause of freedom take rank with those of Washington, Hancock, and Adams.

It is necessary to consider the condition of the country in the spring of 1776. At that time it was truly but the beginning of things for the United States of America. In what is now the center of population, buffaloes browsed in herds and wild deer had naught to fear from the crack of the woodsman's rifle. Even the valleys through which the Mohawk and Genesee flow were almost destitute of white population, and those regions were still the hunting and fishing grounds of the painted warriors of the dreaded

Six Nations of the North. Great cities, the pulsations of whose markets are today noted in the moneyed centers of all Europe, were not yet conceived, and their sites were solitudes of wildernesses.

Eastern and Middle Pennsylvania lay quiet in the shade of a vast and somber forest; Pittsburgh, a mere collection of log cabins, was just becoming known as a point where emigrants built their keel-boats and launched themselves and their fortunes on the waters of the Ohio. Plainfield and Elizabeth were then, respectively, but a hamlet and a small village; while Somerville was not to have an existence for yet a quarter of a century. Newark in 1777 contained but one hundred and forty-one houses, and at no time during the war did it exceed one thousand in population. New Brunswick claimed about the same number. A round cupola capping a square wooden church-tower rising above a few clustering houses was all that marked Brooklyn. Paulus Hook was represented by a ferry-tavern and a few scattering dwellings; it was not till 1820 that it was rebaptised as Jersey City, and even then had but three hundred residents. Only about one-quarter of the lands of East Jersey had been located, and the inhabitants of the entire state numbered less than one hundred and fifty thousand. In the entire country there were but twenty-eight postoffices; as late as 1791 New Jersey possessed but six, and at that time Somerset County appears to have had none.

12

John Malick—Soldier

AND NOW WE FIND the men of Somerset prepared to do their part toward manning the new ship of state, which is at last fairly launched on the turbulent sea of the Revolution. But notwithstanding the ominous notes of war the daily routine of Bedminster life continued. Sun-browned men went to and from the fields, peddlers wandered from village to farm, and women gossiped as they spun or stepped in their short kirtles to the music of their swiftly whirling yarn wheels. There was little or no break in the industries that centered about the Old Stone House. Work continued at the tannery and on the farm, the products of both finding a ready market.

By this time the farm had been considerably curtailed in size. At the death of Johannes a division of his estate was made by will among his children. All the provisions of this last testament are not known, no copy having been found, but references in subsequent deeds show that the tannery, homestead, and two hundred acres fell to Aaron. The southern portion of the farm, embracing one hundred and sixty-seven acres, being all the land fronting on the Bernardsville and Lamington road, was devised to Aaron's youngest brother, Peter. Upon this land, some-time before the Revolution, he erected a house and farm buildings. Here on the breaking out of the war Peter was living with his wife and three children, David, John, and Catherine.

Andrew's share of his father's estate was probably what remained of the four hundred and nine acres of land on the Delaware, which Johannes had purchased in 1747. At any rate, this is where Andrew settled on leaving the homestead, and he continued to be a resident of the township until his death in 1820. On the fourth of July, 1776, he received a commission as captain in the 1st Regiment, Sussex Militia, commanded by Colonel William Maxwell, and throughout the war was active in the services of his country.

At the breaking out of the Revolution, Aaron was beyond the age required by the acts of Provincial Congress for serving in the militia. We know that he did serve as a member of the Bedminster Committee of Observation and Inspection. He did more than this; he buckled the armor on his oldest son John, then a lad of but eighteen, and sent him off with his blessing to fight the battles of his country. It is to be regretted that our knowledge of John's Revolutionary services is not more complete in its details. In General William S. Stryker's *Official Register of the Officers and Men of New Jersey in the Revolutionary War*,[1] he appears as a private in Captain Jacob Ten Eyck's company of the First Battalion, Somerset Militia, and also as a private in one of the New Jersey regiments of the Continental Line.

At the outset of the war this First Battalion was commanded by William Alexander—known to history as Lord Stirling—a son of Somerset in whose Revolutionary record the people of the county justly take much pride. While in England in 1756 he laid claim to the earldom of Stirling, which had been in abeyance for a number of years. Although he was successful in establishing a direct descent, the House of Peers, before whom his claim went for final adjudication, decided against him. The title, however, seems to have been allowed in this country

---

[1] Published in Trenton, 1872. Stryker was the compiler.

at least by courtesy. Washington, in his correspondence, invariably addressed him as "My Lord," and always spoke of him as "his lordship."

On his return to America in 1761, he settled at Basking Ridge on the estate that had been acquired by his father. Here he made improvements which for taste and expense were much greater than anything of the kind ever attempted in the province. His grounds were laid out in the manner of an English park, and the spacious mansion possessed all the characteristics of a gentleman's seat in the old country. This large dwelling, together with its connecting offices, stables, and coach houses, was ornamented with cupolas and gilded vanes, and surrounded a paved court or quadrangle. There was a grand hall and an imposing drawing room, with richly decorated walls and stuccoed ceilings. Jones, the Tory historian,[2] who, of course, bore Lord Stirling no love, states that while living here "he cut a splendid figure, he having brought with him from England horses, carriages, a coachman, valet, butler, cook, steward, hairdresser and a mistress." Here this American noblemen lived the life of a country gentleman of fortune; he rode in a great coach with gilded panels emblazoned with coronets and medallions, and altogether affected a style and splendor probably unequaled in the colonies. He was a member of the King's Council, a colonel in the militia, and was naturally the most conspicuous figure in the county.

At the first sign of a severance of the relations between the colonies and the home government, Lord Stirling warmly espoused the popular cause. On the thirteenth of October, 1775, the Provincial Congress of New Jersey, acquiescing in a recommendation of Continental Congress, organized two battalions consisting of eight companies of sixty-eight privates each. This was the first

[2] Thomas Jones, *History of New York during the Revolutionary War, and of the Leading Events in the Other Colonies at That Period* . . . (New York, 1879).

call on New Jersey and, together with a third battalion organized in February, 1776, was known as the "First Establishment" of troops from the colony for the Continental Army. The men were enlisted for one year, and Lord Stirling was commissioned as colonel of the First Battalion. He was soon promoted to be brigadier general. His appearance was imposing, and it has been said that next to Washington he possessed the most martial presence of any commander in the army.

That John Malick should have enrolled himself in this regiment cannot be charged to any special spasm of patriotic virtue. He had no choice. As early as the third of June, 1775, the Provinical Congress declared that the time had come for the people of the province to arm for defence. On that date, and in August and October of the same year, acts were passed making it obligatory on all citizens between the ages of sixteen and fifty to enroll themselves into militia companies that the several Committees of Safety were directed to form. These companies were then embodied into regiments which were distributed throughout the state. Each man was obliged to furnish himself with a "good musket or firelock, and bayonet, sword or tomahawk, a steel ramrod, worm, priming wire and brush fitted thereto, a cartridge box to contain twenty-three rounds of cartridge, twelve flints, and a knapsack." Militiamen were also required to keep in readiness at home one pound of powder and three pounds of bullets.

The only men of proper age who could avoid militia service were those employed by the province, or who were occupied in the manufacture of government supplies. Of course there were instances of individuals of cowardly nature or weak patriotism who were glad to take advantage of this exemption and seek such employment. In March, 1778, the Hibernia Furnace in Morris County was engaged in producing shot and shell, and consequently offered itself to such persons as a refuge.

The superintendent of the works, in speaking of the exemption of his employees, thus wrote to his principal, Lord Stirling:

> My Lord, this is the only thing that induces the greater part of the men to work here, as they are farmers and have left their farms and come here solely to be clear of the militia and from no other motive. I find they are determined to shuffle the time away they are exempt and do as little business as they possibly can. Could not your Lordship send us some of the Regular and Hessian deserters? I will do my endeavour to make thirty or forty of them serviceable.

The militia law of August, 1775, in compliance with the recommendation of Continental Congress, authorized the raising of minutemen; Somerset furnished four companies formed in one battalion. They were uniformed in hunting shirts, took precedence over other militia, and were required to be in constant readiness to march to any point for the defence of New Jersey or a neighboring colony. So many of the minutemen joined the Continental Army—as it was their privilege to do—that the battalions became much reduced, and before the first of March, 1776, they were disbanded and incorporated in the militia. The first service that the Somerset troops were called upon to perform was in answer to an application of the New York Committee of Safety for a force to aid in suppressing Tories on Long Island. Seven hundred militiamen were consequently ordered to march under field officers Colonel Nathaniel Heard, Lieutenant Colonel Edward Thomas, and Major John Dunn. Of this command one hundred were minutemen from Somerset, and there are reasons to believe that John Malick was among the number.

The battalion marched from Woodbridge on the seventeenth of January. On reaching Manhattan Island they were reinforced by three hundred men, among whom was a New York City volunteer organization, which, it is said, was composed of the most abandoned part of the population. This reinforcement was under the command of Major De Hart of New Jersey, and on the twenty-ninth instant the combined forces crossed to Long Island and proceeded at once on the object of the mission, which was the apprehension of violent Loyalists and the disarming of the disaffected of the inhabitants.

The political aspect of affairs on the western end of Long Island was very different from that of its neighbors, patriotic New England, New Jersey, and the rest of New York. Loyalty and rebellion blended, the balance of power before the arrival of troops being largely in favor of the former. The rich aristocrats and the phlegmatic Dutch, who were also well-to-do, were averse to disturbing the peace and order of the communities. This was especially so in Queen's County, which was largely Tory, and the County of King's was almost equally reluctant to show its influence on the side of the Revolutionary movement. The march of this invading force through these two counties spread dismay among the inhabitants. Colonel Heard was well fitted for his ungrateful mission, and was indefatigable in pursuit of the objects of the movement. So far as lay in his power he treated friend and foe with civility and kindness. He found it difficult, however, to control his auxiliary force, especially the company from New York City; their excesses caused him much pain; and acrimony and bitterness were engendered among the residents of the island against the military representatives of the colonists.

The New Jersey militiamen stand as distinct figures on the Revolutionary canvas. They well deserved the liberty for which they fought. It must be acknowledged that for a short sixty days, or maybe forty, at the close of the year 1776 they faltered in their faith, and, discouraged by the fearful adversities of the hour, many were inclined to abandon the cause and seek protection for their homes and families from a victorious enemy. But it was a temporary disaffection. Henceforth the militia of the Jerseys stood preeminent among the defenders of the liberties of the people. On this head we have the testimony of Washington. In a letter written to the Pennsylvania legislature in October, 1777, he says: "The exertions of the New Jersey militia have kept the enemy out of her limits, except now and then a hasty descent, without a continental regiment. Besides doing this, she has sent, and is now sending reinforcements to this and the northern army."

In August, 1776, the militia was divided into two divisions—that is, every organization was divided into two parts. One was ordered to report immediately to General Washington for one month's tour of duty, as it was termed; the other was required to be in readiness to relieve the first. In this manner, until the close of the war the two divisions did alternate service. They also, when not on a tour of duty, were frequently called upon to defend their homes and communities in the fights and skirmishes known as Quinton's Bridge, Hancock's Bridge, Three Rivers, Connecticut Farms, and Van Nest's Mills (Weston).

Although early in 1776 campaigns were being prosecuted in the North and South, the main theater of war continued to be in the East. But in April it was transferred to New York. On the third of June the Continental Congress called upon the colonies for thirteen thousand eight hundred militia to reinforce the army at New York. New Jersey was required to furnish thirty-three hundred men, and eleven days thereafter the Provincial Congress ordered that the force be raised to serve until the first of December, and to be formed of five battalions. When this command marched away, John Malick carried a musket in its ranks. The five battalions formed a part of Washington's army, which on the eighth of August was composed of seventeen thousand two hundred and twenty-five men, mostly raw troops, of whom thirty-six hundred and fifty-eight were sick and unfit for duty. Of this force eight thousand lay on Long Island between Bedford and the East River, the rest on Manhattan Island, the line extending as far as King's Bridge, the extreme points being seventeen miles apart. The command with which John Malick was connected was on Long Island.

On the twenty-seventh of August this little army of poorly armed, undisciplined militia, that was stretched thinly along an extended line south of Brooklyn, received the shock of a vast, thoroughly equipped body of British and Hessian soldiers, supported by a great fleet. Defeat was an almost foregone conclusion; in the light of subsequent knowledge it seems extraordinary that the American army was not entirely annihilated. The total loss of the enemy was three hundred and sixty-seven men, of whom but twenty were killed, five being officers. The estimated loss of the Americans in killed, wounded, and prisoners was two thousand, among the latter being Generals Sullivan and Lord Stirling, and one who served his country with equal ardor on that day, though in the more humble position of the bearer of a flintlock—John Malick.

John Malick's campaigning for the time being was at an end. A few days later he was taken over to New York and delivered with many other prisoners to the tender mercies of Provost Marshal Cunningham, of infamous memory. He was thrown into one of the New York sugar-houses, and his sufferings in that pest-prison can better be imagined than described. Lieutenant Robert Troup of the Long Island militia, in an affidavit made before Gouverneur Morris, gives a distressing account of the treatment of himself and other prisoners taken at the Battle of Long Island. They were allowed no fuel, and the provisions were so scanty and of such an inferior quality that, as he expressed it, "He doth verily believe that most of them would have died if they had not been supported by the kindness of some poor persons and common prostitutes who took pity on their miserable situation and alleviated it."

The miseries endured by the prisoners were made much greater by the inhumanity of their jailor, Provost Marshal Cunningham. He it was who, on the twenty-second of September of this year, executed with unnecessary brutality young Nathan Hale, the "patriot spy," whose last words were, "I only regret that I have but one life to lose for my country." Notwithstanding Hale's appeals, he was denied the services of a clergyman; and even a Bible for a moment's devotion was refused him. The provost destroyed letters that the sufferer left for his mother and friends, under the plea that it would not do to let the rebels know there was a man in their army who could die with so much firmness. For the benefit of those who take comfort in compensations it may be well to state that this same Cunningham was hanged in London in 1791 for forgery. In his dying confession he acknowledged that when provost in New York he had executed many prisoners on his own responsibility and without trial. How long John Malick remained in the clutches of this monster is unknown. Tradition speaks of his having been taken from prison by a British general whom he was forced to serve until included in a cartel. When finally exchanged he enlisted in the Continental Line, but of his additional Revolutionary record nothing has been preserved.

Our future interest in the American army lies in its experiences on New Jersey soil. We may therefore pass over Washington's masterly retreat from Long Island under the cover of a dense fog; the evacuation of New York City; the successful stand made by the Continental Army at Harlem; the indecisive action at White Plains on the twenty-eighth of October; and the fall of Fort Washington on the sixteenth of November, which may be considered the greatest disaster that befell American arms during the war. Before the latter catastrophe the main British army had moved to the east side of the Hudson, in the vicinity of Dobb's Ferry. Washington, feeling uncertain as to the designs of the enemy, dispatched Heath to Peekskill with three thousand men to guard the approaches of the Highlands, and, leaving Lee with over five thousand men at Northcastle, crossed the Hudson with what was left of the army and encamped in the vicinity of Hackensack. General Greene was already in New Jersey with a considerable force, garrisoning Fort Lee, immediately opposite Fort Washington.

On the nineteenth of November Cornwallis's army, six thousand strong, crossed the Hudson in two hundred boats, and scaling the precipitous heights of the Palisades at old "Closter Landing," the scarlet-coated column with bristling bayonets moved rapidly on Fort Lee. On the approach of Cornwallis the garrison at Fort Lee abandoned that post and fell back to Hackensack, joining the main body of Washington's army, which had made a stand on the right bank of the river. Couriers were dispatched to General Lee, directing him to make all haste in joining the main army with his command.

From this time up to the cessation of hostilities, the soil of New Jersey was the board upon which many of the most desperate Revolutionary games were played, and her territory was much of the time the fighting ground or plunder of the enemy. It is claimed that her losses in proportion to wealth and population were greater than that of any other state save South Carolina. With the exception of the winter of Valley Forge and the Virginia campaign against Cornwallis in 1781, the Continental troops were constantly in or on the confines of the state. In addition, her militia was constantly called upon by the Commander in Chief for special services or to swell the number of the American army.

But we must proceed with the disheartening tale of the retreat across the Jerseys. On the twenty-second of the month Washington reached Newark, Cornwallis having forced him to withdraw from Hackensack. On the following day his army was mustered and found to contain but fifty-four hundred and ten men fit for duty, of whom the enlistments of twenty-four hundred and one extended beyond the coming January. One brigade, that of General Bradley, reported but sixty men present. Washington remained at Newark for six days, when, the van of the enemy appearing, his column was set in motion for "Brunswick."

The British troops rested for several days at Newark, and their stay was marked by desolation and ruin. Its citizens received their first lesson in the miseries of being under the heels of a conquering host. Tory and patriot were alike plundered, women and young girls were much worse than insulted, and, as a witness of that time writes, those only escaped robbery and murder who were fortunate enough to procure a sentinel to guard their doors. He further recites that "there was one Captain Nutman who had always been a remarkable Tory, and who met the British troops on Broad Street with huzzas of joy. He had his house robbed of almost everything. His very shoes were taken off his feet, and they threatened to hang him."

On leaving Newark the Americans moved in two columns to New Brunswick. Washington had hoped to make a stand on the south bank of the Raritan, having confidently expected to receive reinforcements at New Brunswick. He was doomed to disappointment. Lee, who had been repeatedly ordered to hurry forward his command, had not yet come up, and the militia did not respond to the calls of the Governor. In addition, a general spirit of insubordination pervaded the army, and hundreds, deserting the cause, went home believing that a further struggle against the superior organization, arms, and discipline of the British troops would be unavailing.

Cornwallis, on the other hand, on approaching New

Brunswick was largely reinforced by Howe, and Washington's weary, way-worn, shattered battalions were again obliged to take up their hurried flight toward the Delaware. The retreat was by way of Princeton and Kingston, and the inhabitants of lower Somerset had an unhappy first view of the Continental Army. They had good reason for despairing of the patriot cause when they beheld their country's defenders, many of them barefooted and all illy protected from the wintry weather, dwindling away with each mile of their disheartening march, while being chased across the state by a well-clad, victorious force, "tricked out in all the bravery of war." During the night that the column marched from New Brunswick the rain fell violently, and the roads were deep in mud caused by the passage of artillery and wagons. About daylight on the following morning the rear guard passed through Rocky Hill, every step of the exhausted men being above the ankles and often to the knees in mire.

Washington, anticipating the possible necessity of abandoning the state to the enemy, had collected at Trenton all the boats of the upper Delaware. He reached that place with the main body of what was left of the army on the third of December, having left Lord Stirling with a detachment at Princeton to watch and endeavor to check the enemy until the baggage and stores could cross the river. On the seventh the enemy advanced in such force as to necessitate the hurried retreat of the entire American army. By midnight, Washington with all of his men was west of the Delaware; as the troops disembarked from the last boat the music of the pursuers could be heard as their advance entered the town that had just been evacuated. What remained of the army—less than twenty-five hundred men—were now safe. The enemy, after vainly endeavoring to obtain boats, showed no disposition to continue the chase, but went into winter quarters in the different towns, content for that campaign with the occupation of the state and, as they thought, the annihilation of an army. The rebellion was believed to be crushed. Howe and Cornwallis returned to New York, and the latter, thinking his services to be no longer required in America, decided to sail for England.

13

Captured Province

FOR THE TIME BEING New Jersey was a captured province. While many of its citizens made their submission to the victors, the cruelties perpetrated on the inhabitants by the occupying army were such as to greatly increase among the masses the feeling of hatred toward British rule. The sufferings of the people were not only caused by their being forced to impoverish themselves in furnishing billets and forages to the British, but by such marauding and plundering by the troops as would have graced the followers of an Eastern satrap. General Howe's army was at this time given up to indiscriminate and universal thieving, the officers not only countenancing the outrages, but participating as well. The men were licentious and permitted to commit every manner of rapine, violence, and cruelty; consequently, the tartaned Scot with his flowing skirt, the natty grenadier, and the dashing dragoon with scarlet coat and bright yellow short-clothes looked upon a Jersey rebel as legitimate prey.

While many instances might be given of the sufferings visited on the Jersey people at this time, a few illustrations will suffice to excuse or warrant so wholesale a condemnation of the occupying army. Of course, those citizens most active in the patriot cause were especially marked for the vengeance of the British and their partisan allies. No feud so deadly as one between brothers. General Greene, in writing to his wife from New Jersey on the sixteenth of December, thus speaks of the sufferings of the inhabitants:

The tories are the cursedest rascals amongst us—the most wicked, villainous and oppressive. They lead the relentless foreigners to the houses of their neighbors, and strip the poor women and children of everything they have to eat and wear; and after plundering them in this sort, the brutes often ravish the mothers and daughters, and compel their fathers and sons to behold their brutality; many have fallen sacrifices in this way.

In the line of the writer's maternal ancestry are the Middlesex families of Ayres, Dunn, and Dunham. Of the last-named, fifteen members served in the army, nine of whom were spoliated by the British. David, David, Jr., and Samuel of Piscataway had their houses and barns burned; and Elisha, Jonathan, Josiah, and John of Woodbridge also suffered great losses. Azariah—of the Committee of Safety—was robbed of many valuables, and even his aged father, the Reverend Jonathan of Piscataway, was plundered by the thieving soldiery. Samuel, Jacob, and Reuben Ayres, who were in the army, had their Woodbridge houses pillaged: Samuel lost cattle, sheep, hay, and women's clothing, among the last being "one black Calamanco Cloak lined, new," and "one Scarlet Cloak, part worn"; Reuben's house was burned, and his horses and a "good gun" appropriated.

Fifteen members of the Dunn family were in the army, ranging in grade from a private to a colonel. Eleven of them were despoiled by the English and Tories. Captain Hugh Dunn of the First Middlesex Militia at the outbreak of the war had just completed a new house. When the enemy overran Middlesex County, many of the inhabitants deserted their homes. Not so Captain Hugh, who determined to stay on his lands and defend his possessions. He was forced to give up his new dwelling to British officers and to move with his family into the kitchen part of the old house, in the main body of which was quartered a company of Hessians. In the end he fared much better than did some of his neighbors who moved back into the country, his losses being confined to furniture, cattle, grain, and other personal effects, among them being—as he recites in his statement preserved at Trenton —a "new coat for my Negro." He and his wife paid dearly in another way, however, for just then a baby was born to them, and when the little girl began to talk, a stammering tongue and an impeded speech which lasted through life told the story of the excitements and fears of that turbulent period.

Sturdy Hugh Dunn did valiant service in the cause of freedom. His convictions were of the strongest character, and they are illustrated by many curious stories preserved by his posterity. After the famous Boston Tea Party, throughout his long life he never permitted himself to taste the "cheering cup." He even held his own brother in contempt, who at the outset of the war sold his farm and moved to Canada. Many years afterwards, when this same brother sent him from the British possessions a present of a barrel of fish, he would not even grant it storage, but set it out on the roadside, giving all passers-by permission to help themselves.

A son of Somerset prominent at this period for valuable services rendered his country was that able scholar and statesman, Richard Stockton, one of the signers of the Declaration of Independence. He was a man of wealth and lived on a handsome estate near Princeton, which had descended to him from his forefathers. His homestead was repeatedly plundered by the enemy, and while visiting a Mr. Cowenhoven, he and his host were dragged from their beds by a party of refugee Loyalists. They were carried to New York, and Mr. Stockton was treated with such barbarity as to bring on illness which in 1781 resulted in his death.

A neighbor of Richard Stockton, and also a signer of the Declaration of Independence, was John Hart— "Honest John Hart." He was a substantial farmer living in the vicinity of the village of Columbia, in Hunterdon (now Mercer) County. Though an illiterate man and quite wanting in the cultivation and accomplishments which with a few exceptions distinguished the members of the Second Congress, he possessed sound sense, strong will-power, and great tenacity of purpose. Hart's devotion to the interest of the revolted colonies brought upon him the malignant hatred of the Tories and the persecutions of the enemy. His sufferings during the first year of the war were most severe; his property was destroyed, his family dispersed, and he himself, driven from the deathbed of his wife, was hunted through the woods and from cottage to cave. His hardships probably hastened his death in 1780.

Although Bedminster Township lay far north of where the British cantonments were located, it did not escape the miseries inflicted on the communities by the enemy. A squadron of British cavalry suddenly appeared in Pluckamin, and visited all manner of indignities upon the place and people. Women were grossly insulted, dwellings robbed, and stock driven off. The doors of the Lutheran Church were battered down, the pews broken up, and the pulpit hacked and disfigured with saber strokes. The object of this raid was to secure the person of Captain Isaac Van Arsdale, who had made himself obnoxious because of his activity in behalf of the colonists. On learning of their approach he escaped to the woods and, in conjunction with some neighbors, succeeded to some extent in harassing the marauders. At least one man was known to have suffered from their musket balls, as he was brought to Eoff's Tavern, where sheets were torn up to make bandages to stanch his wounds. William McDonald, who owned the mills on Chambers Brook, was probably in sympathy with these cavalrymen, as they treated him with consideration; he, in return, rolled out a barrel of "applejack," and regaled them with bread and cold ham.

On another occasion a troop of light-horse seized Elias Van der Veer, well known to the enemy as an active patriot, and carried him off to Trenton. It is not strange that innumerable experiences of a like character, together with the fact of Washington having been driven from the state, should have produced a profound feeling of despondency. The stoutest hearts began to despair of the future, and many commenced to think only of the safety of their families and property. The victorious enemy, recognizing this growing sentiment, offered amnesty to soldiers and protection to citizens if they would return to their allegiance. Disaffection spread, and as many as two hundred persons came in one day to the British headquarters and pledged their faith to the Crown; among these were Samuel Galloway, a member of the First Continental Congress, and Samuel Tucker of Trenton; the latter had presided over the Provincial Congress of New Jersey when the state constitution was adopted, and was Justice of the Supreme Court and treasurer of the state.

The members of the family in the Old Stone House did not waver in their sympathies, and Aaron showed no hesitation in his fealty to the best interests of the building nation. So it was with all his brothers excepting the youngest. Peter took advantage of the proclamation of the "Right Honorable Lord Howe, and his Excellency, General Howe," and received a protection paper whereby he was assured protection "both for himself, his family and property, and to pass and repass on his lawful business without molestation." Peter's disaffection does not appear to have been permanent; he was never classed as a Loyalist. In making his submission he was doubtless influenced by his business relations with James Parker, the printer. Mr. Parker sometime before the Revolution purchased of the executors and heirs of John Johnstone extensive bodies of land lying within the Peapack Patent. He appointed Peter Melick his agent for its care, improvement, and sale. Peter was obliged to make frequent journeys to Perth Amboy in order to consult with his principal. It is fair to presume that he imbibed more or less of the loyal sentiment there openly and almost universally displayed. A large element of its population, especially among the wealthier citizens, were dominated in their sympathies by the ever-present influence of royal power. General Washington, on the fourth of July, 1776, in a communication to Congress thus refers to Perth Amboy: "The disaffection of the people of that place and others not far distant, is exceedingly great, and unless it be checked and overawed it may become more general and very alarming."

It does not appear that James Parker openly evinced hostility to the new order of things. He endeavored to occupy the middle ground of neutrality. Though in 1775 he was chosen a delegate to the Provincial Congress, he did not take his seat, and in November of that year he located his family on a farm in Hunterdon County, his Perth Amboy home not being re-established until 1785. His property escaped confiscation, though he himself does not seem to have remained at all times beyond suspicion; in 1777 he was placed under arrest by the authorities and for a time was confined at Morristown. Mr. Parker's wife was a daughter of the Reverend William Skinner, rector of St. Peter's Church. Her family was pronounced in favor of a continuance of British rule, and at its overthrow the rector's son, Courtlandt, had for seven years been Attorney General for the Crown. In 1776 he was commissioned a Brigadier General and authorized to raise five battalions among those men of New Jersey who adhered to the King. He succeeded in obtaining at that time but five hundred and seventeen recruits, although later in the war the number in his command was largely increased.

The strong reluctance shown by James Parker and other leading citizens of that portion of the state to support the Revolution may be ascribed somewhat to their extreme feeling of loyalty to the Church of England. They found it difficult to dissever church and state. The clergy, by their oaths of conformity and allegiance, felt themselves bound to sustain the Crown, and the communicants of the church, in a great majority of instances, were influenced by their spiritual guides. In 1775 Doctor Tucker, Dean of Gloucester, addressed a circular letter to the ministers of the "Established Church in North America," warning them against teaching principles as to a civil government drawn from Mr. Locke rather than from the gospel. This admonition was scarcely needed. Both before and after that time the rectors from their pulpits pelted their people with Paul; cried out that "the powers that be are ordained of God"; did not hesitate to preach that "they that resist shall receive to themselves damnation"; and so, in their weekly discourses, rang all the changes on the first eight verses of the thirteenth chapter of the Epistle to the Romans. The apostle Peter, too, helped them with texts as to the duty of obedience and nonresistance to the higher powers, enabling them to show their parishioners that those who "despised government, presumptuous are they."

The dissenting ministers fought under the banner of Saint John and declaimed with equal vehemence against the idolatrous reverence paid to tyrants. They did not hesitate to draw comparisons between the King of England, in his rage against his American subjects, and that horrible wild beast with seven heads and ten horns of Revelation, which was ordained by the devil for the destruction of mankind.

The attitude assumed by both clergy and laity of the Anglican Church resulted most disastrously to the sect, and throughout the war its adherents were ever under the ban of suspicion; the people of other denominations maintained—to quote a writer of that period—"that a churchman and a foe to American liberty were synonymous terms." The effect of such a feeling drove the ministers from their pulpits and brought ruin upon the congregations. When the British evacuated Philadelphia in 1778, Doctor William White, chaplain of Congress and after the peace the first bishop of Pennsylvania, was the only Episcopal minister who remained in that state. When the war was over, in many of the northern states not a church was left; and in all New Jersey Doctor Abraham Beach, rector of Christ Church, New Brunswick, was the only minister who had been able to maintain regular services during the struggle. Throughout the Revolution the chaplains of American refugee regiments were mainly ministers of the Church of England.

Another sect that suffered severely was that of Methodism. Its adherents were yet a feeble folk; they did not number at the outset of the war over one thousand souls, the American communion having been established in New York as recently as 1766. It is claimed that previous to 1771 there were not over fifty Methodists in New Jersey. Bishop Asbury records that in that year there were about two hundred and fifty in Philadelphia, about three hundred in New York, and a few between the Hudson and the Delaware. Probably the first church edifice of that denomination in New Jersey was the one erected just before the Revolution in Trenton. Methodists were objects of suspicion during the war, and it was not uncommon for their preachers and class leaders to be tarred and feathered. The feeling against them was due in a great measure to a pamphlet published by Wesley entitled "A Calm Address to the Americans." It claimed on moral and legal grounds that Parliament had a right to tax the colonies, and it held that American subjects opposing this right were actuated only by a desire to overthrow the government.

Still another body of Christians that suffered much in

the Revolution were the Quakers, and both amusing and pathetic stories are told of their experiences growing out of their adhering to noncombatant principles. The Quaker was ever between the upper and nether millstone. His government drafted him into the ranks; his "meeting" disciplined him for either bearing arms or for procuring a substitute. The old recordbooks of the Society of Friends furnish curious information as to what was considered a falling-away from Quaker grace. Benjamin Harris was cut off from communion with the "Plainfield meeting" for refusing to give any "satisfaction for his misconduct" in that he signed a paper for independency and "suffered his apprentice to go into the army." Another Friend—Marmaduke Hunt—makes confession, when disciplined by the "meeting" that while confined in Morristown jail his distresses were so great that, as he says, "liberty was offered me on condition of my taking the affirmation of fidelity to the states, which through unwatchfulness I submitted to." Several Mendham Quakers were summoned, and made to confess their fault and show penitence for having redeemed goods which the authorities had taken from them for refusing to train with the militia.

On the twelfth of December there were tumult and excitement on the southern border of the Old Farm. Late on that afternoon, through the woods that stretched away beyond the North Branch of the Raritan toward the Bernard Hills, could be heard the rat-ta-ta of drums and the shrill cry of fife. At first faint and in the distance, but soon louder and clearer; then there fell on the ear the tramp of troops, the ring of hoofs on the frozen ground, and the heavy roll of artillery. It was the little army of General Charles Lee that Washington was so impatiently expecting, and which had been so many days on the march from the Hudson. The men trudged along the narrow road in columns of fours and in route step, each one carrying his gun as he liked. They were brown and weatherbeaten; their many bivouacs on the Westchester and Jersey hills had left marks on their uniforms and accoutrements showing the dire effects of wear, wind, and weather—more properly speaking on clothing, not uniforms, as many of these Continental soldiers were without stripe, plume, or color, and often a sash or a corded or cockaded hat was all that distinguished the officer.

The Revolutionary soldiers of "Seventy-Six" knew little of neatness or of the picturesque in dress. With the exception of an occasional militia coat of ancient design, coarse hunting shirts and rough linsey-woolsey suits were the rule for the first year or so of the war. Their guns were of various patterns, the ordinary carbine, fowling-piece, and rifle not being uncommon, all having powder pans and flintlocks. Powder was generally carried in a cow's horn swung over one shoulder, while from the other hung a leather pouch for bullets. All the ideas prevailing at the outset of the war as to soldiers and weapons were very crude. Even the generally astute Franklin held peculiar views and gave curious advice, as is shown by the following extract from a letter written by him to General Lee on the eleventh of February, 1776:

I still wish with you that Pikes could be introduced, and I would add bows and arrows. Those were good weapons not wisely laid aside. First—Because a man may shoot as truly with a bow as with a common musket. Second—He can discharge four arrows in the time of charging and discharging one bullet. Third—His object is not taken from his view by the smoke of his own side. Fourth—A flight of arrows seen coming upon them terrifies and disturbs the enemy's attention to his business. Fifth—an arrow striking any part of a man puts him *hors de combat* till 'tis extracted. Sixth—Bows and arrows are more easily provided everywhere than muskets and ammunition.

The clothing furnished the privates of the two battalions forming the first establishment of the Jersey line was to each man one felt hat, one pair of yarn stockings, and one pair of shoes. The monthly pay of the men was five dollars, but they were obliged to find their own arms; the enlistment was for a single year. The second New Jersey enlistment, authorized by Congress in September, 1776, was composed of four battalions to serve for the war unless sooner discharged. In addition to their monthly pay, the privates and noncommissioned officers received one hundred acres of land and an annual kit of clothing comprising two linsey hunting shirts, two pairs of overalls, a waistcoat of wool or leather, one pair of breeches, a hat or leathern cap, two shirts, and two pairs of hose and shoes. Some of the militia—notably those of Pennsylvania—often made an attempt at a more dashing apparel. The term "Jersey Blues" had its origin in a volunteer company from the vicinity of Springfield. Its uniform, furnished by some patriotic women of the township, consisted of two frocks and breeches dyed a bright blue. In the matter of arms there was within a year a marked improvement, as the agents abroad became able to make purchases in behalf of the young republic. When Washington's army entered Philadelphia in 1777, previous to the battle of Brandywine, Graydon stood on the Coffee House corner, and thus spoke of the appearance of the troops as they passed down Front Street: "They amounted to but eight or nine thousand men; though indifferently dressed they held well-burnished arms, carried them like soldiers, and looked in short as if they might have faced an equal number of men with a reasonable prospect of success."

14

The Surprise Was Complete

At the close of this twelfth day of December, 1776, when Lee's army crossed the North Branch of the Raritan and entered Bedminster, his battalions with clank of arm and swing of saber pressed on along the Lamington highway until the head of the column had passed a considerable distance beyond the crossing of the Peapack Road; the troops then deployed to the right and encamped, the greater part of them occupying the lands of Peter Melick. When the moon climbed the heavens that night it illumined with its mellow gleam a strange spectacle for this quiet Bedminster country. The roads and fields were encumbered with cannon and baggage-wagons, and stamping horses were tethered to trees and fences. Campfires gleamed on the hillsides, around which were stretched tired, bronze-faced men with ragged blankets for a covering and with knapsacks and bundles for pillows. Sorry-looking soldiers they were, with their patched clothing, worn shoes cobbled with strings, and antiquated cross-belts and cartouch boxes. A strange spectacle, indeed, upon which the moon looked down, with naught to break the stillness of the sleeping camp save now or then the whinneying of a picketed horse or the occasional challenge of a pacing sentry.

Poor Peter's protection papers proved of but little

avail at this juncture. He did not think it wise to remain at home to welcome these military guests; his neighbors did this for him, at the same time informing the troops that the owner of the land upon which they had bivouacked was an "exempt." As was the fashion of the time, vengeance followed. Peter's fence rails fed the campfires, and his recently filled smokehouse fed the troops, as did his chickens, shoats, and cattle. Altogether he was forced to make a very handsome contribution to the needs of the Continental Army. My knowledge of the incidents of that night is gained from Peter's oldest daughter, Catherine, then a child of nearly five. She afterwards became the wife of Enos Mundy.

As is well known, Lee did not continue this far with his troops, but stopped for the night with a small guard and some of his aides at a tavern kept by Mrs. White at Basking Ridge. It is probable that General Sullivan, who was second in command, quartered that night at Aaron Malick's house, as it was among the most substantial of the neighborhood. At least family traditions aver that the house was full of officers, who arrived mounted. It is pleasant to learn something of the personality of the leaders of the Revolution who campaigned in this Bedminster country. Sullivan at this time was thirty-seven years old; possessed a well-proportioned and commanding figure, animated by the ruddy hue of health. His voice was deep and melodious, and in his military career he used it to great advantage, for it was always quick to respond alike to stern and gentle emotions. In the morning an officer came in great haste to the Old Stone House and announced the capture of the commanding general. Mrs. Mundy expresses it in her statement: "There was a great fuss in the morning, because a big officer had been captured or killed, or something of that sort, and Grandfather Malick had to go to Germantown with the soldiers on horseback, and he did not get home again until in the afternoon . . . Quite a number of big officers staid at Grandfather's, and an officer came in the forenoon and told of this officer being captured or killed."

There is no doubt that Lee was a brave and brilliant officer, possessing superior mental qualifications. He hated oppression and scorned meanness. Though when stirred by violent impulses his personal animosities were intense, he is said to have ever been an open and honest enemy. Yet at such times both in action and word he was too governed by his angered passions rather than by reason. He was intemperate in language and always over-zealous as to his personal rights. One readily discovers from his correspondence that he was constitutionally what might be in vulgar parlance termed a sorehead. He fully coincided with the assurances of his admirers that he was the greatest general in the country, and the rock upon which his career was shipwrecked was a headstrong nature that could not brook command. The yellow-eyed serpent of jealousy coiled in his heart, and his unceasing vengeful feelings toward Washington were too great for his naturally generous nature to overcome. Could he have brought himself to the occupation of a second place in the hearts and admiration of the people, his name would probably have been remembered as one of the leading and successful generals of the war.

Lee was at this time forty-five. By birth an Englishman, he first becomes known to us in 1757 as a captain of grenadiers in Abercrombie's fatal assault upon Ticonderoga. Three years were then spent in campaigning in the northern wilderness, when, as a lieutenant colonel, he went with Burgoyne to Portugal to aid in repelling the attacks of Spain. He next figures as an impetuous liberal politician in England, and then for two years as a staff officer of the King of Poland at Warsaw. Then we find him with a company of Turks, almost perishing on the Bulgarian mountains while guarding the Grand Seignior's treasure from Moldavia to Constantinople. For successive years he was on the Bosporus, at Warsaw, and in England, in which latter country he grew turbulently indignant on failing to obtain army promotion. As a major general in the Russian service he next campaigned in command of Cossacks and Wallachs, when the fighting was of the severest character. And now we hear of him in Hungary, where he killed an Italian in a duel, and in the following winter in England, deep in the vortex of politics and violent in his opposition to the government. The year 1772 was spent in France and Switzerland. In 1773 he came to this country.

After reaching America Lee became a violent supporter of the provincial claims against England, and his fearless spirit, his enthusiasm and brilliant wit, together with the romance of his life, soon gave him a prominence hardly equalled by any man in the country. He advised with members of Congress and interviewed deputies; always feeding the flames of opposition, he finally was recognized as a leader in the Revolutionary movement. To more closely ally himself with American interests he purchased a Virginia estate, whereupon, hostilities having commenced, Congress commissioned him as major general in the Continental Army. He was intensely chagrined at not being named for the chief command. When Washington was commissioned, Lee naturally scouted the idea that a man who knew nothing of a greater campaign than had been Braddock's could vie with him, a veteran of many wars, as commander in chief of an army. Yet, at this time at least, his love of liberty seems to have overshadowed his ambition. He threw up his commission in the English army and ran the risk of losing all of his possessions across the water, which were considerable, in order to accept the position offered him by Congress. In the beginning he was indefatigable in his endeavors, and his accomplishments as a soldier were so great as to seem to secure for him a brilliant future.

The disasters of Long Island, White Plains, and Fort

191

Washington he falsely ascribed to the incompetence of Washington. Upon this belief he fed his jealousy until it absorbed his whole being and wrecked his whole career. While Washington was making his heroic retreat across the Jerseys, Lee not only failed to hurry to his support, but deliberately disobeyed the commands of his chief. While the army that was being pursued by Cornwallis was anxiously looking for the appearance of Lee's corps, that General delayed crossing the Hudson for several weeks, and then advanced in a most leisurely manner, as if fearful of being a help or advantage to the retreating force. His dilatoriness cannot be charged to his being lukewarm in the cause, or to an altogether determined disobedience on his part. He builded on the hope that the continued delay might furnish him with an opportunity for striking a blow on the flank of the enemy independent of his chief, thus performing a service that would redound to his individual honor. Like too many men before and since who have occupied public trusts, his patriotism was dwarfed by personal ambition.

At four o'clock on the morning of the thirteenth there arrived at White's Tavern one Major James Wilkinson, a staff officer of another Continental general who felt sore because of Washington's superior position—Horatio Gates. The sudden and unexpected retreat of Sir Guy Carleton from before Ticonderoga to Canada had enabled General Schuyler to send several regiments to aid Washington. This force having entered New Jersey, Wilkinson, who was barely nineteen years old, had been dispatched by its commandant, Gates, with a letter announcing his proximity, but on learning that the Commander in Chief was already beyond the Delaware, the Major had turned aside and taken it to Lee as next of rank. Lee received the letter in bed, promising to give an answer after breakfast, whereupon Wilkinson lay down on his blanket before a comfortable fire until daylight.

The General remained in bed until eight o'clock,

when he came downstairs, half dressed and in his slippers. Major Scammel of Sullivans's staff called to obtain orders for the morning march. After a map had been spread on the table and examined, Lee said, "Tell General Sullivan to move down towards Pluckamin." The General then spent some time in listening to complaints from soldiers in his command. He was indignant at many of their demands, especially at those coming from members of Colonel Sheldon's Connecticut light-horse, whom he charged with the desire to go home. These militia troopers were without doubt but poor apologies for soldiers. They were dressed in antiquated state uniforms much the worse for long service, wore old-fashioned, full-bottomed wigs, often awry, and all their accoutrements were of a most ancient and obsolete order. Many of their horses had left the plow to enter service, and together with their trappings they presented anything but a military appearance. One of these "nutmeg" horsemen being captured at the Battle of Long Island, some British officers amused themselves by forcing him to canter up and down in front of their quarters while they made merry over his ridiculous appearance and quaint replies to their questions. On being asked what special service had been required of his troop by the Americans, he answered, "To flank a little and carry tidins."

Lee did not breakfast before ten, and then sat down to write to General Gates. A single quotation from this letter will show its general tone, and the attitude toward Washington: "*Entre nous* a certain great man is most damnably deficient." Meanwhile, Major Wilkinson had his horse saddled and brought to the door, and then sat down at a window and awaited with patience the letter. At about high noon he suddenly saw a troop of dragoons turn from the highway and dash down the lane toward the house, which in a few seconds they reached and surrounded. "Here," cried the Major, "are the British cavalry!" "Where is the guard," exclaimed Lee, "why don't they fire? Do, sir, see what has become of the guard!" As careless as the General, the guards, with arms stacked, were sunning themselves on the south side of the house. They were soon overcome, two brave fellows who resisted being killed by saber strokes. A very short but spirited defense was made by Lee's suite, who, firing from windows, killed several of the dragoons, including the cornet. So near was Harcourt their commander, to being killed that a ball carried away the ribbon of his queue. The British called upon Lee to surrender, threatening that five minutes delay would insure the burning of the building. A discomfited officer almost immediately appeared at the open door, saying: "Here is the General, he has surrendered!" He was hastily placed on Wilkinson's horse, his legs being firmly bound to the stirrup leathers; the trumpet sounded assembly, and, just as he was, without a hat, and in slippers and dressing gown, they hurried him off to New Brunswick.

History furnishes but few examples of a general officer presenting a meaner appearance than did Lee, as surrounded by his exultant captors he clattered through Somerset. His small and restless eyes lost their haughty glances—his usually satirical mouth drooped at its corners with humiliation—his large nose was red with cold—his long, lank, thin body shivered in the December blasts—while his soiled shirt and fluttering dressing gown gave him an air quite opposed to that of a military chieftain.

Lee had supposed himself to be at least twenty miles distant from the enemy, and much surprise was felt that his proximity had been discovered by the British. On the previous afternoon Aaron Malick had occasion to visit New Germantown and did not return till late in the evening. This was a time when no one was above the suspicion of disloyalty. When Wilkinson, or some other officer, reached the Old Stone House the morning of the thirteenth and found that Aaron had been absent the previous night, he was at once suspected of having informed the enemy of Lee's whereabouts. He was placed under arrest and rigidly examined, and was finally sent under guard to New Germantown to prove himself clear of any conspiracy. He had no difficulty in doing this, and was consequently released. On his way home, at the "round hill" about half a mile west of the Larger Cross Roads, he met what was now Sullivan's command pushing on towards the Delaware. While he was talking with some of the officers, the discharge of cannon was plainly heard which announced the arrival of Lee at New Brunswick.

The capture of Lee was discovered later to have been in a measure accidental. It seems that Elder Muklewrath of the Mendham Presbyterian Church had been with the general line the night before, complaining that the troops had stolen one of his horses. On the following morning he fell in with a detachment of the Sixteenth British Light Dragoons under the command of Lieutenant Colonel, the Honorable William Harcourt, which was reconnoitering in the neighborhood. In some manner the elder divulged the proximity of Lee, and, it is said, either voluntarily or involuntarily guided the enemy to the General's quarters. This regiment of Harcourt's—called the Queen's Own— was considered the crack cavalry corps of the British forces. The men were mounted on fine horses sixteen hands high, and in addition to sabers were armed with carbines, the muzzles of which were thrust in a socket at the stirrup. Uniformed in scarlet coats faced with white, bright yellow buckskin breeches, black boots, and jangling spurs, their dashing and formidable appearance was heightened by polished brass helmets, from which chestnut hair flowed to the shoulders.

Washington's magnanimous soul could not see in Lee either a rival or an enemy. He had great confidence in his talents as a soldier and deeply deplored his capture, deeming it a serious loss to the country. Many of the people also held extravagant notions as to Lee's merits, and the affair altogether was considered a public calamity. His exchange and subsequent downfall are well known.[1] As he and his affairs have no further relations with Somerset County, the only additional reference I shall make to this singular man will be to cite the following extraordinary clause found in his will at his death, seven years later: "I desire most earnestly that I may not be buried in any church or churchyard, or within a mile of any Presbyterian or Anabaptist Meeting House; for since I have resided in this country I have kept so much bad company when living, that I do not choose to continue it when dead." Perhaps Lee had the Mendham elder in mind.

As the close of the year 1776 drew near, our state's cup of misfortune would seem to have been full and overflowing. Its legislature had been driven by an approaching enemy from Princeton to Trenton, from Trenton to Bordentown, then on to Pittstown, and from there to Haddonfield, where it had dissolved on the second of December. The army, almost destroyed, had abandoned the state; a general, high in the estimation of the people, had been captured; and the citizens in great numbers were going over to the enemy. That so few made their submission to the Crown is the wonder, not that so many should have proved faint-hearted and lost faith in the cause that seemed so promising but a short year before. It must be remembered that in the bays and harbors rode a lordly fleet, flying the flag that had been an object of affection and reverence to the colonists. Distributed throughout New Jersey was a thoroughly equipped and disciplined army, officered by veteran soldiers and supported by the prestige of a stable and powerful government.

But the people believed in Washington. Two days after crossing the Delaware the number of his men was

---

[1] Lee was court-martialed for disobedience and "misbehavior" before the enemy at the battle of Monmouth, July 28, 1778. He was suspended from command for a year and later dismissed.

reduced to seventeen hundred, of whom hardly more than a thousand could be relied upon for effective service. But at once, with apparently unabated ardor and by the most indefatigable exertions, Washington proceeded to build upon this nucleus of an army. By the twentieth of December his force had been augmented to nearly six thousand men. Proffered bounties and personal solicitation and influence had retained in the service soldiers whose time had expired; the Pennsylvania militia had turned out in force; regiments from Ticonderoga united with the army; and General Sullivan had brought up Lee's division. The British were distributed in cantonments from the Raritan to the Delaware. About fifteen hundred Germans and a squadron of English cavalry were posted at Trenton under command of Colonel Rall (Rahl), and another body of Hessians was stationed at Bordentown under Count von Donop. No fears were entertained of the Americans, and the foreign officers, jubilant over recent successes, were preparing to spend the Christmas holidays with great jollity.

And now, happily, a rift appears in the black cloud of disaster that has so long enveloped the American arms. On the cold and sleety night of the twenty-fifth of December, when the Delaware was chocked with ice, Washington crossed the river with twenty-five hundred men and twenty field-pieces. The command was divided into two divisions under Generals Sullivan and Greene, which took up their line of march for Trenton eight miles away. Owing to delays occasioned by the ice in the river and the slipperiness of the roads, it was eight in the morning before Greene reached the outposts of the enemy. Sullivan's division entered the westerly part of the town about the same time, and both commands pushed forward, keeping up a running fire on the retreating outposts.

The surprise was complete. The Hessian officers, still in the midst of their Christmas festivities, were hardly in a condition to repel so sudden an attack. Colonel Rall had

197

been engaged in playing cards with a convivial party of officers at the residence of a rich merchant. A short time before the attack he had returned to his quarters considerably the worse for his night's festivities. On being aroused by his aide and apprised of the approach of the enemy, the dumbfounded Colonel was quickly in the saddle and at the head of his troops, but before they could be completely formed the Americans were on them with cannon and bayonet. A short and decisive engagement resulted in a complete success for Washington's army. His troops were so disposed as to surround the enemy, who must choose between being cut to pieces and surrender. The British light-horse made their escape, but the less fortunate Hessians grounded their arms. According to an account published in the Philadelphia *Post* of the twenty-eighth of December, the capture included one colonel, two lieutenant colonels, three majors, four captains, eight lieutenants, twelve ensigns, two surgeon mates, ninety-nine sergeants, twenty-five drummers, nine musicians, twenty-five servants, and seven hundred and forty privates. In addition, the victorious Americans carried back with them to Pennsylvania three captured standards, six fine brass cannon, and about one thousand stand of arms. The Continental forces had but four casualties, while the enemy's dead amounted to thirty men and six officers. The colonel commanding, who was badly wounded, was placed on parole; he died a few days later.

On that cold day after Christmas, when the story of the battle of Trenton went flying from hamlet to farm over the hills and valleys of Somerset, the startling news was a matter of peculiar interest to the members of the family at the Old Stone House. Their rejoicing over the victory of the Americans was tempered somewhat by the knowledge that the vanquished were Germans, and that some of them with but little doubt had been Aaron's fellow-townsmen in the old country. It was the custom for German princes, in filling the ranks of battalions intended to be bartered to foreign governments, to secure recruits when possible from their outlying possessions rather than from their home dominions; it is fair to presume, then, that Bendorf was obliged to furnish its full quota to the forces destined for America. Aaron was probably well informed of these facts by his correspondents abroad, and though the news of the affair at Trenton may have added much to the happiness of the holiday season, yet he would have been quite wanting in sensibility had he reflected without concern upon the possibility of there being among the unfortunates who had been killed, wounded, or captured men who in their youth had been his playmates on the streets of his native town.

Just here it would seem eminently proper to say a few words in vindication of the memory of these overmaligned Hessians. It is quite time that the name of the German auxiliaries of the English army in America was severed from the odium attached to it for over a century past. Most of the barbarities and cruelties practiced upon the citizens of New Jersey by the entire British forces have been charged against the so-called Hessian troops.

Hessians! How they have been hated by the Jersey people! The very name is still spoken by many with a prolonged hiss. For generations the word has been used even as a bugaboo with which to frighten children, and by the imperfectly read the German troops have been stigmatized as "Dutch robbers," "blood-thirsty marauders," and "foreign mercenaries." While many of them were not saints, neither were they the miscreants and incendiaries, bent on excursions of destruction and rapine that the traditions fostered by prejudiced historians would have us believe. Many of these Germans were kindly souls, and probably the most abused people of the time. Individually they were not mercenaries, and a majority of the rank and file without doubt objected as strongly to being on American soil fighting against liberty as did their opponents to have them here. Some idea

199

may be obtained of their repugnance to coming to this country from Schiller's [2] protest against the custom of his countrymen's being sent across the seas in exchange for the gold of foreign governments. He tells how on one occasion upon orders being published directing a regiment to embark for the colonies, some privates, stepping out of the ranks, protested against crossing the ocean and demanded of their colonel for how much a yoke the prince sold men. Whereupon, the regiment was marched upon the parade, and the malcontents there shot. To quote Schiller, "We heard the crack of the rifles as their brains spattered the pavement, and the whole army shouted, 'Hurrah for America!'"

Germany's despotic princes justified their human traffic with the specious plea that it is a good soldier's duty to fight when his country requires his services—that whether it is against an enemy of his own government or that of another should not be considered or enter into his conception of allegiance. They argued that there is no boon so great as a full treasury, and when a subject contributed by enlistment to that end, he was fulfilling the highest duty of citizenship. Their people did not respond to such views of patriotism; consequently, in securing recruits the most severe measures were necessary. Impressing was a favorite means of filling the regimental ranks; strangers as well as citizens were in danger of being arrested, imprisoned, and sent off before their friends could learn of their jeopardy, and no one was safe from the grip of the recruiting officer. As every conceivable method of escape was devised by conscripts, desertions were punished with great severity, though as a rule not with death, as the princes found that their private soldiers had too high a monetary value in European markets to be sacrificed by the extreme penalty.

When the news of the capture of the Hessians at

---

[2] John Christoph Friedrich von Schiller, German poet, playwright, and author.

Trenton spread through New Jersey and Pennsylvania, the inhabitants thronged from every direction to view these beings whom they had been led to believe were monsters; they were very much astonished to find them like ordinary men of German extraction. The people were filled with wonder, however, at their strangely martial appearance. Their officers, with embroidered coats and stiff carriages, were in strong contrast to the easy-going commanders of the Continental forces, while the men in their dress and accoutrements presented a very different appearance from that of the generally poorly clad and equipped soldiers of the young republic. This was especially true of the grenadiers. They wore very long-skirted blue coats which looked fine on parade, but were ill-calculated for rapid marching; a yellow waistcoat extended below the hips, and yellow breeches were met at the knee by black gaiters. A thick paste of tallow and flour covered the hair, which was drawn tightly back and plaited into a tail which hung nearly to the waist. Their mustaches were fiercely stiffened with black paste, while above all towered a heavy brass-fronted cap. When in full marching order they must needs have had stout legs and broad backs to have sustained the weight they were forced to carry. In addition to cumbersome belts, a cartouche box, and a heavy gun, each man's equipment included sixty rounds of ammunition, an enormous sword, a canteen holding a gallon, a knapsack, blanket, haversack, hatchet, and his proportion of tent equipage.

It would be interesting to learn just how so deep-seated an aversion to the Hessians first became planted in the minds of the people, particularly in those of Pennsylvania and New Jersey. It could not have been because of their nationality, as among the populations of those states were many Germans, who had always been appreciated as a worthy folk, quiet rather than bellicose in character. Yet, for some mysterious reason, these German soldiers were looked upon with great dread by the inhabitants, especially by those who knew the least of them. The terror they inspired was often dissipated by a better acquaintance, as the private soldiers were found to be—with of course individual exceptions—simple-minded souls, and more afraid of their officers than of anything else. Mr. Onderdonk in his *Revolutionary Incidents* [3] speaks of them as "A kind, peaceable people, inveterately fond of smoking and of pea coffee; their offences were of the sly kind, such as stealing at night, while the British and new-raised corps were insolent, domineering, and inclined to violence and bloodshed."

[3] Henry Onderdonk, *Revolutionary Incidents of Suffolk and King's Counties* . . . (New York, 1849).

15

Assunpink and Princeton

THE CHRISTMAS HOLIDAYS of the year 1776, which will ever be considered one of the great epochs in American history, completely changed the aspect of the Revolutionary contest. Sir William Howe and Lord Cornwallis, astounded at the news from Trenton, were at once alive to their error in thinking that American independence was a matter of the past. Abandoning his proposed home voyage, Cornwallis hastily marched his troops toward the Delaware, being joined on the way by Count von Donop's force from Bordentown. The British column, five thousand strong, reached Trenton late on the afternoon of the second of January. Washington was already there with nearly an equal number of men, although his army was largely composed of undisciplined, un-uniformed militia. Intent on reoccupying New Jersey, he on the thirtieth of December had again crossed the Delaware.

It was nearly dark before the British faced the main body of the Americans at Trenton. After sunset the enemy advanced in two heavy bodies to the north side of Assunpink Creek in order to force the bridge, but from the opposite shore the American dogs of war barked from their iron throats a dubious welcome. The enemy's attempt to force a passage of the stream was defeated by the effective manner in which General Knox handled his artillery, which was advantageously planted on the high southern bank of the creek. Owing to the lateness of the hour Cornwallis retired to the rear of the town, on the Princeton Road, deciding to await daylight before renewing the attack, and when, he boasted, "he would catch that old fox Washington." From time immemorial a fox has been the most uncertain of all game, and Lord Cornwallis had quite neglected to remember that it was not uncommon for that wary animal, when just about trapped, to quietly steal away.

Frederick the Great, on being told that a distinguished general had never made a mistake, replied, "Then he must have fought very few campaigns." If Washington could ever be charged with a lack of military judgment, it was when he placed his army in the position it occupied on this night of the second of January. Realizing his dangerous situation, he was full of anxiety. Should an engagement follow the dawn, defeat would mean the destruction or capture of the entire Continental force, the troops being so disposed as to render a retreat impracticable. An engagement was certainly to be expected, the chances of success lying almost wholly with the enemy as opposed to the raw levies of the Americans was the flower of the British army. Washington's decision was promptly reached, a decision that was probably as important in its immediate results and in its future effect upon the destinies of the country as was any he was called upon to make during his entire career. The British had left at Princeton the Seventeenth, Fortieth, and Fifty-fifth Regiments of infantry and three squadrons of dragoons. They were to join Cornwallis in the morning, but could they be reached by the Americans before that time their destruction was not impossible. Washington, calling his generals together, disclosed his plan, which was to move quietly around the enemy's flank and, marching rapidly on Princeton, strike a telling blow in that unexpected quarter.

Assunpink and Princeton

The impedimenta was sent off silently in the direction of Bordentown, the campfires were brightened, and pacing sentinels were left on guard, whose frequent challenges deluded the outposts of the enemy. Soon after midnight the ragged army broke camp. They pushed out far east of and around the sleeping British soldiers; in the deep stillness of the night, along a narrow new road through the woods, the troops silently defiled over the frozen ground, their departure entirely unsuspected by the enemy.

The morning of the third of January was clear and cold. A white hoar frost sparkled and glittered on the fields, and the branches of the trees were gemmed with buds of ice. Soon after daybreak the people in the vicinity of Princeton were awakened by the noise of musket shots. File-firing commenced pattering like drumbeats, followed by a regular fusillade of platoons; then came the roaring of cannon. The citizens soon discovered that war in its full flower was at their very doors. General Mercer with his brigade, which on nearing the town had been detached from the main column, came upon the British advance at Samuel Worth's mill, near where the King's Highway crosses Stony Brook about one mile southwest of Princeton. He would have been overwhelmed, but Washington with the Continentals and militia promptly came to his support; a sharp and decisive engagement followed; in less than thirty minutes victory perched upon the American banners, and the enemy, horse and foot, were in full retreat.

I do not propose to weary the patience of my readers with an account of this famous battle. Able historians have made us all familiar with the miraculous escapes of Washington when exposed to a cross fire of friend and foe; have told over and over again of General Mercer's having been pinned to the earth by the fatal thrusts of British bayonets; of how the smoke rose above the combatants and hung in air, a clear, white, cumulus cloud, as if weighted with the souls of those who had just closed their eyes on the radiance of that winter morn; of the appearance presented by the British commander, Lieutenant Colonel Mawhood, who in the heat of the action rode at the head of his men on a little brown pony, with two spaniels playing before him; of Knox's training his artillery on Nassau Hall to dislodge a portion of the Fortieth Regiment which had taken refuge in the college building; and of the many other incidents crowded within the short space of time occupied in completely routing the British forces. Taking into consideration the number of troops engaged, no action during the war was so fatal to American officers. One general, one colonel, three captains, one lieutenant, and an ensign were killed; but then, officers were so numerous in this little army that, even in so short an exposure to the enemy's fire, that number of casualties was fairly to be expected. All told, the American loss was but thirty, while the British left one hundred dead on the field and nearly three hundred men in our hands as prisoners, including fourteen officers.

The Americans had no cavalry to follow the fleeing enemy, and the foot soldiers were in anything but a condition for pursuit. After the fight Washington was sorely tempted to push on to New Brunswick in the hope of securing the British stores. It was impossible, owing to the condition of his men; for much of the past thirty-six hours they had been marching and fighting, many of them had had neither breakfast nor dinner, and the entire army was completely exhausted. He was thus forced to seek the hill country where his victorious troops could without molestation obtain the rest and refreshment they so much needed. Reforming his column, the general pressed on along the King's Highway to Van Tilburgh's Inn at Kingston. Here, turning to the left on the narrow Rocky Hill road, he marched his way-worn soldiers down the valley of the Millstone.

The first information that Cornwallis had of the affair

at Princeton was the booming of cannon on the break of that cold day which he had expected to devote to catching "the old fox." He was much chagrined at Washington's escape, but was soon in full pursuit. Much time was lost in crossing Stony Brook, the bridge having been destroyed. On nearing Princeton a cannon shot from a small redoubt brought the British to a halt, their generals thinking that the Americans had fortified themselves in the town. This gun was fired by a few militiamen who had then hastily retired, but an hour was lost before Cornwallis discovered this and was again on the march. Having great fears for his military chest and supplies at New Brunswick, he hurriedly passed on through Princeton and Kingston without learning that at the latter place his foes had filed to the left.

Meanwhile, let us follow Washington, who was for the first time penetrating Somerset County. Arrayed in the Continental blue and buff, as he sat his horse with all that martial dignity peculiar to himself, he came as a conqueror, welcomed by the enthusiastic greetings of the populace. The little army toiled along the east bank of the Millstone, the men in high spirits over the experiences of the past twenty-four hours, but yet so weak from cold, hunger, and fatigue that they defiled along in dispersed order, with heavy steps, guns carried in whatever way was easiest, and their eyes almost glued with sleep. Many fell out by the way, and stretching themselves on the frozen ground sought that repose which exhausted nature refused longer to await. But few of the men were decently clad, much less amply protected from the wintry air, while some were without covering for their feet.

It is told that Washington while riding by the side of his troops noticed that William Lyon, a Continental soldier from Middlesex County, was without stockings and almost, if not entirely, without shoes. As he trudged sturdily along, his bare and bloody feet left their marks on the ice and gravel of the roadway. The General, checking his horse, tapped Lyon gently on the shoulder and said, "My brave boy, you deserve a better fate." "Ah," replied the young soldier, "there is no danger of my feet freezing as long as the blood runs." Rumbling along in the midst of the column were country carts containing that sad contingent of all victorious armies, the wounded—poor wretches who rested wearily against the sides of the wagon bodies, their countenances making mute appeals for human sympathy; some with arms in slings, some with heads bandaged, some with limbs and jaws shattered, while others lying in the straw were pale and wan, with eyes fast glazing.

Much of interest appertaining to this march to Morristown is to be learned from the manuscript diary of Captain Thomas Rodney of the Dover light infantry. When the van of the American army reached the bridge which then spanned the Millstone near Griggstown, British cavalry appeared in considerable force on the opposite bank. Just then the condition of Washington's men was such that he desired neither to pursue nor to be pursued, so, riding forward, he ordered Rodney to halt and break up the bridge. The captain recites that on this being done the enemy were forced to retire. Commissaries were sent forward to notify the inhabitants of the coming of the troops, and to direct that food be prepared for their refreshment. This demand met with a fair response, and when the army at dusk reached Somerset Courthouse—Millstone—where it encamped for the night, a considerable number of rations were in readiness.

Washington and some of his staff quartered at the residence of John Van Doren, just south of the village. Mr. Van Doren's military guests were not always of so distinguished a character. Some months later it was soldiers of the enemy that took possession of this old homestead. Upon their approach the men of the household thought it wise to disappear, but old Mrs. Van Doren

208

pluckily stood her ground and defied the intruders. She refused to give up her keys or tell where the family treasures were secreted, whereupon the brutal soldiers, after ransacking the house, hung her up by the heels in the cellar. After their departure she was released by her neighbors, but not until black in the face and almost lifeless.

During the night many laggards came into camp, and in the morning the column was again pushing northward, and continued to Pluckamin, which place was reached during the afternoon. The wounded were distributed in the houses of the village; the Lutheran Church as a temporary prison received the captured men, while in the Matthew Lane house it is said that the thirteen captured officers were placed under guard. The troops encamped on the bleak hillside just south of Pluckamin, the top of which, as Rodney writes, was covered with snow. Torn with the shock of conflict, weak from need of nourishment, and enfeebled by cold and exhaustion, the little army was most grateful for this place of security and the prospect of rest. Commissaries had been busy; within a few hours the camp was pretty well supplied with provisions, and before the drums beat tattoo nearly one thousand men, who had been unable to keep up on the march, rejoined their commands. When the darkness of night closed around Pluckamin Mountain, the ruddy glow of campfires shone among the trees near the foot of its northern slope. The flames, flashing up, illumined groups of soldiers, stacks of arms, and tethered horses; near by, baggage wagons, caissons, and cannon were parked in military lines, while here and there the shadowy forms of sentinels could be distinguished. There is no such comfort as fullness and warmth after cold and hunger. It was not long before most of the tired men were full-length at the foot of the trees, forgetting the travail of a soldier's life in needful sleep.

Sunday the fifth of January was a great day for

Pluckamin. The news of Washington being in Bedminster had rapidly spread, and, while it was yet early, on the roads and lanes leading to the village numerous parties of country people could be seen, all hurrying to visit the soldiers and learn for themselves the latest news of the campaign. Throughout the entire day the place was astir with an animated multitude, and excitements of all kinds ruled the hour. Squads of infantry and artillery men were everywhere. Farmers' wagons laden with provisions came rolling in from the neighborhood of Peapack, Lamington, and the valley. Stern, brown-visaged officers in heavy boots and tarnished uniforms were mounting here, dismounting there, and clattering through the streets in every direction. Foraging parties were being dispatched; couriers and express messengers rode off in hot haste; horses neighed, men shouted, and on all sides were handshakings and congratulations. The martial instinct of the people seemed alert; eyes sparkled and all hearts beat quickly. Every little while brought new arrivals of country people, and the details of the famous victory must be gone over again and again. Although the war was yet young, the soldiers had plenty to tell of marches and countermarches, of camp life and bivouacs, of attacks, routs, wounds, and hardships. And then the newcomers were carried off to the Lutheran Church, which was surrounded by a cordon of sentinels. And through its doors and windows, what a brave show!—two hundred and thirty British soldiers; broad-shouldered, big-boned Scotchmen, stalwart grenadiers, and dragoons brilliant with color—caged lions, who looked with gloomy stares upon the inquisitive and rejoicing Americans, whom the experiences of the past few days had taught them to better appreciate as soldiers and freemen.

And so the day wore on! Everywhere were motion and confusion. Eoff's Tavern kept open table, and on its porch Continental and militia officers of all grades mingled. It was *cling-clang! cling-clang!* all that Sunday on the anvil of the village forge, for from sunrise to the gloaming honest John Wortman and his brawny assistants were busy with hammer, sledge, and tongs, shoeing army horses and repairing army wagons. "Captain Bullion," too, was robbed of his usual Sunday quiet, being obliged to expose his wares for the benefit of impatient soldiers and visitors. Surgeons hurried from house to house, drums beat for guard mount, subalterns marched reliefs to the different sentry posts, and the din of war was in the very air.

Amid the bustle and animation, in fancy, I can see Aaron Malick, clad in his Sunday breeches of blue cloth, his red waistcoat with flapping pockets showing from under an amply skirted coat adorned with metal buttons. He had come down from the Old Stone House with the hope of learning something of his boy, John, but that poor lad was still in the grip of Provost Cunningham and knew nothing of the happy close of a campaign which had commenced for him rather ingloriously. In after years Aaron often told of the aspect Pluckamin presented on those memorable days. He especially delighted in reminiscences of the generals whose names grew greater as the war progressed—of Greene, tall and vigorous, with the air of one born to command; of Sullivan, alert and soldierly; of Knox, whose broad, full face beamed with satisfaction; but above all, of the conspicuous figure of Washington, who seemed a king among men as he moved amid the throng, with high-born eye, lofty but courteous port, and a calm, strong face reflecting a mind full of the tranquillity of conscious power.

Visitors to Pluckamin on that eventful Sunday were treated to an unexpected affair of ceremony. About midday a detachment of forty men from Rodney's regiment marched into the village, and drew up in line with its center opposite the entrance to the building in which lay the dead body of Captain Leslie. This young British officer was about to be buried with the honors of war, the light infantry being selected as escort because of their soldierly appearance and superior uniform. At the beat of muffled drum and wail of fife the men presented arms as the corpse was borne from the house to the flank of the line. The escort then broke into a column of fours and, reversing arms, marched in slow time and with solemn step to the Lutheran churchyard, where they filed to the left, forming in line opposite an open grave which had been dug near the head of that of Johannes Moelich.

There were wet eyes and true grief at that sepulcher. Among the citizens and military clustering about the bier were the captured British officers, whom Washington had generously permitted to be present in order that they might bid a final adieu to a comrade in arms who had been much beloved. And then the solemn hush was broken by the voice of the chaplain, saying, "I am the Resurrection and the Life, saith the Lord." As the simple service continued, the body of the young warrior slowly descended to its gravelly bed, the troops, meanwhile, resting their bent heads on the butts of their muskets, the muzzles being pressed to the ground. When the icy clods fell on the rude coffin, the escort fired three volleys over the open grave, and then shouldering arms, marched away, the drums and fifes striking up a lively tune on reaching the highway. The prisoners were returned to their quarters, the crowd dispersed and again contributed to the village tumults, leaving Leslie to sleep in his remote and retired tomb until its deep silence shall be broken by a majestic reveille, ushering in that eternal day which shall proclaim the full brotherhood of man, and in which such distinctions as friend and foe shall be no more, forever.

Captain Rodney tells us that these high military honors were accorded because of the desire of the American army to pay "due respect to bravery, tho' in an enemy." Leslie's gallantry in action at Princeton had won the admiration of his opponents; indeed, this may be said of the entire Seventeenth British Regiment. In the height of the engagement, Washington, on witnessing the courage and discipline of this command, could not forbear exclaiming to his officers, "See how those noble fellows fight! Ah! gentlemen, when shall we be able to keep an army long enough together to display a discipline equal to our enemy's?"

The attention of Surgeon Benjamin Rush to the son of his friends in Scotland did not end with the funeral. He marked the grave with a brown headstone. This soldier's grave is a connecting link between our Somerset village and the busy life of one of the most gifted Americans of the last century. When Doctor Rush died at the age of sixty-eight, few men in the United States were better known, were held in higher esteem for genius and learning, or were more sincerely beloved for philanthropy and good works. When at Pluckamin with Washington's army, he was thirty-one years old, his Princeton degree having been gained at the early age of fifteen. In person he was above middle stature, with a slender but well-proportioned figure. His combined features bespoke a strong and an active intellect, and though his whole demeanor was thoughtful and grave, expressive blue eyes illumined a highly animated countenance.

Doctor Rush was a man of wide and varied knowledge, with a talent for imparting it to others that was singularly felicitous. It is claimed that no one long remained in his presence without feeling conscious of an intellectual refreshment; and a contemporaneous writer has recorded that "his conversation was an attic repast, which, far from cloying, invigorated the appetite of those who partook of it." Before the end of the month he had taken his seat in Congress, which was then sitting at Baltimore. His figure soon became a familiar one to Somerset people, as in April he received the appointment of surgeon general of the hospital in the middle department, and in July was made physician general of the army.

Another interesting incident connected with the stay of the army at this time in Pluckamin was the arrival in camp of the gallant Captain John Stryker's troop of Somerset horse, laden with spoils from the enemy. Cornwallis in his hurried march toward New Brunswick was so unfortunate as to disable a number of his baggage wagons. He left them at the side of the road in charge of a quartermaster with a guard of two hundred men. Captain Stryker, though having with him but twenty troopers, resolved upon the capture of these stores. In the darkness of night he distributed his small force in a circle, completely surrounding the camp. The guard was suddenly astounded by a volley of musket shots and the whistling of bullets, while from under the black arches of the bordering trees came loud and repeated shouts, as if from a countless host. Demoralized by recent defeats, the men incontinently fled, thinking that they had been attacked by a large force of the Americans. Their fright was not so much caused by the roar of musketry as by the unearthly yells of the lusty troopers which so suddenly broke the stillness of the night. Captain Stryker was not long in so repairing the wagons that they could be hauled to a place of safety; he lost no time in making his way to Washington's camp with his treasures. The joy of the troops was unbounded when it was discovered that the wagons contained woolen clothing, of which the men stood in sore need.

Early on the morning of the sixth of January Pluckamin lost, as suddenly as it had gained, the distinction of being the headquarters of Washington's army. Soon after sounding reveille the drums beat assembly, and the men were under arms. The different commands filed out of camp and passed through the village, taking up their line of march northward. It was probably the most peaceful and satisfactory march experienced by the Continental Army since leaving Hackensack, three months before, with Cornwallis at their heels. Secure from pursuit, the little army trailed slowly along the narrow road, breaking in upon the country quiet with rattle of scabbard and snort of charger, with champ of bit and jingle of harness, with rumble of baggage and gun wagons, and with the crunch on the frozen ground of thousands of marching feet. Just before sunset it reached Morristown, where we, after having piloted Washington and his men in safety through Somerset County, may leave them to go into winter quarters.

16

Elegant Silks and Ruffles

IN RINGING UP the curtain on the next act of our local drama, a scene is disclosed very different from any heretofore shown on these Bedminster boards. In life, as on the mimic stage, startling and unexpected changes are not only always in order but frequently come as unannounced surprises. And so it is with the era we have reached in telling the story of the Old Farm. Its familiar environment of country quiet is transformed—its accessories are all of a different pattern. In the place of the fir tree and the myrtle have come the thorn and the bramble; ploughshares and pruning hooks have literally been beaten into swords and spears. Though war and rumors of war had now long been rife, its alarms and incidents had not been a portion of the daily life of this agricultural community.

When Breed's Hill trembled under its cannonade, Bedminster repose was not disturbed; and when the Battle of Long Island raged, the family in the Old Stone House was affected thereby only as it touched its members personally in their love of country or in their anxiety for those engaged in the conflict. Even when the tide of combat, crossing the Hudson, rolled over the level plains of the Jerseys, and the American army, sullen and dispirited, fell back to the Delaware before an exultant enemy, Bedminster was too far distant to have the spell of war overturn its usual routine of existence. At times during the month of the year just gone its rural calm had been broken by military turmoil, as, for instance, when Sullivan came marching through with Lee's division. But such occasions had not been many, nor for long, and the homesteads, fields, and folds had quickly relapsed to their accustomed quiet.

Now, however, all this was to be changed, and the beat of drum and blare of trumpet were to become familiar sounds. The Old Farm bordered a military thoroughfare, for in establishing the American camp at Morristown for the winter other cantonments had been located in the south, east, and west. There was constant going and coming between the different posts, and the highways and byways were alive with soldiers. Farmer lads on their way to mill with sacks of corn athwart their horses' backs rode cheek by jowl with spurred and booted troopers, and listened with open-eyed wonder to their warlike tales. The rattle of farm wagons was supplemented by the heavy roll of artillery trains, and squads of infantry were met at every hand.

At this time many a Continental officer whose name now ornaments the pages of history dismounted at the Old Stone House for rest and refreshment, or for a draught from the deep well of its flanking dooryard. This dwelling lays no claim to the possession of a bed upon which Washington has slept; exhibits no chair upon which he has sat or table at which he has dined; but it is fair to presume that more than once its walls have reflected that august presence. As at that time this house ranked among the most important of the township, it is not probable that the Commander in Chief could always have passed it by. His papers and correspondence show him to have been that winter constantly on the road, visiting the different outposts and making the acquaintance of the country and people. We shall, therefore, not be charged with trespassing beyond the boundary line of possibility when in fancy we see him giving a dignity and grandeur to the homely interior of the Old House, as he stands, erect, serene, majestic, before the great fireplace in the living room. He is questioning Aaron, perhaps, as to the character of some of the inhabitants thereabouts, or receiving at the hands of Charlotte a hospitable mug of cider or a cup of cream, while the family and friends look with love and respect upon the illustrious man.

Washington had great fondness for horses. Having from boyhood been at home in the saddle, he presented when mounted a singularly graceful appearance. During the winter and spring of which we are now writing he was frequently seen trotting along the Bedminster highways, accompanied by members of his staff and a small guard. A chronicler thus describes his impressions, received a few years afterwards, on unexpectedly coming upon the General riding over the Somerset hills:

As I walked on, ascending a hill suddenly appeared a brilliant troop of cavaliers. The clear sky behind them equally relieved the dark blue uniforms, the buff facings and glittering military appendages. All were gallantly mounted—all were tall and graceful, but one towered above the rest. I doubted not an instant that I saw the beloved hero. . . . Although all my life used to the pride, pomp, and circumstance of glorious war, to gay and gallant Englishmen, the tartaned Scot, and the embroidered German of every military grade, I still think the old blue and buff of Washington and his aids, their cocked-hats worn sidelong, with the union cockade, their whole equipment, as seen at that moment, was the most martial of anything that I ever saw.

And we may readily believe that the inhabitants looked with delight on these chance meetings with the Commander in Chief.

We may suppose that Aaron journeyed frequently to Morristown during the winter; visitors were made very welcome at the American camp, especially if they brought supplies. Farmers soon found that they had an excellent market near at home, and that commissaries were eager to pay fifteen cents for beef, forty-five cents for butter, and eight shillings for geese and turkeys. The main part of the army lay in the Lowantica or Spring Valley, which stretches from Morristown toward Green Village. The main street of this military village was about eighty feet wide and bordered with large officers' tents. It was well graded and used as a parade ground, a large liberty tree being planted in its center. On parallel streets, about forty feet wide, were the soldiers' huts built in blocks of four or five together, and in addition there were log storehouses and large cabins for the use of sutlers and commissaries. Both officers and men were in splendid spirits, and the sentiments of all had undergone a marvellous change, an almost jubilant confidence having taken the place of the despondency of the close of the year.

The pendulum of public opinion had swung to the other extremity of its arc. The people expected that the American army, small in numbers, poorly clad, badly fed, and with but little training, would prevail against Howe's well-appointed force of veteran soldiers. That at times the Americans did successfully cope with the enemy, and that, though often suffering privations hitherto almost unknown in the annals of warfare, they continued to harass the foe, and ultimately triumphed, can largely be charged to the fact of superior generalship. In addition, the extent and variety of the country with its inimical population and alert militia made a British success barren of results. There always remained an army— though a ragged one—in the field. It was not like European fighting where often one great action would be decisive and end the war. As General Greene wrote at this time: "We cannot conquer the British force at once, but they cannot conquer us at all. The limits of the British government in America are their out-sentinels."

Washington's headquarters in Morristown were at a tavern, which, together with the old courthouse with its wooden cupola and shingled sides, faced the village green. At the outset of the war Morristown had but about two hundred and fifty inhabitants. Its two church edifices, Presbyterian and Baptist, on the arrival of the American army were converted into hospitals, in which use they continued for about eighteen months. The Presbyterian congregation was forced to worship, even in the cold weather, in the open air, assembling in an orchard.

The Commander in Chief appointed the light infantry to be his personal guard, requiring twenty-six men to mount sentry around the tavern. That this guard might always be within a more convenient distance than the general camp, the entire regiment was installed about one mile away in the large Ford mansion, now the well-known "Headquarters." General Greene quartered with a Mr. Hoffman, whom tradition mentions as a good-natured man, whose charming wife was a great lover of the clergy. It is said that Mrs. Hoffman was often perplexed with doubt and difficulties on religious questions raised by the General's aides, especially by the merry, restless, witty Major Blodget.

Early in January Mrs. Washington, Mrs. Knox, and other ladies joined their husbands in camp; after that the officers of the army knew many comforts and not a few pleasures. Visits were exchanged between hospitable, blazing hearthstones, merry sleigh rides were enjoyed over the snow-covered Morris and Somerset hills, there were dinners at the different generals' quarters, little dances were frequent, and occasionally a subscription ball —or assembly as it was termed—was given. The latter affairs put the rural as well as the army society agog, invitations being extended in the neighborhood. These more important dances were held in a large room over the commissary's storehouse, which faced the square.

General and Mrs. Washington were much attached to each other and, so far as was possible, avoided long separations. It was the custom of the Commander in Chief to dispatch an aide-de-camp each winter to escort his wife to headquarters. Her arrival was a noted event, and her plain chariot with neat postilions in scarlet and white liveries was always welcomed with great joy by the army. After the war Mrs. Washington used to say that she nearly always had heard the first and last cannon-firing of each campaign. Mrs. Elizabeth F. Ellet, in her *Domestic History of the American Revolution*,[1] states that on this, Mrs. Washington's first visit to New Jersey, she was met by her husband some distance from camp, probably at Pluckamin, he having come from Morristown for that purpose. The lady at whose house the General awaited the arrival of his wife was much astonished when the carriage stopped at seeing so plainly dressed a woman descend. She at first thought her to be a servant, but the idea was soon dispelled by seeing Washington hasten to aid her in alighting, and by noticing the tenderness of his greeting. After satisfying himself as to her health and the comforts of the journey, his first inquiries were for the favorite horses he had left at Mount Vernon.

This was a time for ladies of monumental headgear and exceedingly elaborate toilets; but Mrs. Washington was very quiet in her tastes, and except on occasions of ceremony always dressed with much plainness. In many respects the first lady of the land afforded an excellent example to the women of America. Lossing [2] depicts her at home as looking after every detail of the household, going about with a bunch of housekeeper's keys depending from her waist and personally directing her many servants. While at Morristown, one day a number of the ladies of the village called upon her. Considering the occasion one of great importance and wishing to create a favorable impression, they arrayed themselves in their

---

[1] Published at New York in 1850.
[2] Benson J. Lossing, *The Pictorial Field-Book of the Revolution* (New York, 1851–52). There were several editions.

best gowns. One of the ladies, in her old age, gave the Reverend Doctor Joseph F. Tuttle, Morristown's historian,[3] the following account of their visit:

> We were dressed in our most elegant silks and ruffles and so were introduced to her ladyship. And don't you think we found her with a speckled homespun apron on, and engaged in knitting a stocking! She received us very handsomely and then resumed her knitting. In the course of her conversation she said very kindly to us, while she made her needle fly, that American ladies should be patterns of industry to their country women. . . . We must become independent of England by doing without those articles which we can make ourselves. Whilst our husbands and brothers are examples of patriotism we must be examples of industry!

"I declare," said one of the visiting ladies afterward, "I never felt so rebuked and ashamed in all my life."

Mrs. Washington used to entertain intimates of Morristown camp society with accounts of her home life, and how there were always sixteen spinning wheels going. She showed the ladies two morning dresses which had been made in her own house from ravelings of an old set of satin chair covers. This material was carded, spun, and woven with cotton yarns in alternate stripes of white cotton and crimson silk.

Life has many sides. Mrs. Washington must have appreciated this to the full in the strong contrasts presented by her alternate experiences of quiet home life at Mount Vernon, with its comforts and luxuries, and of the excitements, discomforts, and dangers incidental to camp life each winter. She, however, always gladly braved the latter in order to enjoy her husband's society, and that she might aid him by counsel and consultation in the care of his distant estate.

The buoyancy of feeling pervading the community was much enhanced during the month of January by a series of military successes. On the seventh of the month

---

[3] Author of various historical articles in the *Proceedings of the New Jersey Historical Society* and other publications.

General Maxwell, with a considerable body of Continentals and militia, fell suddenly upon Elizabethtown, capturing fifty Waldeckers and forty Highlanders, and making a prize of a schooner loaded with baggage and blankets. About the same time a detachment surprised Spanktown—Rahway—driving out the enemy and securing a thousand bushels of salt. On the twentieth a foraging party of the enemy came out from New Brunswick to obtain flour from the mills on the Millstone. They were attacked with great spirit by four hundred Jersey militia and fifty Pennsylvania riflemen, who completely routed the enemy, killing and wounding a number, making nine prisoners, and securing forty wagons and nearly one hundred English draught horses.

These many satisfactory enterprises, coming so soon after the affairs of Trenton and Princeton, still further increased public confidence. Washington deemed it expedient to take advantage of this prevailing sentiment by endeavoring to counteract the effect of the Howe's exemption proclamation. He consequently issued a counter one, directing all persons who held British protection papers to deliver them at headquarters or some other designated point and there take the oath of allegiance to the United States. Thirty days from the twenty-fifth of January were allowed in which to do this, and those failing to comply within that period were required to withdraw themselves and their families within the British lines. Probably it was at this time that Peter Melick experienced his second change of heart toward the American cause, for he certainly remained in New Jersey, and we hear nothing more of his disaffection. With detachments of the American army lying on his north, south, and east, and with squads of Continental soldiers passing and repassing almost daily on their way to and from the various posts, Peter could not have highly valued his British protection papers and doubtless was glad enough to recover the good opinion of his neighbors by again ranging himself on the side of those who supported the government.

The result of this order was much as Washington had anticipated. Some citizens in the vicinity of Elizabethtown, New Brunswick, and Perth Amboy, unable to resist the dominating influence of the proximity of the English army, adhered to their belief in the uselessness of continuing the contest and, therefore, were forced to abandon their homes. But the majority of the inhabitants, now feeling secure in the protection afforded by American arms, were very ready to disavow their recent submission to the emissaries of the Crown. This was particularly the case in Somerset and Morris, and for the rest of the war Tories were few and silent in those counties.

All this time the British were quiet within their lines, and seemed content to await warmer weather before undertaking further operations. This gave to the Americans a much-needed opportunity for recuperation and for recruiting a new army, the terms of the enlistments for the old one, which had been for a single year, having expired. Meanwhile it was necessary that a close watch should be kept upon Howe's force lest he should steal unawares in the direction of Philadelphia or of Burgoyne's northern army. For this purpose different cantonments were established extending from the Highlands on the north under Heath to Princeton on the south under Putnam. This last General's command of about six hundred men served as a corps of observation.

During the winter and spring the graceful figure of Putnam's chief aide was often seen galloping across the country; and more than one Somerset maiden learned to look with fluttering heart and mantling color for a passing smile from the dangerously handsome Major Aaron Burr. If Dame Rumor wags a truthful tongue, this young staff officer was not always content with paying a passing tribute to rural beauty. Whatever ambitions, worthy or otherwise, may have attacked this extraordinary man in civil life, they do not seem to have affected his military career. The Major wrote to a friend from Princeton on the seventh of March that he was well contented, neither expecting nor desiring promotion, and, as he expressed it, "I am at present quite happy in the esteem and entire confidence of my good old general."

During the few months that Putnam was stationed at this point he was very active in scouring the country, and he took from the enemy nearly one thousand prisoners and about one hundred and twenty wagonloads of baggage and other booty. Sullivan's command lay in the vicinity of Scotch Plains, from which place he constantly sent out scouts to watch and report on the movements of the foe, and Dickinson, with the Jersey militia, did the same service in the vicinity of Somerset Courthouse, now Millstone. General Lincoln, with a considerable force, guarded the Raritan ford at Bound Brook. A blockhouse or fortification was erected near the mouth of Bound Brook Creek; an earthwork connected it with the river.

To be within easy support of these various posts, in February Greene's division moved down to Basking Ridge, where it remained until the opening of the next campaign. "Great men," says the hero worshipper, Carlyle, "taken up in any way are profitable company." If General Nathanael Greene was not great he at least did great things, and not the least by any means of his achievements was his having so educated himself as to rise in a few years from a very ordinary social plane to be the friend and companion of Washington, and from a private in a Rhode Island company to the rank of major general in the American army. The personality of Greene made a strong impression on the people of Somerset. Vigorous in mind and body, he was ever actively alert in behalf of the cause for which he had drawn his sword, and was much beloved by his friends while feared by his foes. Being enterprising and full of resources, he was considered as dangerous as his chief, and Cornwallis is reported to have said that he never felt secure when encamped in his neighborhood. In case of Washington's death it was generally admitted by the country that Greene of all others was most fitted for the chief command.

At Basking Ridge this General's headquarters were at Lord Stirling's handsome residence, where Lady Stirling and her attractive daughter, Lady Kitty, made most agreeable hostesses. At this time this manor house was the seat of hospitality, refinement, and luxury; great sociability prevailed, and many friends were welcomed with old-fashioned heartiness. There was no lack of excellent society in the neighborhood. Altogether, we may imagine that General Greene and the young men of his staff discovered that their lines had fallen in very pleasant places.

When the British overran Union County, Governor Livingston was forced to abandon his Elizabethtown residence, Liberty Hall. While he was here, there, and everywhere, serving the state and aiding Washinigton, his family spent the winter with Lady Stirling, who was Governor Livingston's sister. In the spring the Governor established a home on a farm at Parsippany to which he could retreat when necessary. But even there several unsuccessful attempts were made by refugees to capture the chief magistrate, for whom a standing reward was offered by the enemy.

The Livingston young ladies were exceedingly popular and highly considered by the best people of that day, their many physical and mental graces often acting as social oil upon the troubled waters of that turbulent time. Their experiences during the war, both while visiting the army as the guests of Mrs. Washington and while at home in Elizabethtown, were of the most varied character. On one occasion Susan, the second daughter, by her cleverness, aided perhaps by her personal charms, was the means of preserving her father's most valuable papers; this was at a time when a marauding band of the enemy were ransacking Liberty Hall. She was considered a wit in Revolutionary circles, and many of her bright sayings have been preserved. It was in New York at the time of the evacuation that in conversation with Major Upham, one of Lord Dorchester's aides, she expressed the hope that the English would soon depart; "for," said she, "among our incarcerated belles the scarlet fever must rage till you are gone." The Major cleverly replied that he feared the ladies would be tormented by a worse malady, the "blue devils."

To return to the Continental Army! In this year, 1777, matters were at the lowest ebb in February; at one time in that month it is claimed that fifteen hundred men could not have been mustered in Washington's camp. But this condition of affairs, which the enemy happily did not discover, rapidly mended. As the spring advanced the force at Morristown was gradually augmented by recruits who had been enlisted for the new army by the different states. The second establishment of eighty-eight battalions, of which the New Jersey quota was four, had been authorized by Congress in the preceding September.

By the last of April the army rejoiced in the possession of new muskets of a uniform pattern, two vessels having arrived from France bearing twenty-four thousand stand of arms. In that month there reached camp a man who had already won golden opinions as a soldier, and who was destined to do yet greater things for the country. This was Colonel Daniel Morgan, who appeared at the head of one hundred and eighty stalwart riflemen, a command that was afterwards recruited to a regimental standard and known as "Morgan's Rangers." This officer was long of limb, possessed great strength and muscular activity, with a face which, though scarred by an ugly wound received in the French and Indian War, plainly indexed a character full of inherent strength, good humor, honesty, and self-reliance. He was a Jerseyman, having been born in Hunterdon of Welsh parentage in 1736.

227

He early left home to seek his fortune, and finding his way to Virginia became a teamster. As such, Morgan with his own wagon and horses accompanied Braddock on his unfortunate expedition. This made him a soldier, for his military instincts soon caused him to exchange the reins for a musket.

After the fall of Yorktown, Morgan, then a brigadier general, was invited to dine with some of the captured British officers at Winchester, who were in his charge. In conversation with Captain Samuel Graham the American officer playfully remarked that the British still owed him a lash from a whip. On being asked for an explanation, he told of his having driven a wagon in the early days of the French and Indian War; for some irregularity he was sentenced by court-martial to receive five hundred lashes. He got but four hundred and ninety-nine, as he counted them himself as they fell, and afterwards convinced the drum major, who wielded the whip, of his mistake.

Private Morgan's bravery in 1758 secured for him an ensign's commission from the governor of Virginia. At the outbreak of the Revolution he raised in that colony a company of ninety-six young marksmen, all skilled in woodcraft, and with them joined the army that assailed Quebec. He proved a brave and an adroit fighter, winning even British encomiums for the courage displayed in the assault. After the wounding of Arnold he was captured, and so marked had been his conduct in that affair that the enemy offered him a command, which he indignantly declined. After eight months' captivity he was exchanged and joined Washington's army. Thenceforward he shared in the hardships of every campaign until the summer of 1779, when his shattered health forced him to resign. When the unhappy tide of war, flowing southward, rose to a flood in the Carolinas and Gates exchanged his northern laurels for the willow of defeat at Camden, Morgan again offered his services to the country. He became

Greene's most trusted lieutenant, and in January, 1781, covered himself and the southern army with glory by winning the battle of Cowpens without the aid of a single piece of artillery. The "old wagoner" fulfilled the promise he made his men "that he would crack his whip over the head of Ben Tarleton in the morning as sure as he lived."

17

A Time to Fight

THERE WAS FIGHTING at Bound Brook on Sunday, the thirteenth of April. The enemy, four thousand strong, marched from New Brunswick at nine o'clock on Saturday night, and the expedition was conducted with so much secrecy that but few of the inhabitants knew of their departure until Sunday morning. It is said that the British, in marching, avoided the roads; at all events they reached the American outposts, and there lay on their arms until daylight, their proximity entirely unsuspected. On Sunday morning long before breakfast the garrison of the blockhouse were greeted by a rattle of musketry and a rain of ball clattering against the wooden walls of their stronghold. General Lincoln, whose troops did not number one-quarter those of Cornwallis, had no opportunity of forming his men, and barely time to get in the saddle and order a hasty retreat; indeed so close was the foe that one of the aides fell in their hands before he could mount his horse. Some desultory, defensive firing was continued for a time by a portion of his troops, but eventually they fell back to the mountain in the rear of the town, with the loss of two pieces of artillery and sixty men killed, wounded, and prisoners.

This sudden onslaught of the British filled the Bound Brook villagers with dismay, and, as panic-stricken as the troops, they deserted their homes and sought safety in flight. When the firing ceased and the smoke cleared away, the enemy found no one to dispute with them the possession of the place; its only occupants were a dead soldier stretched in a pool of blood on the blockhouse floor, with a few more of the slain and some of the wounded lying singly or in heaps on the streets and in the adjoining fields. Considerable booty was secured, comprising a quantity of arms, two wagons loaded with ammunition, several horses, and about one hundred head of cattle and sheep. In addition several hundred barrels of flour were destroyed, together with a lot of whiskey, rum, and other stores that the Continental Army could just then but illy spare. General Greene hurried to Lincoln's support, but Basking Ridge being twelve miles distant, it was after midday before his division reached Bound Brook; by that time the enemy had evacuated the place and retired to Raritan Landing.

This affair at Bound Brook caused much concern to the Commander in Chief; it showed conclusively that the post was one of exposure and danger, and great anxiety was felt lest a second attack should be attended with even more disastrous results. It had been hoped that an advance on the enemy might be made to advantage, but after Greene had reconnoitered their position and examined the condition of the American posts it was deemed unwise to make the attempt.

Although his vigorous and usually judicious military efforts were as a rule requited by the frowns of fortune, General Lincoln never lost his popularity or the confidence of the army, Congress, and the Commander in Chief. He had been a farmer until over forty years old at Hingham, Massachusetts, and all he knew of the soldier's art before the war was gained as a militia officer. At the outset of the Revolution, after serving in the Provincial Congress and as one of the Committee of Correspondence, he was appointed major general by the Council of Massachusetts, and in October, 1776, at the

231

head of the militia of his state joined the main army at New York. He soon displayed great ability as a commander, which, together with his upright character and undoubted merit, induced Washington to recommend him to Congress, whereupon in February, 1777, that body created him a major general in the Continental establishment. Though his inherent qualities and superior powers were pronounced, his military misfortunes were proverbial.

The General was long remembered at Bound Brook as an erect, broad-chested man, having a frank, open countenance with an aspect rather venerable and benign. His indefatigable perseverance and unconquerable energy won the citizen's admiration, and, though genial by nature and easily approached, his mere presence invariably provoked respect. It is said that, always himself correct and chaste in conversation, none dared when with him to indulge in profanity or in levity on serious subjects.

There was another arrival from Virginia that spring at Morristown, which excited great interest. It was that of Brigadier General John Peter Gabriel Mühlenberg, who had left New Jersey in 1772 as an humble Lutheran clergyman. He was warmly welcomed by the Germans of the New Jersey hill country, but they found it difficult to grow accustomed to his Continental blue and buff and military trappings. So much glitter and sheen seemed a strange metamorphosis from the modest canonicals of their old German pastor; but it was the same man with the same great affections and merry heart that had left them five years before, and he found many friends who delighted in his return. We may be sure that the General went out of his way to visit his old parishioners living in the Bedminster Stone House. He could not have had other than pleasing remembrances of his past intimacy with Aaron Malick, who had been an active and leading member of his congregation at Pluckamin, and two of whose children he had baptized. From these circumstances we may fairly fancy the warm reception extended to the parson-soldier as his burly form darkened the doorway of the living room and his hearty tones called down, in the good old German pastoral fashion, blessings on all in that house.

The attachment felt by the people of Zion and St. Paul's congregations toward their former rector was not only due to the faithfulness with which he had ministered his holy calling; he had endeared himself to them by the sympathy and affection with which he had entered into all their daily affairs. He was a part of their life—of their pleasures as well as of their pains. With them he fished the streams, with them he roamed the hills for game; he could dance as well as pray, and no festive occasion was complete without his presence.

He had occupied Zion's pulpit for the first time in 1769, and continued to supply that and St. Paul's at Pluckamin for three years. In 1772 his father had been applied to by Germans of the valley of the Blue Ridge, Virginia, for a minister for their new church at Woodstock, they asking that his son might be sent. This request had been acceded to, and the young minister made his way beyond the Potomac.

When Mühlenberg reached his parish in the Old Dominion, his personal qualifications and high character soon won from his new people the same love and respect that he had enjoyed from those of New Jersey, and it was not long before his popularity throughout the entire valley of the Blue Ridge was unbounded. By his skill with the rifle he shot his way into the affections of many a frontiersman, and his love of hunting brought him the companionship of not a few of the leading men of that hunting-loving province—among them Patrick Henry and Washington. With the latter he often explored the mountains with horses, hounds, and horns in search of deer, and it is said that in the use of his favorite weapon he found himself the peer of his illustrious companion. The friendship thus formed proved lasting and was probably largely influential in transforming the country parson into a Revolutionary soldier. Mühlenberg became the political as well as the religious leader of the Germans in the colony. He was untiring in his endeavors to quicken the patriotic impulses of his people, and when the clouds of discontent and apprehension began to darken the political horizon, the prominent Whigs of Virginia found in him a most important and valuable ally. He was made a member of the Virginia Convention, became the chairman of the Committee of Correspondence for his county, and in December, 1775, was commissioned as colonel of the Eighth Battalion—known as the German Regiment.

When bidding good-by to his congregation in January, 1776, at the close of his sermon he announced that he believed with the Holy Writ that there was a time to preach and a time to pray, but that those times had passed away; then, with increased emphasis, he cried out with dramatic fervor that there was also a time to *fight* and that time had now arrived! Thereupon he suddenly threw off his gown and stood before his people in the full uniform of a Continental colonel. At a signal, drummers, who had been stationed outside the door, beat a stirring march, and Mühlenberg, displaying a list, solicited recruits. Nearly three hundred German Lutherans enrolled their names. In February, 1777, Colonel Mühlenberg was appointed a brigadier general and was ordered to report to Washington at Morristown.

As the spring advanced, the British were displaying more activity in their camps, and an important movement was evidently in contemplation. At New Brunswick they were constructing a portable pontoon bridge, and in many ways their operations indicated an intention of soon attempting the passage of the Delaware. Washington deemed it wise to post his army in a stronger position so as to be better able to check the enemy in any overland endeavor to reach Pennsylvania. He selected the heights in the rear of Bound Brook, and directed that an encampment should be laid out on the side of the hill below Chimney Rock, to the right of the gorge through which Middle Brook descends.

The troops were disposed so as to guard against surprise and to deceive the adversary. We find Washington biding his time, watching from his eyrie for every sign or incident indicating on the part of the enemy an intention to advance. Meanwhile both officers and men found plenty to do; earthworks were thrown up, cannons so mounted as to sweep the plain below, huts and storehouses erected, and much time was devoted in endeavoring to transform raw recruits into something approaching disciplined soldiers. Commissaries were soon flying around among the farmers, and for some weeks to come Middlebrook Camp was an excellent market for sheep and cattle. Farm kitchens and cellars were ransacked for cider vinegar—then considered a sovereign remedy for camp fever produced by a too continuous flesh diet. The supply soon became exhausted, and a substitute was made with rum, molasses, and water, a little flour being added to produce fermentation. So, two weeks or more passed away, until the army was just beginning to wonder whether Howe purposed summering on the Raritan, when suddenly the campaign opened.

On the night of the thirteenth, General Howe, leaving two thousand men at New Brunswick, marched, nearly fifteen thousand strong, in the direction of the American camp. In the morning the troops came to a halt with the right of the army at Millstone, while the left rested on the river. This was indeed an advance in force. There no longer seemed any reason for questioning that the objective point was to be Philadelphia. But the British General, profiting by past experiences, was wary, and his first desire was to cripple the American army. So instead of marching southward and exposing his flanks, he presented his front to Washington, hoping that the American general would come down from his stronghold and give him battle.

On the morning of Sunday the fourteenth of June the inhabitants of Franklin Township were made acquainted with the pictorial effect of war to an extent not before enjoyed—if such a word can be used in speaking of a display made by an enemy. All through the previous night, along the Amwell Road and along the road following the west bank of the Raritan, had been heard the hollow tramp of marching men—the rumbling of artillery —the sound of countless hoofbeats—the blast of bugles —and the sharp tones of military command.

At daybreak rank upon rank of soldiers with guidons and pennons fluttering were seen sweeping along these highways and occupying the country that intervened between Millstone and New Brunswick. Everywhere were troops, and still troops! They stood in compact masses—they bivouacked in the fields—the eye swept down long lines of color and along ranks of glittering steel; the rising sun, flashing on helmets of brass and bathing royal standards proudly floating over well-equipped battalions, illumined a scene unusual indeed for Somerset people. This was no army formed of men, hungry, tattered, worn out by the marches they had made, but a well-fed, gaily apparelled force, strong with the refreshment of long quiet. Here were Anspachians and Waldeckers, the first somber in black leggings and dark blue uniforms, the second gaudy with many hues and tricked out in foreign finery. There, a regiment of Scotch, stalking by as if on their own breezy highlands, national and picturesque in bare knees, flowing kilts, and tartaned bonnets. Neat, graceful English grenadiers offered a complete contrast to the more heavily accoutred German foot-soldiers; while sturdy Hessian yägers with yellow housings and dangling scabbards and squadrons of British dragoons in all the splendor of glint and color added to the brilliancy of the picture. Such soldiers seemed only to need the word of command to make their way to the Delaware or to any other point to which they might be ordered.

With the approach of the English all was stir and bustle in the American camp. The army paraded on the hillside, prepared to receive the enemy should an attack be attempted but declining to abandon its strong position for the uncertainties of an engagement on the plain below. So the adversaries confronted and watched each other for five days, the British entrenching themselves somewhat, throwing up earthworks at Millstone and Middlebush. Meanwhile the militia flew to arms and, distributed in small squads, made the stay of the enemy as uncomfortable as possible. Marksmen lurked behind the trees or lay concealed under the fences. Unhappy the lot of the redcoat who wandered too far from camp, the forager who straggled too far from his party, or the picket who occupied a too extended line. Morgan's men were also ubiquitous; like so many wasps they stung the foe at every turn.

Howe continued to maneuver in front of the Americans, hoping to bring on a general action, but Washington was too wise to permit his raw troops to cope with this veteran force unless it should be in the strong position he occupied. Some of the junior generals, quite willing to test the mettle of the new army, were eager for the fray. Among them was Brigadier Anthony Wayne, an officer who was full of nervous energy and who always felt within himself the potentiality of great deeds; he urged that at least some sidestroke should be attempted. The Commander in Chief, however, would not permit any movement to be made; his desires were all accomplished in barring the enemy's southern progress. On the nineteenth of June, Howe, despairing of attaining his purposes, suddenly retired with his army to New Brunswick. Three days later, on Sunday the twenty-second, the

British entirely evacuated that place, retreating to Perth Amboy.

When Howe fell back to Amboy, Washington, in order to be within supporting distance of Greene, moved with the main army to Quibbletown (now New Market). On Thursday the twenty-sixth Howe hurriedly marched in the direction of Westfield, hoping to push around to the rear of the Americans and thus prevent their again reaching the heights. But Washington was too alert to be the victim of such strategy.

On Monday, the thirtieth of June, Howe and his army crossed to Staten Island on the pontoon bridge constructed for use on the Delaware. Thus ended the first invasion of New Jersey. Seven months' occupation of the state by a thoroughly equipped foreign army had resulted in nothing. The undisciplined forces of the Americans had defeated every effort made by the enemy to penetrate beyond the Delaware, and most of the time had restricted them to the vicinity of the Raritan.

Soon after crossing to Staten Island the British embarked on two hundred and seventy transports that were lying in the Lower Bay. What Howe would next do was now the question in the American camp. Washington was at a loss whether to continue in Somerset, so as to move quickly toward Pennsylvania should the British sail for the Delaware capes, or whether to march to the Highlands of the Hudson, fearing that the enemy might ascend the Hudson River in order to combine with Burgoyne. There was, at least, no reason for longer perching on Middlebrook Heights. Early on the morning of the second of July was heard the shout and din of breaking camp. Huts were dismantled, baggage wagons were loaded, and guns limbered. Soon the woods about Chimney Rock were echoing for the last time that year to drumbeats for assembly, and the men, with knapsacks packed and strapped, were hurrying to their companies. Horses, ready saddled, pawed the ground in front of officers' quarters, and troops were in motion in every part of the camp. Washington had decided to march farther northward so as to be better able to move in either direction when Howe's intentions should be known.

On the afternoon of the fourth the troops encamped at Morristown, where they remained for one week. Meanwhile the English fleet was under sail, now heading up the Hudson, now cruising in the Sound, now bearing away for the Hook, each change of direction adding to the uncertainty and anxiety of mind of Washington and his generals. On the eleventh it was determined to continue the march, but on the following day the army was arrested at Pompton by a drenching rainstorm. Washington was ill at ease. This watching an enemy that was on board a fleet he found a very different business from standing on the brow of the "Blue Hills" and surveying the foe on the plains below. He chafed sorely at this delay, but it was unavoidable; the descending floods continued, the roads were choked with mud, and the Pequannock and Ramapo rivers were swollen into rapid torrents. A long halt not having been anticipated, a concentrated camp had not been pitched, the troops bivouacking as best they could in an extended line under the dripping trees that bordered the road. And so two very uncomfortable days were passed. The rain was incessant, the men were soaked to the skin, water trickled, dripped, and splashed from caissons, wagons, and saddles, while from the horses' sides and flanks rose a thick steam, which mingled with the aqueous vapors exuding from the soaked and spongy ground.

On the fourteenth the column was again in motion, toiling over the miry and slippery Ramapo Hills and pushing on through the Clove to the Hudson, which was reached on the twenty-second. The Commander in Chief, though full of perplexity, was ever watchful of the enemy, and as their latest move pointed seaward he again fell back with the greater part of his army to Pompton.

Two days later the mystery seemed solved, for on that day he wrote General Lincoln: "I have just received information that the fleet left the Hook yesterday, and as I think the Delaware the most probable place of their destination I shall move the army that way."

And now we again see the Continentals swinging their hurried way along the Somerset roads, which a hot July sun and thousands of trampling hoofs and feet had already made dusty. On Sunday the twenty-eighth the eyes of Bedminster people looked with delight upon the conspicuous and well-known figure of Mühlenberg mounted on a tall white charger with rich housings, riding at the head of four thousand troops. General Greene being absent on a few days leave, Mühlenberg had command of the division. How the old parishioners of the German General must have marvelled at his strangely martial appearance! As his erect form amid his soldier comrades passed along the familiar highways, what comparisons must have been made with former days: with those days when he rode this same country on errands of mercy and love astride a modest cob, wearing instead of epaulettes of bullion the livery of a Lutheran domine, and when in place of the swinging sword and warlike holster were peaceful saddlebags stuffed with Bibles, prayer books, and sermons.

On the thirtieth, Mühlenberg's division was resting at Coryell's Ferry on the Delaware. To expedite crossing the river, the divisions of Stephen and Lincoln, which followed Mühlenberg's, reached the Delaware four miles above at Howell's Ferry, while Lord Stirling's division, debouching south, rested at Trenton. On the thirty-first a courier was dispatched to hurry forward Sullivan's division, an express having brought the news of two hundred and twenty-eight sail of vessels being at the capes of the Delaware. The next day, to Washington's great surprise and dismay, a second express announced that the fleet had sailed eastward. The clouds of doubt and uncertainty which had so happily seemed dissipated again gathered, darkening the horizon. Once more it became necessary for a portion of the army to take up its line of march in the direction of the Hudson, Washington remaining in Pennsylvania so as to be near Congress until Howe's intentions should be fully disclosed. This was a trying time for the troops. The heat was extreme, and the men suffered much fatigue and injury from their continuous and hurried marching along the dusty roads and over the many hills that intervened between the Hudson and the Delaware.

Congress and the Commander in Chief were now kept for many days in a state of suspense, the complete disappearance of the fleet rendering it uncertain whether Howe's next stroke was to be in the direction of the upper Hudson, of Philadelphia, or of Charleston. If in the latter, it was felt that the Continental Army was too distant to be of any avail; consequently its different divisions were distributed in Pennsylvania and New Jersey, ready to move quickly should time divulge that either of the other points was to be the destination of the fleet. To the great joy of everyone, on the twenty-eighth of August Howe showed his hand—all doubts were set at rest, for transports and convoys were discovered within the Virginia capes and, with their canvas wings wide spread, standing fairly up Chesapeake Bay. And so this extraordinary chase, unparalleled in the chronicles of warfare—a chase of an army on the sea by an army on the land—drew near to a finish. The Continental divisions were quickly brought together; and the concentrated force, now largely increased by regiments from the south and by Pennsylvania militia, marched down the Delaware, the men elated that there was no longer any uncertainty as to the intentions of the enemy.

18

A Machine of Delicate Adjustments

B UT, AS THEY ARE HURRYING on to the inevitable colli-
sion, you and I, reader, must cry, halt! We have for
some time been drifting together on the tide of national
history. This was all very well while that tide ebbed and
flowed within our own state; but now that it has sought
channels beyond the borders of New Jersey it behooves
us to abandon the great historic figures in whose excellent
company we have been, and turn again to the contemplation of a simpler form of humanity. Ours the simple duty
of writing the story of an old farm, and as fascinating as
the greater theme may be, we must not devote too much
time to the historic interest of those wonderful years
when a great nation was in the throes of its birth, and
thus neglect those minor personal interests in which rest
the foundation of our work. We confess, however, to a
feeling of regret at turning our backs upon the Continental Army. There is a singular charm in either witnessing or participating in scenes where men contend together for mastery, and it is undoubtedly true that all
human nature retains its primitive savage love of conflict.
The army will come again to Bedminster, when it will
once more properly be within our province to delineate
its fortunes.

Upon returning to Somerset County we find it
strangely quiet after the military turmoil of the preceding

seven months. While some of its citizens had been bent on killing and maiming men, others more peacefully occupied had not neglected nurturing the land, ploughing, planting, and tilling the fields. In a great clock the small wheels seem of minor importance, yet did they fail to make their revolutions the entire mechanism would be useless and the hands could no longer mark off on the dial the seconds, minutes, and hours of life.

Society is a machine of intricate construction and delicate adjustments. Mankind, with its many-sided characters and greater and lesser capacities, furnishes the motive power. Thus we find that all this time Bedminster men, when not under arms on their monthly tours of militia duty, were engaged in turning the smaller social wheels, occupied themselves with their ordinary pursuits, performed their daily duties, and sought pleasure and amusement as if war were not. Those pleasures, it would seem, did not always keep strictly within legal bounds, for we find that in 1778 the October term of Somerset courts convicted John Schenck of breaking the law against horse racing and fined him ten pounds.

While Washington and his men were at the front assailing the enemy with lead and steel, the patriotic citizens at home were guarding the rear against the attacks of a much more insidious foe. Between the sessions of the legislature the Council of Safety kept a zealous oversight of the conduct of the citizens, sitting for that purpose at short intervals in different parts of the state. Then would be summoned to the presence of this august body both suspected and unsuspected persons—the one to explain as best they could their attitude toward the new republic, the other to testify as to what they knew regarding the daily walk, conversation, and behavior of the people of their respective vicinities. From the fifteenth to the twenty-sixth of July (1777) the Council of Safety sat at New Germantown. The minutes of the Council meeting, held on the twenty-fifth instant recite:

Doctor Aaron Craig and John Teeple Tavernkeeper, appd. before the board pursuant to citation and severally took and subscribed the Oaths of abjuration and allegiance agreeably to law . . . Philip Meelick appeared before the Board pursuant to citation, and produced proof of his having taken the Oath agreeably to Law, on the 12th of this instant, whereupon he was dismissed.

Nothing is said of Peter Melick having presented himself before this Council. It is reasonable to suppose that he was absent from the county, as no proceedings were instituted either against his person or to confiscate his property. Citation before the Council was not necessarily evidence of disaffection, as all male adults were required to take the oath of allegiance, and some of the firmest of patriots were peremptorily summoned to repair their negligence. During the few days that the Council of Safety sat at New Germantown, one hundred and eighty-three citations were issued, and one hundred and fifty-seven oaths administered.

On examining old Somerset records we are led to believe that to some extent this county escaped the religious blight that fell upon many communities during the Revolution; and that social morals were not permitted to sink to the low level of those of many other localities. That Bedminster Township was preeminently favored in this regard is beyond dispute, and it can be attributed to the far-reaching influence on its people of its strong Dutch Reformed and Presbyterian congregations and their able ministers. During the early years of the eighteenth century the state of religion in New Jersey was at an exceedingly low ebb. Professing Christians were very lax in the outward observance of the forms of their faith, and in their daily lives gave but little evidence of the belief that was supposed to be theirs. All kinds of error and practices prevailed in the churches; conversion in the present sense of the term does not seem to have been a necessity for membership, and in many instances even ministers do not appear to have been overzealous in spiritual matters.

A Machine of Delicate Adjustments

Among the dissenting congregations it was the crying aloud in the wilderness of the ministers Theodorus
Jacobus Frelinghuysen of the Dutch churches of the
Raritan Valley and Jonathan Dickinson of the Presbyterian congregations in the vicinity of Elizabethtown that
had first aroused the people to sense their need of a more
vital piety. The efforts of these divines were supplemented in 1740 by the earnest and what was considered
almost inspired preaching of Whitefield, Tennent, Edwards, and other eminent pastors of that time. A religious
awakening ensued which had a most marked effect upon
the morals, character, and daily walk of the people. The
churches were invigorated, and for a generation afterwards religion occupied a place in the thoughts and lives
of the people that it had never known before.

Interesting testimony regarding the severe opinions
prevailing at that time as to frivolous and dangerous
recreations is furnished by the record of a meeting in 1767
of the consistories of the Bedminster, Raritan, and North
Branch Dutch Reformed churches—then under one ministry. The fathers of the congregations had come together
to suspend a member for attending a shooting match, for
dancing, and playing cards. They inscribed in Dutch on
their book of minutes—as is shown by the translation
made for the Reverend Henry P. Thompson's *History of
Readington Church* [1]—the following as the result of their
deliberations:

> Shooting matches are illegal, and contrary to the laws of
> the land, and afford inducement for the assembling of many
> idle and fickle persons, where nothing is ever transacted ex-
> cept that which is utterly useless, and usually ungodly . . .
> Inasmuch as dancing is a wantonness unbecoming Christians,
> and a temptation to fleshly lusts, and besides an offence to the
> pious, especially in their time of need, therefore, those who
> indulge therein are to be admonished . . . Those who, after
> admonition, continue to play with dice and cards must not

[1] *History of the Reformed Church at Readington, N. J., 1719–1881*
(New York, 1882).

245

be allowed to come to the Lord's Supper, and if contempt for this discipline be manifested, they must, at last, be cut off from the church . . . The conduct of —— —— is thus of great offense to this church; and in addition thereto, he has shown contempt of that ecclesiastical oversight to which he solemnly promised to submit himself. Therefore, this consistory, because of the said —— —— continuance in such conduct, consider him an unworthy partaker of the Holy Sacrament, and hereby forbid him the use thereof, and lay him under censure until he shall manifest sorrow and repentance.

From the records of the Morristown Presbyterian Church can also be obtained some interesting information as to what manner of social offences were visited with ecclesiastical condemnation. In 1760 a man and his wife were disciplined for eating stolen watermelons—we are not informed who purloined the fruit. In 1766 a man was adjudged guilty of a "premeditated first quarrel"; and in 1772 another contentious brother was before the church "for taking hold of an antient man, a member of ye church, and shaking him in an unchristian and threatening manner." For "ye premature marriage of wife's sister after first wife's death," the newly married pair were brought before the session in 1786, but we are left in ignorance as to just what measure of time the worthy elders and deacons considered premature.

With the outburst of anger and acrimony engendered by British tyranny that precipitated the Revolution, the Christian zeal and fervor that had distinguished the members of the dissenting congregations received a serious check. The outbreak of hostilities exerted a most unfriendly influence on religious opinions, and the inhuman practices of war had a deadly effect on moral character. Tory and Whig were alike too intolerant of each other's convictions to square their conduct by Christian teachings. Both in social and political life hatred took the place of that broad and generous spirit which the laws of God demand shall govern citizens in considering the interests of a common brotherhood. The disintegration of society, the scattering of the members of congregations, and the frequent of church edifices for military purposes, all tended to prostrate religious affairs and to give them a minor rather than a paramount importance. The business of the time was to kill, not to save, men. Campaigning dulled those finer feelings that had been bred under domestic influences and church teachings, profanity increased, cruelty and lawlessness usurped the place of brotherly affections, and scepticism and unbelief grew and became widespread. In some localities a community of Christian feeling was nearly exterminated, and the abandonment of all Sabbath observances was the rule rather than the exception. This was especially true of neighborhoods lying in the track of contending armies. The Presbyterian church buildings of Princeton, Mount Holly, Elizabeth, Westfield, Newark, Springfield, and Connecticut Farms; the Dutch edifices of New Brunswick, Millstone, and Raritan, and many others, were either entirely destroyed or so injured as to be unfit for service.

Bedminster's religious interests did not suffer so much as the county's less fortunate and more southern townships. St. Paul's Lutheran congregation at Pluckamin, which had grown feeble, seems to have ended its existence, and its house of worship was alternately used as a prison and a stable; but the other two strong congregations held firmly together and continued to present a bold front to the wickedness of the times. The Dutch Reformed congregation at this period was prospering under the pastorate of Jacob Rutsen Hardenbergh. He was now in the prime of his years and usefulness, and not only completely filled all the requirements of a spiritual shepherd, but so preached practical politics and the duties of citizenship as to imbue his hearers with the spirit of lions in the defence of their liberties and in their resistance to oppression. Tories were not to be found among his regular auditors. Mr. Hardenbergh was a member of the convention that formed the constitution of the state, and Washington frequently found in him a valuable counsellor as to men and affairs of the vicinity. So ardent was this clergyman in the cause of freedom that the enemy early in the war offered a reward of one hundred pounds for his apprehension, and for several months he always slept with a loaded musket at his bedside.

Late in the century the minister was a much more important personage in the New Jersey communities than now. About him centered not only the religious but the intellectual and educational influences of the neighborhood. Books were rare and costly, newspapers were few and did not reach regularly the interior country; it was, therefore, from the pulpit that intelligence was disseminated. But it was not only preaching that was expected from the clergyman; pastoral visits were an important part of his duties and considered occasions of much consequence by the families of his congregation. At such times great preparations were made for receiving the man of God, who was looked upon with peculiar awe and veneration. The good man of the house put on his Sunday clothes, the good wife spread her most attractive board; the children's brown feet were encased in shoes, and, dressed in their best with their faces polished, they awaited with great fear and trepidation the severe ordeal of catechism and religious instruction. Prayers were offered at each visit, and with the coming and going of the minister a special blessing was felt to have fallen on the household.

At this time Mr. Hardenbergh's services were still divided between Bedminster, Raritan, and Readington, but each congregation had a lay preacher who conducted services on the days of the pastor's absence. On the Sunday that the minister officiated at Bedminster the people awaited his coming on the church green. We may fancy him alighting from the conveyance in which he had

248

driven over from the parsonage on the Raritan. With Dinah Van Bergh on his arm and followed by a colored servant bearing the Bible and hymnbook, he made his way in a stately fashion amid the respectful and expectant throng to the church door. His people followed him in, but did not seat themselves until the domine, standing for a moment at the foot of the tall pulpit stairs with his face buried in his hat, had breathed a silent prayer for help and guidance. When in his high perch, he looked down on a very plain congregation.

Many of his hearers had walked from home barefooted, putting on their shoes only when nearing the church, and in summer weather the men did not hesitate to take off their coats and listen in their shirt sleeves. But they paid close attention to the long sermon—too often, perhaps, as was the manner of the age, composed of dogma and polemics—and stored away each point in their minds for more leisurely digestion and for use as arguments during the week in discussions in the fields, stores, and blacksmith shops. Hymnbooks were few in those days; the precentor, or "lining-deacon," still stood under the pulpit to "raise the tune" and to read out in sonorous tones two lines of each hymn, the singing consequently being of a ludicrously disjointed and disconnected character. In their forms of worship the Dutch were tenacious of original methods and strenuously resisted all efforts at reform. Before this time some endeavor had been made to introduce hymnbooks and continuous singing, but without avail, and it was not till after the close of the century that the "lining-deacon" ceased to be an institution in that denomination.

Long before the Revolution the Congregationalists and Presbyterians had introduced singing by note in their churches, but this innovation had been brought about only after long controversies and much bitterness of feeling. The objections advanced against the change were many and curious, not to say absurd. In the front rank, of course, stood that well-worn argument of all conservatives, "that it was needless, the old way being good enough." But many honest people with "dimly lighted souls" were fearful that the whole idea was a scheme of the evil one to undermine true religion. It was claimed that to abandon the ancient melodies in favor of new tunes would cause disturbances in the churches, grieve good men, and make the young disorderly because taking them away from home influences while occupied in learning the new way of singing. In fact, the proposal created a great stir among the dissenters, and many of the pamphlets and articles published on the subject displayed much rancor and ignorance. Said one writer, "Truly, I have a great jealousy, that we once begin to sing by note, the next thing will be to pray by rule, preach by rule, and then comes popery."

In the Mendham Presbyterian Church singing by note was introduced during the pastorate of Francis Peppard, which commenced in 1764. To many of his people this innovation was a great offence; one of the elders—Cummins, by name—ever after showed his repugnance to the choir by stalking out of church when singing began, not returning until its conclusion. Notwithstanding the opposition this reform, like many others before and since under the enlightenment of free discussion, finally prevailed in Congregational and Presbyterian denominations. But all this did not disturb the more phlegmatic Dutch, who at this time were well enough content with their fathers' ways. In Bedminster Church it was not until the year 1790—when a new generation had largely outgrown not only the usages but the language of Holland—that the people would even consent to do away with having preaching at stated intervals in the Dutch tongue.

At the period we have reached it was still the custom of the Bedminster congregation, as it continued to be for many years later, to listen to two long sermons on Sundays, with an intermission of but half an hour between each service. During this interval Mr. Hardenbergh conferred with his consistory and exchanged greetings with members of his flock; while it was the practice of his wife to gather about her certain of the women with whom she would discuss the sermon and hold converse on subjects of experimental religion. Meanwhile, the people generally when the weather permitted, clustered in knots under the trees or rendezvoused beneath the white covers of their farm wagons, and ate the luncheons brought from home. Some of the neighborhood slaves of good repute were given the privilege of having stands on the church green for the sale of root and malt beer, thick slices of buttered rye bread, sugared *olekokes*, Dutch crullers, and gingerbread. It was for these Sunday booths that the children saved their pennies, or eggs, which were equally current. They were the missionary boxes of that time, and constituted about the only ray of sunlight that crossed childhood's path on what must have been—if child nature was the same as now—the gloomiest day of the week.

> *Hush! 'tis the Sabbath's silence-stricken morn;*
> *No feet must wander through the tasselled corn;*
> *No merry children laugh around the door,*
> *No idle playthings strew the sanded floor;*
> *The Law of Moses lays its awful ban*
> *On all that stirs.*

The little Jersey lads and lasses in late Colonial and early Revolutionary days did not, in their Sabbath journeys, find their ways strewn with flowers. There were no Sunday Schools, no attractive Bible stories, no interesting library books. The joyous sound of childish voices was never heard in glad Sunday songs, for the "old, old story" had not yet been told for them in tuneful verse. They had to content themselves with the Heidelberg and Westminster catechisms, and the same strong spiritual food as had their elders—largely composed of stern Calvinistic tenet and dogma.

The Reverend Ashbel Green in his autobiography [2] — though by no means intending so to do — has painted in somber colors the strict and solemn manner in which the Lord's Day was observed under his paternal roof about the time of which we are writing. His father, for forty-five years the Presbyterian clergyman at Hanover, was equally learned in law, medicine, and theology, and also engaged largely in business enterprises. A letter was once addressed to him as "Preacher, Teacher, Doctor, Proctor, Miller, and Distiller."

Doctor Ashbel Green tells that upon his father's family returning from church on Sunday after listening to two long sermons, a short rest was taken, when the children with the mother were brought together for religious instruction and devotion. Each one was asked in regular order every question in the "Westminster Shorter Catechism," besides being expected to make remarks and explanations on the most important questions and answers. When this was finished, the children, of whom there were five or six, were questioned on five Bible chapters that had been given them during the week for study. This was succeeded by their being asked as to the two texts of the day and all that could be remembered of the sermons. This was followed by their repeating sentences of devotional poetry, and the telling of the religious reading they had had during the week other than the Bible; then came prayers and a pious address by the sire.

By the time all this was over the day must have been well on the wane, but still no relief from this religious strain came to the young people. Secular conversation of any kind was not permitted, and no ordinary home subjects were ever broached by the family excepting those relating to the evening milking and the care of the horses and cattle. Shall we be charged with being hypercritical

[2] *The Life of Ashbel Green . . . Written by Himself . . .* (New York, 1849).

of such colorless Sundays if we wonder whether the boys were not occasionally wicked enough to steal out behind the barn and there give one, long, low whistle as a vent to suppressed vitality? In the face of the reverend doctor's testimony we may not marvel at the story told of the little Colonial maid who interrupted the weekly catechetical inquisition by asking if there were to be any Sundays in heaven; and who, on being answered, "Yes, it will be all Sunday, one long saints' eternal rest," replied, "Well, then, father, do you know that I'd a heap liefer go to the other place."

The weight of puritanical Sabbaths which pressed so heavily on childish heads was much lessened by the establishment of Sunday Schools. Strange as it may appear, their introduction was strenuously opposed—not, as one might suppose, by the freethinkers and the ungodly—but by members of orthodox churches and even by ministers. As early as 1747 one was opened at Ephrata, Pennsylvania, by Ludwig Hacker, a German Seventh-Day Baptist; this was thirty-five years before the first one was instituted in England by Robert Raikes. Hacker's pioneer school stood alone in America until 1786, when one was established in Virginia. They soon became numerous throughout the country as individual enterprises. It was not until 1809 that their control began to be assumed by the churches. The first record I have found of a New Jersey Sunday School is of one founded in the congregation of the Presbyterian Church at Hackettstown, on the fifth of May, 1812.

Aaron Malick during his life continued to be associated with the Lutheran Church at New Germantown, but as his children grew to men's and women's estate they connected themselves with the Dutch Reformed Church. Aaron seems also to have had the interest of this Dutch flock at heart, as is shown by his having given his bond to aid it financially. He must have been a liberal Christian and in sympathy with all denominations, as we find his name occasionally among the communicants of the Bedminster Presbyterian Church at Lamington.

In May, 1782, the services of the Reverend Doctor John Rodgers were secured, he remaining in charge until the peace in 1783. Like his brother of the Dutch pulpit, he dealt telling blows from the sacred desk at Tories as well as at unbelievers and earned a national reputation as a patriotic clergyman. His pronounced course in opposition to the Crown necessitated his leaving New York on the advent of the British, who converted his Wall Street church into a barrack for troops. The condemnation of an enemy often rises superior to the best of praise. Judge Jones,[3] in his venomous Tory way, thus describes Doctor Rodgers:

> An incendiary and a person of rigid republican principles, a rebellious, seditious preacher, a man who had given more encouragement to rebellion by his treasonable harangues from the pulpit than any other republican preacher, perhaps, upon the continent. Being a minister he had free access to all the families of the Presbyterian persuasion, consequently opportunities for using his influence and doing a great deal of mischief.

Judge Jones' description grossly misrepresents the character of this worthy man, for he possessed not only the faith and hope but also the charity of a Christian. Despite all the decision with which he thought and the firmness with which he acted during the struggle for independence, he was distinguished for his liberality toward those who adopted a different opinion or pursued an opposite course. In his judgment of others, as has been well said, he showed the liberality of a gentleman, and was not soured by that spirit which assails and sometimes subdues clerical men of great talent and worth. The Bedminster people grew warmly attached to this eminent divine whom the chances of war had exiled to their retired hill country.

[3] See footnote, page 166.

A Machine of Delicate Adjustments

Elders of the last generation remembered him as a large man with an imposing presence, of courtly and gentle manners, but uncompromising in the elucidation of his religious and political views. In making visits he wore his gown and bands on weekdays as on Sundays, and as he walked abroad, carrying a gold-headed cane and arrayed in a buzz-wig, cocked hat, and silver knee and shoe buckles, he presented a distinguished and dignified appearance. It was not uncommon for ministers of that time to wear their gowns when out of the pulpit. The Reverend John Witherspoon during the six years that he was a member of the United States Congress always appeared arrayed in full clerical robes.

Patriotism and Presbyterianism were closely allied throughout the entire Revolutionary contest. In that communion there were few Loyalists, and both clergy and laity not only preached and talked against the surrendering of any of the privileges of freemen, but were ready to, and did, donate their property and lay down their lives to the end that the country they loved so well should be free and independent. On the seventeenth of May, 1775, the synod, then sitting in Philadelphia, appointed Doctors Witherspoon and Rodgers and the Reverend James Caldwell as a committee to present to the churches an appeal on behalf of the country. Though ministers of the gospel of peace, these committeemen in their address deemed it their duty to take a firm stand on the side of war should a continuation of hostilities be necessary to preserve the united interests of the colonies. They further urged upon the people the duty of aiding in the execution of the measures proposed by Continental Congress. From then until 1783, when the synod issued another pastoral letter congratulating the people upon the happy termination of the war, both clergy and laity were marked as special objects for British and Tory persecution.

It was on the clergy that the direst evils fell, for with

the death or running out of a "rebel parson" it was considered that one more of the seditious streams flowing from Presbyterian pulpits had been dammed. Among the ministers who fought with the army, or preached and prayed from drumheads, stands conspicuously in the foreground James Caldwell, pastor of the Elizabethtown Church. His church was considered a hotbed of rebellion, and its congregation has a distinguished Revolutionary record. In it were such sturdy patriots as Governor William Livingston; Elias Boudinot, commissary general of prisoners, president of Congress, and first president of the American Bible Society; Abraham Clark, one of the signers of the Declaration of Independence; Generals Elias and Jonathan Dayton; Colonels Spencer and Barber and forty other commissioned officers, to say nothing of noncommissioned officers, privates, and militia. In this connection it is interesting to note that this is the oldest English-speaking congregation in the state, organized probably previous to the summer of 1665, and, without doubt antedating that of Newark by two years.

Another clerical martyr for upholding his convictions with pen, tongue, and sword was John Rosbrugh of Delaware Forks, the chaplain of the Third Battalion, Northampton (Pennsylvania) militia. He was captured at Trenton by a troop of horse on that January night when Washington stole away from the banks of Assunpink Creek, and was savagely butchered, though incapable of resistance. *The Pennsylvania Evening Post*, in giving an account of the affair, states that after being thus massacred the "dam'd rebel minister" was stripped naked, and in that condition left lying in an open field till taken up and buried by some of the inhabitants. In the following reproduction of one of his last letters to his wife, if not the last, the words within brackets supply the place of those wanting in the original:

[Monday] morning, 10 o'clock, at Bristol Ferry, Decem-[ber thirtieth, My dear wife, I] haven't a minute to tell you [that the] company are all well. We are going over to N[ew

Jerse]y you would think [it] strange to see your Husband, an old man, riding with a french fusee slung at his back. This may be ye la[st] ye shall receive from your Husband. I have committed myself, you [and the dear ple]dges of our mutual love to God. As I am out of doors [I cannot] write more. I send my compliments to you and children [and all our] friends. Pray for us. From your loving Husband.

JNO. ROSB[RUGH].

Mentioning Aaron's having communed with Lamington Presbyterians recalls the fact that the partaking of this sacrament by that denomination was made a much greater occasion than it is at present. At Lamington it was the custom at such seasons to secure the assistance of another minister. The Friday preceding communion Sunday was observed as a fast, and the regular pastor preached in the church at twelve o'clock. On Saturday afternoon the visiting clergyman delivered a preparatory sermon. On Sunday morning came the action sermon, after which the ordinance was administered, often to five successive tables, long addresses being made at each. Then there was the usual half-hour intermission, giving the people an opportunity for regaling themselves with cake and beer at the always well-supplied stand of Betty McCoy. On Monday morning at ten o'clock the visitor preached a farewell sermon, and thus ended the four days' services.

Betty McCoy was an old Scotch woman, and a noted character in the congregation. She acted as a sort of pew-opener, church-cleaner, purveyor, and at times, general exhorter. When not so occupied she was usually visiting and gossiping among the people of the neighborhood, by whom she was welcomed as a worthy creature for over one-third of a century. Many stories are told of the acidity of her tongue, of the innateness of her wit, the excellence of her appetite, and the fervor of her religion. Rumor has it that at one time at Pluckamin she put to flight an entire troop of British horse, one of the men having endeavored to take from her a package of much cherished tea.

There were other ways prevalent among Presbyterian congregations of the last century that would now excite surprise, if not reprehension. Dr. S. W. Boardman, in an address in 1887 at the Centennial of the Hackettstown Presbyterian Church, referred to an ancient custom of concluding the installation services of a minister by giving a ball in the evening, at which the new pastor and his wife were expected to open the dance. Evidently in social customs this denomination was not in accord with the more severe views of their Dutch Reformed neighbors. It is not an agreeable vision, this, of the sedate brothers of the Presbyterian sessions and their wives solemnly advancing and retreating, bowing and curtsying, scraping and tiptoeing through the stately figures of a minuet, while younger and more frolicsome members of the communion cut pigeon wings and *contredanses* and reels.

Many other curious customs and observances connected with churches in Revolutionary days could be narrated. As is well known, the word temperance, as relating to drinking, was not yet coined, and it was considered that liquor was necessary to health. Ministers or laymen would swallow a glass of applejack as unhesitatingly as they would a piece of bread. The story is current in Bedminster that one Sunday a clergyman, who was sent to supply Lamington Church, preached an excellent sermon. On descending the pulpit stairs the elders gathered about him and, as was customary, paid his fee in crisp half-pound notes. "Gentlemen," said the minister, "will you walk out with me?" Whereupon, crossing the road they entered the tavern and, ranging themselves in front of the bar, all took a drink with the clergyman. He then handed the tavernkeeper a half-pound note, saying "Take your pay out of this bank note, I have just received it for preaching the sermon." They then all returned to the church and soon afterwards were engaged in the afternoon service.

19

The Rhythmic Sway of Marching Columns

WE ARE NOW NEARING the close of the year 1778, and such of my readers as are martially inclined may join me in welcoming the return of the Continental Army to Somerset. Much has transpired since we bade good-by to its officers and men on the banks of the Delaware. It is not needful to detail their varied experiences on the Brandywine, at Germantown, at Valley Forge. Though Howe had gained two considerable victories in Pennsylvania, he had neither destroyed nor crippled Washington's army; and by his costly change of base had secured little else than comfortable winter quarters in Philadelphia—quarters which actually weakened and demoralized his command. It was the Americans who really reaped advantage from the Pennsylvania campaign of 1777; it converted their raw force of citizen-soldiers into an effective army, and gave the country an increased confidence in its defenders.

The Americans were not without other causes for satisfaction with the occurrence of the year 1777. Early in October more than one chaplain and clergyman was preaching in exultant tones from the words of Joel: "I will remove far off from you the northern army." This text tells the whole story! A great shout of joy had gone up from the entire country when the wonderful news of

Lesser Crossroads

Burgoyne's surrender came rolling down the broad reaches of the upper Hudson, reverberated through the narrow defiles of the Highlands, and, sweeping on southward, carried an ecstacy of delight to the inhabitants of both banks of the river.

There are somber shadows in the picture displayed by the next slide of the magic lantern of history. It is the vision of cold and hungry soldiers, shivering under tattered blankets in the rude huts of Valley Forge. But when the black clouds of adversity hung lowest over the American camp, almost obscuring hope, suddenly amid the darkness a bright light shot athwart the national heavens. "As cold water to a thirsty soul, so is good news from a far country." It was glad tidings from over the seas that so quickened with joy the patriot pulse. While the woods surrounding Washington's cantonment were still carpeted with snow, intelligence reached headquarters that on the sixth of February, 1778, a treaty of amity and commerce and a defensive treaty of alliance, the essence of which was the absolute and unlimited independence of the United States, had been concluded with France. Great was the happiness of the American people when they learned, later, that the French had agreed to furnish men and treasure to aid in establishing a republic in the western hemisphere. The Revolution no longer partook of the character of a rebellion of rebels, but was to be recognized among the nations of the world as a great political movement, destined to be the agency for the cutting asunder of ancient bonds and, probably, for the establishment of a powerful government.

During the spring, General—now Sir William—Howe went home to explain as best he could the causes for the non-success of his campaigns since leaving Long Island. He was succeeded by Sir Henry Clinton. This General, not relishing the possible appearance of a French fleet at the capes of the Delaware, no longer felt his army to be secure in its comfortable quarters. By the fifth of June

260

he had destroyed his outworks, and the British transports dropped down the river, having on board some of the German troops, the heavy baggage, a part of the cavalry, and a large contingent of Loyalists. With the main army Clinton evacuated the city on the eighteenth, taking up his line of march for New York by way of Haddonfield, Mount Holly, Allenton, and Freehold. Morgan's riflemen were quickly hanging on his right flank, while Maxwell with the Jersey brigade, Dickinson with the Jersey militia, and Cadwalader with Pennsylvania volunteers harassed the left of his long line, which was so encumbered with wagons and bat-horses as to stretch like a narrow, many-colored ribbon over nearly twelve miles of country. With such an exposure the slowly moving column was fearfully galled, which, together with the intense heat, made this memorable march across our state rank among the enemy's most unhappy experiences of the war. It was not a march, but a retreat. With the thermometer marking ninety-two in the shade and the men heavily accoutred, it is not strange that soon many of them, spent with exhaustion, fell by the way.

The major part of the Americans crossed the Delaware at Coryell's Ferry and reached Hopewell on the twenty-fourth of June, when Washington held a council of war with twelve general officers. His advisers were equally divided as to the wisdom of risking a general engagement. Whereupon, as usual, he reached his own conclusions—the result being the Battle of Monmouth on the twenty-eighth, which, to quote the chief's words, "from an unfortunate and bad beginning turned out a glorious and happy day."

One of the unique spots on the American coast is that solitary outpost by the sounding sea which stands guard at the entrance to New York Harbor—that spinal curvature of sand, bristling with stunted trees, which forms what sailor and fisherfolk know as the Horseshoe Cove. On the one side spreads the sheen and sparkle of the glistening bay, whose low murmuring waves lap its yellow strand, while seaward its dunes and beaches offer the first barrier to Atlantic billows that have swept unchecked their imperious way for nearly three thousand miles. Between are hummocks and swales of drifting sand, mostly covered with a maze and tangle of somber cedars and other evergreen trees, twisted, bent, and scarified by many a weary gale. With the exception of a few buildings clustering about the government station and the railroad terminus, it is an uninhabited waste of desolate solitude, where the winds sadly sough through the dense undergrowth, and where the silence is otherwise unbroken save by the wailing of the surge, the cry of the sea-fowl, and the hum of the Jersey mosquito.

On the second of July, 1778, the repose and silence of Sandy Hook was suddenly disturbed by the din of war. The seagulls and fishhawks, startled by the unusual sound of pibroch, bugle, and drum rattle, deserted their accustomed haunts and with loud screams sailed away over the bay to the mainland. On that day General Clinton's army, exhausted by the exploits and discomfitures of the hot field of Monmouth, came pouring across the Shrewsbury River on a pontoon bridge which they had been two days in building. The line of retreat from Freehold was strewn with knapsacks, firelocks, and other implements of war, and with not a few dead men. This sandy neck was soon alive with troops and all the paraphernalia of a great body of soldiers. Amid the dark green of the thickets and undergrowth were to be seen the varied colors of scarlet, blue, and other uniforms, and the glint and glitter of burnished arms. Massed on the shore and at points where the open spaces in the woods were most frequent were red ranks of British grenadiers, gaunt Scots in green and plaid, fierce-looking German yägers, white-wigged Hessians, and buff-breeched light dragoons. Interspersed among the long lines of baggage and artillery trains, which extended for several miles along the beach of the

262

inner bay, were ambulances and country wagons laden with wounded and invalided men.

This phenomenal spectacle was not confined to the land, for Lord Howe's fleet had most opportunely arrived from the Delaware. The Horseshoe presented a scene of naval pageantry that would attract a great array of visitors. Anchored on its surface were innumerable transports, guarded by formidable men-of-war flying from their mizzens the royal cross of St. George. Passing and repassing between them and the shore were great numbers of large scows, long-boats, and yawls, manned by British tars, busy in transporting to the ships the troops, baggage, artillery, and tents of Clinton's army. Some of the wagons that had carried the baggage and wounded were burned near the water's edge; their horses were made to swim to the ships, being towed behind the boats that transported the men. All useless and disabled horses were turned loose and chased back into the open country. After crossing the pontoon bridge some of the regiments were forced to march through the deep sands several miles to the lighthouse at the end of the Hook, and then, to reach the small boats, the men were obliged to wade in the water over their knees. It was the sixth before the embarkation was completed and the last of the fleet weighed anchor and set sail for New York. And so concluded a nearly two years endeavor of a thoroughly equipped foreign host to subdue the Americans. Every effort made by the enemy to destroy the Continental Army had been defeated, and the object for which the British were contending was not one whit further advanced than when in the autumn of 1776 Cornwallis crossed the Hudson and entered the Jerseys.

After the Battle of Monmouth, Washington, leaving Maxwell's brigade and Morgan's rangers to watch the enemy, marched his army to New Brunswick and encamped on each side of the river. After the intense heat and rapid marching of the previous ten days, this refreshing halt was a delightful experience for the army. The men were quick to take advantage of the proximity of the river to wash and cleanse themselves, they being conducted to bathe in squads by noncommissioned officers, who were directed to prevent their bathing in the heat of the day or remaining too long in the water. As Saturday was the fourth of July, the Commander in Chief on Friday thus addressed the army in general orders: "Brunswick Landing, July 3, 1778: Tomorrow the anniversary of the Declaration of Independence will be celebrated by the firing of thirteen pieces of cannon, and a *feu de joie* of the whole line. . . . [T]he soldiers are to adorn their hats with green boughs and to make the best appearance possible. A double allowance of rum will be served out." The festivities were not permitted to interfere with the trial of General Lee for his misconduct on the field of Monmouth. The court-martial, which had been organized two days before, had a sitting in the morning.

On Sunday morning the left of the front line broke camp and by the twentieth the entire army was east of the Hudson, headquarters being established at White Plains. For the remainder of the season the activities of war centered mainly at Newport and Savannah. The lot of the force under Washington was one of comparative peace and comfort, owing to the inactivity of the British in their quarters on the island of Manhattan.

At the end of November the Commander in Chief made his dispositions for the winter. Cantonments were established surrounding New York and extending almost from the Sound to the Delaware. Six brigades were quartered east of the Hudson. West of the river at Smith's Clove the North Carolina brigade was stationed to guard the Highlands, while to protect lower Jersey Maxwell's brigade was placed in the vicinity of Elizabethtown. Early in December Washington came marching through Bedminster on his way to the old camp at Middlebrook Heights.

The Rhythmic Sway of Marching Columns

Reader, if you purpose continuing in the company of the writer, you must follow the soldiers. As sure as sparks fly upward, so sure will a small boy drop bat, top, or marble when he hears the music of a military band. It must be confessed that your scribe is in sympathy with that same small boy; for he has ever been incapable of resisting the fascinations of the rhythmic sway of marching columns, the glitter of drawn sabers that marks the undulating motion of a moving squadron of troopers. Washington had been strongly urged to turn over his command to Greene, and to winter himself in Philadelphia. In his zeal for the service he resisted the invitation, preferring the meager and contracted quarters of camp to the convenience and amusements of the capital in order that the affairs and requirements of the army could receive his constant care and attention. The Commander in Chief, not being able to find a building in the vicinity of Bound Brook or Middlebrook ample enough for his purposes, established his headquarters at the Wallace house, located where the road from Somerville to Raritan crosses the track of the Central Railroad.

The winter encampment at Middlebrook opened with a much happier outlook than had the one at Valley Forge the year before. The embarrassments of this time were the reductions of the battalions owing to expiration of time of service, the difficulty of the country's feeling too great a security after the success of the last campaign, and the rapid decline of the currency, which added greatly to the difficulties of the commissaries in their efforts to supply the needs of the soldiers. Notwithstanding all this, affairs were buoyant as compared with what they had been the previous year. The men were in excellent health and spirits; their commander, in a letter to Lafayette, writes of them as being in better condition than they had ever been since the formation of the army. The weather was unusually mild, and the spring came in early. There was no severe cold after the tenth of January

265

and scarcely any frost, and by the first of April fruit trees were in bud and vegetation began to appear.

Mrs. Washington joined her husband at the Wallace house, and this mansion opened its hospitable portals that winter and spring to many distinguished people. The daily dinner was an affair of ceremony and importance, as, in addition to the visitors at headquarters, the company included a certain number of officers whom it was the General's habit to invite daily to dine. It was, of course, impossible that the Commander in Chief should be personally acquainted with all the officers of his army; his practice therefore was to extend invitations through brigade orders. Often as many as thirty persons were entertained.

From a letter written by the General from Camp Middlebrook to a deputy quartermaster general at Philadelphia we gain some idea of the extensive menage sustained in this Somerset house that winter. The letter ordered purchased for use at headquarters a dinner service of queensware. Among the pieces enumerated as desired were two large tureens, three dozen dishes, eight dozen shallow plates, and three dozen soup plates. Washington's letter further requested that there should be sent him "six tolerably genteel but not expensive candlesticks;" "as much fur as will edge a coat, waistcoat, and breeches;" and "two pounds of starch." He also asked for a new hat, saying, "I do not wish by any means to be in the extreme of the fashion, either in the size or manner of cocking it." The deputy quartermaster general searched the Quaker City in vain for queensware; but Lady Stirling came to the Commander in Chief's relief and informed him that such a service as he desired could be procured at New Brunswick.

Although the dinner from force of circumstances could not abound in superfluities, it was amply provided and handsomely served. General and Mrs. Washington occupied seats at the side of the table, while the honors were performed by Colonel Hamilton or some other member of the military family. Promptness was the rule at headquarters dinners. Washington never permitted that anyone should be waited for longer than five minutes, conceding that time for variance in watches. To guests arriving when the company was seated he would make some pleasant apology, a not uncommon one being, "Gentlemen, I have a cook who never asks whether the company has come, but whether the hour has come."

An officer who was with the army that winter has left a record of his impressions on the occasion of his enjoying the hospitalities of headquarters. He has much to say of the simple and modest deportment of his illustrious host, who, while conversing affably with his guests, preserved a reserve amounting almost to a hauteur, and whose cheerful, open countenance together with great dignity of manner impressed each one present with a combined feeling of love, fear, and veneration. Washington treated all at the table with equal attention; and when the cloth was removed, after a few parting glasses of wine, retired, leaving his guests to the courtesies of his staff officers.

Attached to the line and staff of the army were many brilliant young men. In Washington's immediate military family were Colonels Alexander Hamilton and Tench Tilghman, his two most trusted aides. The manners of the latter, who was at that time thirty-four years old, were distinctly those of one who had always moved in polite circles. He belonged to a distinguished Maryland family and was connected with the best people of that aristocratic province. At the outset of the Revolution his father adhered to the Crown, and Philemon, a younger brother, entered the British navy. But Tench was from the beginning a sturdy patriot, and in 1776 joined Washington's army as captain of a Pennsylvania company that had volunteered for one campaign. His handsome presence, bravery on the field, together with his personal merits and the high social position he was known to occupy, attracted the attention of his superiors, and at the expiration of a short term of service he was invited to be a member of Washington's military family.

Hamilton was a bright star in that military firmament. Though then but two and twenty his dignity of character was such as to insure for him all the consideration due to one who had profited by the experiences of many years; it is said that when he entered a room, notwithstanding his youth, it was apparent from the respectful attention of the company that he was a distinguished person. Colonel Hamilton was slight in figure and rather undersize, but possessed a graceful carriage and courtly manners together with an air of much refinement. His cheeks were as rosy as a girl's, the color mantling a very fair complexion from which the powdered hair was rolled back and gathered in a club behind. On the first of March in 1777, when barely twenty years old, he was appointed aide-de-camp to Washington, and, owing to his intelligence and sagacity, soon gained the full confidence of his chief and was invited to assist in the planning for the concentration and arrangement of the new army then forming. Hamilton's amiability and agreeable presence inspired in all with whom he came in contact the most affectionate attachment.

These two aides divided between them the honors of presiding at General Washington's table and of generally acting as major-domos at headquarters. They must have added much to the pleasure of visitors, especially to those of the fair sex. Perhaps this may partly explain the fact of the Wallace house having entertained so many ladies that spring. Governor Livingston's two daughters, Kitty and Betsy, as they were familiarly called, were Mrs. Washington's frequent guests. The Governor's eldest daughter, Sarah, who had for five years been the wife of John Jay—then president of Congress—was also entertained. Mrs. Jay was both clever and beautiful and considered a social star, not only in Philadelphia but afterwards in Madrid and Paris, when she accompanied her distinguished husband to the courts of Spain and France. It is said that the brilliancy of her complexion gave rise to much speculation in Revolutionary society. Even Doctor Witherspoon, who admired her greatly, used playfully to express to Kitty Livingston his doubts as to the genuineness of her sister's coloring. The French minister went so far as to lay a wager with a certain Spanish don that Mrs. Jay's complexion was artificial. The gentleman from France acknowledged his error by paying the bet.

Another young soldier at headquarters who contributed greatly to the social atmosphere of the army was William Colfax, an officer of Washington's Life Guard. At the outset of the war, when but nineteen, he entered a Connecticut regiment and fought at Bunker Hill. He served until the peace, being three times wounded, once dangerously. He was transferred to the Guard at Valley Forge in 1778. When at Middlebrook, his buoyant nature and engaging appearance won for him many friends. He had dark hair, always well powdered and worn in a queue, a clean-shaven face, a clear florid complexion, and beautiful blue eyes dancing with expression. Colfax was a personal favorite of Mrs. Washington, who presented him with a linen thread net for his queue, knit by her own hands.

It was considered a great honor to belong to the Life Guard of Washington. The men were selected with much care from the different regiments, all states being represented; it was requisite that each member should be American-born, of good moral character, finely formed, from five feet eight inches to five feet ten inches in height, and from twenty to thirty years old. This command was kept thoroughly drilled in all manner of infantry maneuvers that it might stand as a model for the army. While at Middlebrook it contained one hundred and eighty men, but at the end of this year (1779) its number was increased to two hundred and fifty, and Colfax was given the command.

The custom was to have the Life Guard hutted adjacent to the quarters of the Commander in Chief. Upon an alarm being given, the Guard would at once take possession of headquarters and barricade the entrances; then, all the windows being opened, five men would be placed at each one, where with guns loaded and cocked they would remain until troops from the camp surrounded the house. Mrs. Washington in after years used to tell with much amusement how that often, on occasions of false alarms at night, she had been obliged to bury herself in the bedclothes in order to be protected from the winter winds which swept through the open windows of her sleeping rooms while the soldiers stood guard.

Perhaps one of the most popular men in the vicinity of Middlebrook Camp was a swarthy-faced, graceful youth of twenty-three—Henry Lee, afterwards the father of Robert E. Lee. A Virginian by birth, he graduated at Princeton, and when only twenty was captain in the cavalry regiment which later came under the command of Colonel Bland. He early attracted the attention of the Commander in Chief, who at the Battle of Germantown selected his troop as a personal guard. Lee's bravery and soldierly qualities soon won for him a majority, and he was given a separate command of three companies of light-horse. While at Camp Middlebrook Major Lee and several brother officers were quartered at "Phil's Hill," the hospitable dwelling of Philip Van Horne, the father of five handsome and well-bred daughters who were the much admired toasts of both armies. Van Horne, himself, as far as loyalty was concerned, seems to have been a suspicious character, and at one time Washington contemplated his removal to New Brunswick. Indeed, he was arrested and put on his parole, but was permitted to remain at Middlebrook, where he and his bright-eyed girls continued to welcome alike friend and foe.

The Rhythmic Sway of Marching Columns

The division of Major General Israel Putnam lay below Middlebrook Heights, near Chimney Rock. Other brigades occupied nearby and adjoining lands, on which many interesting Revolutionary relics have been ploughed up by former owners of the land. Until within a few years numerous low mounds were to be seen, which when opened revealed large stones and brickbats—the remains of the foundations of chimneys and fireplaces—plainly indicating the site of the log cabins or huts in which the troops were quartered. These huts were constructed of dovetailed tree trunks, no nails or ironwork of any kind being used. The interstices between the logs were filled with clay, and the chimneys, made of small sticks, were similarly plastered. The officers' huts were generally divided into two apartments for four occupants who comprised one mess, but the privates' and noncommissioned officers' huts had but one room and contained ten or twelve straw-filled bunks for that number of men.

Somerset is peculiarly rich in Revolutionary houses. A notable example is the one which was occupied that winter by General Greene, located midway between Bound Brook and Somerville on the banks of the Raritan. Greene at this time was acting as quartermaster general, he having accepted the position in the previous March in order to relieve that department and Washington from great embarrassments. In addition to the official intercourse of Greene, the presence of his lady proved a powerful attraction and drew many to this old Dutch farmhouse.

The troops of General Wayne were encamped south of the Raritan. This General is often mentioned in Revolutionary annals as "Mad Anthony" because of a bravery that was fearless of consequences. Somerset traditions, however, distinguish him as "Dandy Wayne," for the reason of his having been conspicuously handsome, with much magnetism and dash, and always uniformed and appointed with great care and fastidiousness.

271

20

God's Acre

THE CORPS OF ARTILLERY commanded by General Knox lay at Pluckamin. The guns were parked and the men's quarters were erected on the northwest side of the Cornelius Eoff farm, a piece of rising ground a short distance from the road, which displayed the camp to good advantage. A range of fieldpieces, mortars, howitzers, and heavy cannon formed the front line of a parallelogram, while flanking the remaining sides were huts for the officers and privates and other necessary buildings. Facing the parade and standing on a slightly elevated plateau was a spacious and well-proportioned structure, capped with a small cupola. It was called the academy, and enclosed a room fifty feet by thirty, with an arched ceiling and plastered walls. Here from a low rostrum at one end of this room the brigade preceptor delivered lectures on tactics, gunnery, and other military subjects. It may be readily supposed that this capacious hall also furnished an agreeable rendezvous for the officers during the long evenings of that winter.

Altogether, the encampment unfolded itself very attractively to an approaching visitor and was in every respect a superior military village, one of a no inconsiderable population, as the returns of the artillery corps at that time show its total effective strength to have been forty-nine companies, containing sixteen hundred and seven men. Both officers and men of this artillery brigade wore uniform coats of black, turned up with red, jackets and breeches of white wool, and hats trimmed with yellow, the prescribed attire of the Continental artillery.

In the first years of the struggle Revolutionary soldiers were rarely arrayed in martial attire. As the war progressed and enlistments were made for longer terms, uniforms were adopted; and in other ways the regiments presented a much more soldierly appearance. One of the greatest offences against historical verity is the prevalent belief that the Continental troops were uniformed in blue and buff. Such were the colors of the Commander in Chief, his staff, and many of the generals, but the prevailing uniforms of the rank and file were brown, blue, and green, with trimmings of various hues. This popular but erroneous notion has been fostered by artists, who in illustrating Revolutionary scenes have pictured Continental soldiers clad in blue coats with buff facings, buff waistcoats and breeches, top boots, cocked hats, and ruffled shirts.

Of the troops under Washington's immediate command at that time, some of them were uniformed as follows: General Wayne's Pennsylvania division wore blue coats lined with white, ruffled shirts, red flannel leggings, and "a sort of cap dressed up with fur." Among other Pennsylvania regiments, the men of the Ninth had brown coats faced with red, with red cuffs and capes, and cocked hats with white loopings; the Eleventh Regiment, long blue coats faced with red and buff, and small round hats with black feathers. The Third Virginia Regiment was uniformed in light drab coats with pale blue facings, green vests, and linen overalls; the Sixth Virginia wore black coats faced with red, white waistcoats, linen shirts, and overalls; while the coats of the Thirteenth Virginia were blue, cuffed and faced with yellow. The Fifth Maryland Regiment wore brown coats faced with red, spotted swanskin vests, oval brass buttons, brown broadcloth breeches; while the Sixth was arrayed in gray coats faced with green. The prevailing uniform coat of the Jersey line was blue turned up with red.

As for the cavalry, Lee's legion wore cocked hats and "green coatees" faced with white, their waistcoats were white and their breeches black. Colonel Moylan's Fourth Regiment light dragoons, a command well known in Somerset though not with this year's encampment, wore green coats turned up with red, green cloaks with red capes, red waistcoats, buckskin breeches, and leather caps trimmed with bearskin. The artists perhaps found their typical Continental soldiers in the men of Washington's Life Guard; they being near the person of the General wore uniforms that in colors and distinctive features in many respects harmonized with his full dress and that of his staff officers.

General Knox, together with his wife, quartered at the Jacobus Van der Veer house, just below the Bedminster Church. During the winter and spring of 1779 it was the most important house in the neighborhood and the rallying point for both military and social affairs. Scores of people came and went each day, and if this old dwelling is ever in a retrospective mood, it must look back upon those busy months as a very distinguished epoch in its existence. Knox was very popular in Somerset County, and old residents of the last generation delighted in anecdotes and reminiscences of his amiability and good fellowship. When stationed at Pluckamin he was about thirty-four years old, stout but active, possessed great intelligence, and had a most genial presence. He readily made warm attachments, and the villagers all looked upon him with great admiration. Tradition speaks of his walking about with a grand and self-complacent air, greeting in hearty tones those he knew with a strong and decisive voice easily recognized as that of one accustomed to command. His large and full face was brightened by a covert smile, and on removing his hat he exposed a low, broad forehead and short hair standing up in front but long and queued behind.

Mrs. Knox, who shared with her husband the inconveniences and dangers of his campaigns, was nearly as well known as the General and has been called the heroine of the Revolution. She was a woman possessing many graces of mind and person, and though vivacious preserved a most dignified address. Her imposing appearance, independence of spirit, amiability of character, and originality of mind made her a conspicuous figure in Revolutionary society. The following extract from a letter written by General Greene to his wife on the twenty-third of the preceding June would lead us to believe that campaigning agreed very well with General Knox and his lady: "Mrs. Knox has been in Philadelphia and is now gone to Morristown. She is fatter than ever, which is a great mortification to her. The General is equally fat, and therefore one cannot laugh at the other. They appear to be extravagantly fond of each other; and I think, are perfectly happy."

General and Mrs. Knox tasted sorrow as well as pleasure while living in the Van der Veer house. About twenty-five feet west of the Dutch Reformed Church a tombstone is still to be seen, upon which is the following inscription: "Under this stone are deposited the Remains of Julia Knox, an infant who died the second of July, 1779. She was the second daughter of Henry and Lucy Knox, of Boston, in New England." Mrs. Knox was, in all, the mother of ten children. Seven of them died in infancy, without doubt because of the excitements and severe bodily and mental strain incidental to campaigning. Bedminster traditions preserve an unhappy story connected with the death of this Revolutionary babe. Notwithstanding that Knox was in the township defending the homes and liberties of the people, the Consistory of the Dutch Reformed Church refused to allow this little one to be buried in the churchyard. In their ignorance and superstition the Dutch fathers considered the fact of Knox being a member of the Congregational church of New England sufficient to warrant their refusing his child a sepulcher.

The General's host, old Jacobus Van der Veer—himself one of the Consistory—was very indignant at the stand taken by his co-trustees. He, poor man, had suffered from the same bigotry. A few years before, on the death of an insane daughter, a burial place had been denied his child; this, too, in the face of the fact that the church grounds had been a gift to the congregation from the man they were treating so harshly. The worthy elders reasoned that the girl's infirmities would endanger her salvation in the next world, consequently her body in this one could not be permitted to crumble into dust among those of the elect. Van der Veer buried his daughter in a field just beyond the line of the "God's acre." He is said to have taken Knox by the hand, and leading him to the lonely grave outside the fence, ejaculated with a choking voice, "Gen'ral, this is my ground, bury your child here." The prejudice of the church people seems to have lessened, as a few years later the fence was moved so that the burial ground now includes the once excluded graves.

Social intercourse abounded in the military community of Pluckamin and its vicinity, and the officers often extended a generous hospitality to merrymakings at the artillery park. By far the most notable social event in Somerset's Revolutionary history was the grand fête and ball given at Pluckamin. This celebration was in honor of the first anniversary of the French alliance; it should properly have taken place on the sixth, but was deferred because of Washington's absence in Philadelphia. The attendance comprised all the army officers in that part of the country, prominent citizens and their families from this and adjoining states, and a great number of Jersey people as spectators. A large pavilion or temple was erected, one hundred feet long and of excellent proportions, showing thirteen arches supported by columns and illuminated with paintings and mottoes descriptive of the conception and progress of American liberty.

The guests whom it was intended to especially honor having arrived, the celebration was inaugurated by the discharge of thirteen cannon, whereupon the assembled company sat down to a very fine dinner served in the academy. A handsome exhibition of fireworks was given in the evening by Colonel Stevens of the artillery, after which came a grand ball extending far into the night.

After the dining tables were removed, besides the space occupied by dowagers, wall-flowers, and other onlookers there was left a "range for about thirty couples to foot it to no indifferent measure." What a scene it must have presented for staid Pluckamin! Balls in the olden time lacked much of the hilarity and vivacity of the dances of today, but what they lost in the apparent gaiety of the occasion was more than compensated for by the picturesqueness of the costumes and by the stately grace and courtliness of the dancers. Scarlet coats, satin short-clothes, and striped waistcoats added much to the color and beauty of the scene, as their wearers stepped the stately minuet or went down the middle in the popular *contredanse*. The sobriety of this occasion, notwithstanding the joyousness of the event it celebrated, was without doubt enhanced by the presence of Washington. His personality always impressed others with a certain degree of veneration and awe, and even in times of festivity his countenance, while benign, was said to be almost austere and his manner uncommonly reserved.

Mr. Lossing [1] quotes the aged widow of Alexander Hamilton as having said that Washington never danced; that though he frequently attended balls and assemblies and always honored some lady with his hand, he merely walked through the figures. The General's evening dress is said to have been of black velvet, with knee and shoe buckles and a steel rapier, and his hair, thickly powdered,

[1] See footnote, page 221.

was drawn back from the forehead, and gathered in a black silk bag adorned with a rosette. He opened the ball with Mrs. Knox. Cannot you see him, with his imperturbable face and kindly, grave mien, as, holding aloft his partner's hand, with all the graceful dignity of a nobleman of nature he steps with her down the room? More than one beauty of that period, now sleeping under crumbling headstones in Pluckamin and other churchyards, was made happy in after years by the remembrance that she danced that night with the "Father of his Country."

The winter and the spring at the Pluckamin and Middlebrook camps were passed in perfecting the army in tactics and drill under the able oversight of Inspector General Steuben. At the latter cantonment the huts were erected in uniform and compact lines forming successive streets. For a considerable distance facing the front line the ground was cleared and smoothed and freshly swept each morning, thus forming a fine parade for drills and inspections. Here the men were daily exercised in the manual of arms and the school of the company, and the regiments and brigades were frequently reviewed and inspected by General Steuben. This officer was an enthusiastic soldier and exceedingly diligent in his special department. At inspections it was his custom not only to rigidly scrutinize the bearing, uniform, and general appearance of each man, but to take in his hands the muskets and accoutrements, examining them to discover, if possible, a speck of rust or defect in any part. Flints and cartridges were counted, knapsacks unslung, and every article spread on the soldiers' blankets to see if they contained all that had been furnished by Congress.

Major North of Steuben's staff recorded that he had seen the General and his assistants occupied for seven long hours while inspecting a brigade of three small regiments. Such thoroughness was unknown in the Continental Army before the advent of Baron Steuben. He was at this time about fifty years old, of great dignity of deportment, rich and elegant in dress, and wore brilliant decorations. Doctor Ashbel Green, who in his youth campaigned with the Baron, said that his large size, strikingly martial aspect, together with his handsome horse trappings and enormous holsters, made him appear as a perfect personification of the "God of War."

In the old country Steuben had been aide-de-camp to Frederic the Great; of high rank in the service of the Margrave of Baden, from whom he received the "Order of Fidelity"; and grand marshal of the court of the Prince of Hohenzollern-Heckingen. The King of Sardinia sought his services, and the Emperor of Austria endeavored to attach him to his army. All of these brilliant positions with their honors and emoluments were sacrificed that he might fight for American independence. On the thirteenth of July, 1783, he thus wrote to the officers of the New Jersey line: "A desire for fame was my ruling motive for visiting America, but when I saw so many brave, so many good, men encountering every species of distress for the cause of their country, the course of my ambition was changed, and my only wish was to be linked in the chain of friendship with those supporters of their country, and to render that country which had given birth to so many patriots every service in my power." On his reaching the army at Valley Forge in 1778, Steuben was appointed inspector general. From the outset of the war the troops had been in sore need of just such military knowledge as he was peculiarly fitted to impart, and they soon gave evidence by increased discipline and effectiveness of his ability as a tactician and disciplinarian.

The Baron made his headquarters nearly a mile south of the Raritan at a house located at the end of a shady lane running from the New Brunswick Road, then the residence of Abraham Staats. It was during this spring that Steuben issued his famous *Regulations for the In-*

fantry of the United States. When Lossing was in Bound Brook preparing his *Field Notes* in 1848 he found old residents who well remembered the foreign appearance that the dignified officer presented, his magnificent apparel, and the splendor of the gold and diamond decorations he wore when in full dress.

Late in April army society was pleasantly agitated over the arrival at Middlebrook of the French minister, M. Gerard, and Don Juan de Miralles, a gentleman of distinction from Spain. They were met some distance from camp by General Washington, who, accompanied by the Life Guard and a cavalcade of prominent officers, escorted them in honor to headquarters. M. Gerard was already well known to the Commander in Chief and to some of his generals, having been in the country since the preceding July. He was looked upon by all with peculiar interest—not to say affection—because of being the representative of the nation's valued allies, the French. His visit to camp was for the purpose of consulting with Washington respecting some concert of action between the French fleet and the American army.

Don Juan de Miralles was a recent arrival in America, and attracted much attention because of the element of uncertainty that seemed to attach both to his mission and to himself. He was an unofficial Spanish agent who had been dispatched to the United States by the Governor of Havana in order to obtain information as to American affairs which would enable the Spaniards to reach a conclusion on the propriety and wisdom of recognizing and aiding the new republic. He was supposed to be endeavoring to further these ends, but it was subsequently discovered that his personal sympathies ran counter to the attainment of such results. Congress, while showing the envoy every consideration, appeared to be a little afraid of him, and, as he did not directly represent the Spanish court, was careful to treat with him only in an unofficial capacity and through the intervention of the French minister.

Spain was at this time coquetting with Congress, and showed but little disposition to negotiate an alliance except on the basis of the exclusive right of navigating the Mississippi. She was also anxious that her right to conquer and retain Florida should be acknowledged. Though urged by France, she held back from entering into fraternal relations while there was yet a prospect that by offering pecuniary assistance to our struggling country she could allure its legislators into concessions that would greatly inure to the benefit of Spain. To the average American of that day the matter of controlling the commerce of the Mississippi or of claiming the territory beyond that stream did not seem of much moment. This is evidenced by a letter of Gouverneur Morris, who wrote at that time: "As to its navigation"—referring to the river —"everybody knows that the rapidity of its current will forever prevent ships from sailing up it."

While members of Congress from the Middle and New England states considered the country lying east of the Mississippi quite ample enough for the needs of coming generations, southern members fortunately had some conception of the future value of the western territory and its mighty waterways. Thus a congressional discussion was provoked, which continued until the procession of events in Europe had forced Spain into an alliance with France. Our own country was then able to enjoy all the benefits of Spanish assistance without making those valuable concessions which had been demanded.

The presence of these guests in camp added much to the social gaiety, and resulted in an occasion of ceremony and pomp in which old Bound Brook witnessed scenes of military pageantry. Great preparations had been made, and on the morning of the review, crowds of people gathered to enjoy the display. A decorated grandstand had been erected in a large field, on which were seated Mrs. Washington with two young lady visitors from Virginia, Mrs. Knox, and Mrs. Greene. Dignitaries and leading families arrived in carriages from all parts of the state.

The local color and picturesqueness of the scene were not entirely contributed by flying banners, pacing sentinels, and uniformed officers hurrying here and there in their efforts to further the preparations of the commandant of the forces. The "quality" added not a little to the picture, for the age of fine dress had not yet gone out, and the line between the gentry and the masses was still strongly drawn by the apparel of their respective classes. Ladies at festive gatherings were decked in lofty, round hats with tall feathers and wore satin petticoats, taffetas, and brocades. Gentlemen of the old school still were crowned with full-bottomed wigs, though younger men, more in the mode, had their own or false hair drawn in a queue, stiffened with lard and powdered with flour. This custom provoked Sir Joshua Reynolds in his *Discourses* [1] to compare a man of fashion with a Cherokee Indian who daubs his face with red and yellow, saying that, on meeting, whichever of them laughed first at the other's fashion was the barbarian.

Neither had the stately courtesy of Colonial days yet disappeared. In fancy we can see the Jersey gallant with his cocked hat under the arm of his varied-hued coat, in knee breeches, striped silk stockings, and pointed buckled shoes, bowing low by the open door of the lumbering vehicle of that time, and with grace and ceremony handing its fair occupant to a seat on the reviewing stage. The lady, before seating herself, salutes the gentleman with a very low, well-posed, and stately curtsy; whereupon the gallant not only raises his heavily laced cocked hat and

---

[1] *Discourses Delivered at the Royal Academy* (Boston, 1821, and other editions).

bows low, but waves his leg and scrapes the floor with his foot.

Let us, in imagination, mount the grandstand and witness with the expectant throng the approaching display. And now salvos of artillery announce the arrival of the generals and their distinguished guests. They enter the field splendidly mounted, forming a brilliant cavalcade. In the advance is Major Lee with his legion of graceful Virginians clad in green and white. Superbly horsed, gay with nodding plumes and noisy with clanking sabers, champing bits, and jangling spurs they prance proudly by, making way for the Commander in Chief on whom all eyes are turned. Washington at this time is forty-seven years old. Uniformed in blue and buff, with epaulets of bullion, varnished boots, ivory-hilted short-sword, and a three-cornered hat with a black cockade, he sits his bright bay with the grace of a perfect horseman.

Then come the generals, their staffs and orderlies, and the foreign guests—the courtly Don Juan in his suit of crimson and aiguilette of gold, and the French minister in an embroidered coat rich with jewels and foreign decorations. On they come amid the *rat-ta-ta* of snare-drum, the *bum-bum* of bass, the shrill cry of fife, and the blare of trumpet! On they go—past the grandstand—flashing in the bright sunlight.

Meanwhile, the infantry and artillery, having taken possession of the spacious field, are formed on its two sides, the regiments in line of masses, in columns by divisions. The Commander in Chief, with his general officers and the foreign envoys, passes in front of the troops from right to left in review, receiving the drum ruffles and military honors due his rank. The generals then dismount at the grandstand and witness with their ladies and guests the evolutions and field maneuvers of the army, together with musketry and cannon-firing. At the sound of a bugle the line wheels into column, and the men come swinging down the left of the parade in cadenced step, their burnished arms shining in the sun. On reaching the color marker they change direction, bring their guns to a carry —and now, with pennons fluttering and flags waving, the battalions go sweeping by in division fronts and quick time, each officer saluting and each soldier bearing himself as if proudly conscious of being under the eye of the commander. Here in these ranks are men who shivered on that bitter December night at Trenton, who bled on the banks of the Brandywine, who fought desperately in the fogs of Germantown, who suffered with hunger and cold at Valley Forge, and who thirsted through the intense heat of the bloody field of Monmouth. What wonder that the air is rent with acclamations! that cheer after cheer rises from the throats of the vast concourse of spectators!

When the review ended the generals, their staffs, and the distinguished guests remounted their horses and left the field. Joined by some of the regimental colonels— making a party of sixty in all—they rode through the village and, clattering over the Raritan bridge, soon turned down a grassy lane and drew rein in front of Steuben's quarters at the Staats house, where a bountiful repast was spread in a marquee under the trees. The entertainment was intended to especially honor the French minister, who was warmly attached to the Baron, their friendship having begun in Europe.

Steuben was a genial host. On this occasion he was ably assisted in entertaining his guests by the group of clever young men forming his military family. Among them was Captain Peter S. Duponceau, a jovial French lad only nineteen years old, who was always ready to frolic and laugh. He came from France as the Baron's secretary, and he must have brought with him abundance of Gallic assurance, for on landing at Portsmouth he celebrated his arrival in this country by kissing the first pretty girl he met on the street. Probably no one present at the banquet under the trees on this May Day did more to promote the

284

merriment and hilarity of the company than Steuben's aide-de-camp, Captain James Fairlie, a youth of twenty-one. His amiability and wit always enlivened any society in which he was thrown, and it is said that even the taciturn Washington was not proof against his drolleries.

On the fourteenth of the same month there was another parade and review, with its attendant ceremonies. This time it was not in honor of representatives of the civilized courts of Europe, but of the savage and un-tutored sons of the forest, to whom the authorities deemed it good policy to pay some attention and courtesy. General Washington was mounted on a fine gray horse, and in addition to his customary retinue was followed by his servant "Bill." As the cortège passed in front of the line and received the salute, it was accompanied by a band of Indians mounted on mean horses without saddles, some of them with old ropes and straps for bridles. The faces of the red men were painted, they wore dirty blankets, tufts of hair were their only head covering, and from their ears and noses barbaric jewels were suspended. Altogether, as a witness has recorded, "They exhibited a novel and truly disgusting spectacle."

The reverse of the medal! It was not all pride, pomp, and parade at the Middlebrook camp. On the twentieth of April a great assemblage of people and a detachment of troops surrounded an open space, wherein five soldiers sat on their coffins with halters around their necks under a gallows. They were condemned to an ignominious death for desertion, and for a crime that the Commander in Chief always found it hard to forgive, that of robbing the inhabitants. With their open graves in full view and while standing under the beam of death awaiting the final preliminaries preceding their plunge into eternity, three of them received a pardon and were conducted from the gallows more dead than alive; the other two were obliged to submit to their fate.

The presence of an occupying army in the community

must of necessity entail upon the inhabitants much inconvenience, and often distress and loss. It was Washington's endeavor to protect the people of Somerset from all unlawful and marauding acts of the more disorderly element in his army. Thieving and the destruction of property at all times met with condign punishment. Domine Hardenbergh, on behalf of the consistories and people of his several congregations, addressed a long letter to General Washiington expressing the grateful sense of the community for his own and his officers' vigilance in maintaining strict discipline throughout the army, whereby the good people of the neighborhood had been protected in their persons and property, and their calamities sensibly relieved.

It was here at Middlebrook that Washington completed his plans for an active campaign against the northern Indians. The expedition, which was placed under the command of Sullivan, had for its objects the chastisement of the natives for the atrocities committed in Pennsylvania and the destruction of the cohesive power of the confederated Six Nations. This Indian campaign came at a very inopportune time for the officers of the Jersey brigade, they being just then indignantly dissatisfied with the authorities for making no reply to their petition for relief, which had been submitted to the legislature on the seventeenth of April. The pecuniary distress of both officers and men was great, for not only had their pay long been in arrears, but when paid, owing to depreciation, that of a colonel would not supply his horse with oats, and the four month's pay of an enlisted man was only enough to furnish his family with a single bushel of wheat. Notwithstanding this discontent immediate steps were taken to put the different commands in a condition for marching; fortunately, before breaking camp the anxieties of both officers and men were relieved by the former receiving two hundred dollars and the men forty dollars each.

The Somerset encampment did not break up till June

and July, when the troops marched northeasterly over the hills to Morristown, and from there to the Highlands of the Hudson. On the fifteenth of July "Mad Anthony Wayne" made his famous charge on the rugged heights of Stony Point; and on the nineteenth of August Major Lee attacked and captured the fort at Paulus Hook (Jersey City).

21

Queen's Rangers

WHEN THE CONTINENTAL ARMY marched northward to the Hudson it did not altogether deprive Somerset from being a locality on which public interest centered. Before the close of the year 1779 several events transpired in the county which were important enough to attract much attention.

On the twenty-seventh of July there were great festivities at Basking Ridge, the occasion being the marriage of William Duer to Lady Kitty Alexander. The spacious Stirling mansion was filled with guests, including many prominent officers of the army and civil and social magnates from New York and New Jersey. Family traditions aver that the soldiers from a nearby camp assembled in front of the house and clamored loudly for a view of the bride. Whereupon the dainty Lady Kitty, in full bridal array, stepped in her satin slippers out on the lawn, and there received the congratulations of her father's fellow-campaigners. This is about the last mention we have of this family in our state, for in a few years their handsome seat with its broad surrounding acres passed into the hands of strangers.

A writer who had visited Lady Stirling's household at the time it counted General Greene among its number, and who returned to Basking Ridge ten years later, speaks in a pathetic way of the scene of neglect and decay that met her eye. Its grand hall and decorated drawing room were used as a storehouse and piled with sacks of corn and wheat. Pigs and poultry roamed at will in the paved quadrangle, and its surrounding stables and coach houses were fast going to ruin. Through the unhinged door of the latter was to be seen the great family coach; its glory had departed, for the medallions, coronets, and gilt were bespattered and stained, hens made their nests on its formerly sumptuous cushions, and roosted at night on the high dash and huge leathern springs.

Lord Stirling's earthly reward for his valuable services to the country was an early grave, and the affectionate and grateful remembrance of his countrymen. At the outset of the war his landed property in New York and New Jersey was estimated to be worth one hundred thousand colonial pounds, above encumbrances. When public tranquillity was first disturbed, he at once recognized that he should be forced to neglect his private affairs while discussing with his sword the great questions at issue. Lord Stirling's poverty at the time of his death was not due to want of forethought, but was the outcome of the general prostration of the country at the close of the war and the great changes in currency values. On entering the army he obtained from the legislature an act which empowered commissioners to sell the most of his New Jersey lands and, after paying indebtednesses, to invest the proceeds for his benefit. The properties were sold while the Continental money was yet a lawful tender, but before the debts could be paid the tender act had been repealed. The currency rapidly depreciated, and before his death in 1784 he had to face the fact that his efforts to provide for the future of his family had resulted in his being left without his estates, without any value to the proceeds of their sales, and without his debts being paid. Creditors within the British lines attached and sold his New York property, his obligations soon swallowed up the homestead, and he was thus stripped of everything.

Another occasion of that year was the college commencement held in September at Princeton, when six students received their diplomas. These were the first graduates since 1775, as until this year there had been no classes since early in 1776, although partial instruction had been given to a few students by the president and one of the professors in the summer of 1778. Previous to 1779 Nassau Hall had been used as a barrack by both armies, which, of course, left it in a very dilapidated and polluted condition. The chapel, together with the library, was stripped of furniture and ornaments, Governor Belcher's portrait was stolen, and all the books disappeared, some of them being afterwards found in North Carolina, where they had been left by Cornwallis's men.

How many of the undergraduates and alumni of the "College of New Jersey" are aware that their being able to sing of the glories of "Old Nassau" on campus and at annual banquet is due to the humility of a colonial governor? In 1756, one year before the death of Governor Jonathan Belcher, that dignitary presented his library to the college. In gratitude for the gift the trustees requested that they might be allowed to give his name to the now venerable building, then being erected, which for so many years housed the faculty and students of the ancient seat of learning. His excellency declined the proffered distinction. He requested that it should be named to "express the honor we retain in this remote part of the globe, to the immortal memory of the glorious King William III, who was a branch of the illustrious house of Nassau." And so it was that the trustees decided that the new collegiate building, "in all time to come," should be called "Nassau Hall."

This was not the "beginning of things" for the College of New Jersey. The sturdy oak of alma mater was planted in Presbyterian soil in Elizabethtown in the year 1746. Its founder and first president was the Reverend Jonathan Dickinson, for forty years the pastor of the First Presbyterian Church of that town, whose congregation was the earliest organized in the colony for the worship of God in the English language. An old academy, which was burned by the enemy during the Revolution, contained the class recitation rooms of the new college, while the students, twenty in number, boarded with families in the village.

President Dickinson's duties were many and various. He and an usher were the only teachers of the college, and his ministerial work was severe, as the members of his large congregation were scattered over the country as far as Rahway, Westfield, Connecticut Farms, and Springfield. In addition to the labors of so extended a parish the pastor was compelled, owing to his meager salary, to cultivate a farm. He also practiced medicine, and obtained a high reputation as a physician. A copy of a pamphlet published by him in 1740 gives his views of the "throat distemper," a disease since known as diphtheria. It was not uncommon in Colonial days for the clergy to attempt the healing of the bodies of the people as well as their souls.

At this time the Reverend Aaron Burr, father of the slayer of Alexander Hamilton, was the Presbyterian minister at Newark and eminent both as a scholar and as a divine. On the death of Mr. Dickinson the trustees of the college confided the students to his care. Under Mr. Burr's presidency the institution flourished at Newark for eight years, when, the undergraduates having increased to seventy in number, it was decided to locate the college permanently at Princeton. After much opposition on the part of the congregation of the Presbyterian Church, who protested against the loss of their pastor, Mr. Burr and his young men in October, 1757, betook themselves southward. At this time Princeton was already a village of some importance. Being located on the thoroughfare between New York and Philadelphia—the "King's Highway"—its vicinity was well peopled while the greater part of New Jersey was yet mantled in continuous forest.

Students under the presidency of Aaron Burr would have been aghast at much of the required and elective work of the present curriculum; " 'ologies" were largely unknown, metaphysics, psychology, biology, and even applied chemistry were not thought of, and the course of studies was mostly confined to those that would now be considered fundamental. Even college presidents of the early days had but a limited knowledge of what would now be included in a broad education; their most pronounced strength lay in the direction of polemic and didactic theology.

The course was short at Princeton. Among its students we find that Doctor Benjamin Rush of the class of 1760 graduated at fifteen; Aaron Burr of the class of 1772 at sixteen; Adjutant General Joseph Reed, whose local knowledge contributed so greatly to Washington's success at the battle of Princeton, of the class of 1757 graduated at sixteen; and "Light Horse Harry Lee," of the class of 1774 at seventeen. In fact, most students received their parchments at an age when now they would be thinking of matriculation.

A third event that especially marks the year 1779 in New Jersey's Revolutionary history is the noted raid of the Queen's Rangers in October through Middlesex and Somerset counties. In cleverness of conception and in rapidity and dash of execution this military enterprise was considered by both armies as being among the most brilliant of the war. The germ or nucleus of this command was to be found in a corps of partisan rangers, half hunters, half woodsmen, who were held in high repute in Colonial times. Their first commander was Major Robert Rogers of New Hampshire, and under him they performed many arduous and valuable services on the French and English fighting ground between Ticonderoga and Crown Point. This officer disciplined his men until they were equally at home in the open country or on forest trails, in whaleboats, canoes, or on snowshoes, in civilized or in savage warfare. He was thoroughly versed in all the arts of woodcraft, his endurance and fearless bravery were phenomenal, and until the Revolution he and his Rangers were never mentioned without honor.

At the breaking out of the Revolution Rogers, adhering to the Crown, was commissioned a major and authorized to raise a corps of hussars and infantry to be called the Queen's American Rangers. He procured his men mainly from among the refugees of New York and Connecticut, and did excellent service during the early part of the war. In 1777 he resigned and went to England. While there he was appointed, with the rank of lieutenant colonel, to the command of the King's Rangers, another refugee corps.

When Rogers resigned from the Queen's Rangers, John Graves Simcoe, a young officer who had distinguished himself at the Battle of Brandywine, applied for and received the command with the rank of major. The Queen's Rangers under his control was always in the advance or on the flank of the British army and became the most efficient legionary corps in the English service; its men won laurels for themselves and their young commander in many well conducted raids and brilliant actions. Simcoe, who was soon promoted to be a lieutenant colonel, was ever on the alert; he infused into his men his own spirit of tireless energy, and Sir Henry Clinton in one of his reports to his government asserts that the Rangers, within three years after this dashing young officer had taken command, killed or made prisoners twice their own number. Simcoe was an honest fighter and a good hater, and never outgrew his antipathy to anything and everything American. In his orders he did not hesitate to characterize his foes as a "mean and despicable enemy," and his journal [1] invariably speaks of the

---

[1] This journal was privately printed at Exeter, England, in 1777 under title of *Journal of the Operations of the Queen's Rangers*

American army as "the rebels," and its Commander in Chief as "Mr. Washington."

It was on the morning of the twenty-sixth of October that this famous raid of the Queen's Rangers through the Raritan Valley occurred. Its object is said to have been twofold—the capture of Governor Livingston, whom Simcoe had been falsely informed was staying with Philip Van Horne at "Phil's Hill," Middlebrook; and the destruction of fifty large flatboats which he had been told were at Van Veghten's Bridge, on their way to the army. These boats had been built on the Delaware by Washington's orders so as to be ready to aid in an attack on New York City, which he was then meditating. They held seventy men each, and had been hauled across country on wheels to the Raritan. Simcoe's plan was to move with his cavalry from Amboy to Bound Brook and Van Veghten's Bridge; and then hastily return on the opposite side of the Raritan. When nearing New Brunswick he purposed bearing off to the south, in the hopes of being able to entice the militia and others that by this time might be following him, into an ambuscade near the South River, where a supporting force of his infantry were to lie in wait for the expected victims.

To execute this purpose Major Richard Armstrong, who commanded the foot, was dispatched to South Amboy, from which place he was directed to march with haste and in silence six miles to the bridge crossing South River, the point where his troops were to await in ambush the arrival of the cavalry with, it was hoped, the Jersey militia in pursuit. The raiding column embraced forty-six men of the Ranger hussars, twenty-two of the Buck's light dragoons (a Pennsylvania refugee corps) commanded by Captain Sandford, and a few guides and volunteers under Lieutenant James Stewart. This last officer was a Loyalist Jerseyman, and was well known

. . . It was republished in New York in 1844 as *Simcoe's Military Journal* . . .

and hated in Middlesex and Somerset as "Tory Jim."

Simcoe moved with great rapidity through Piscataway Township to Quibbletown, taking pains on the way to impress everyone met with the idea that his force was a body of Americans. This he was the better able to do because the uniform of his command differed but little from that of Lee's legion, the men wearing green coatees, leather breeches, and cocked hats bound with white braid. Indeed, Lee, who greatly admired Simcoe, says in his memoirs [2] that the Colonel with the most successful audacity stopped during the march at a depot of forage and announced to the commissary that his force was the Virginia light-horse. He drew the forage he needed, paying the customary vouchers therefor, signing them in the name of Lee's quartermaster. Before reaching Quibbletown one Justice Crow was overtaken, whom the Colonel, in order to make him believe that the raiders were from Washington's army, charged with being a Tory; to further the belief the justice for a time was carried along under guard with the detachment, notwithstanding the protestations of the countryman that he had "only been a-sparkin'."

A short halt was made at the Quibbletown Tavern, ostensibly to look for Tories; then the troopers hurried on to Bound Brook where they rested for a while at a public house kept by Peter Harpending. Its boniface was a stanch patriot and one of the men of Somerset whom the Howes stigmatized as "archtraitors" and excepted from the general amnesty offered in 1776. On leaving Bound Brook Colonel Simcoe, having secured a guide in a country lad, made his way up the heights toward Chimney Rock to Washington's camp of the year before. According to an account published in Rivington's *Gazette* by a junior officer accompanying the expedition it was intended to destroy the huts and buildings, but on learn-

---

[2] Henry Lee, *Memoirs of the War in the Southern Department of the United States* . . . (Philadelphia, 1812, and other editions).

ing that they had been sold to some of the inhabitants the Colonel decided to leave them standing. The raiders' next stop was at Philip Van Horne's, Middlebrook, where they were disappointed at not finding Governor Livingston. The troops then continued their march to Van Veghten's Bridge on the Raritan. The greater part of the boats they expected to find there had been sent forward, but with hand grenades brought for that purpose they destroyed eighteen that were left, together with their traveling carriages, an ammunition wagon, some harness, and a quantity of forage and stores. Here they burned the Dutch Reformed Church building.

The Rangers were not over one hour at Van Veghten's Bridge; they then crossed the Raritan and pushed on to Hillsborough. There they burned the Somerset courthouse, after first releasing from jail three Loyalist prisoners, one of whom, according to Simcoe's report, "appeared to have been almost starved and was chained to the floor." While burning, its flames ignited and consumed two nearby dwellings. By this time the country people were up in arms and the militia gathering, so the column was soon again in motion. Filing to the east, it crossed the river and hurried along the Amwell Road in the direction of New Brunswick.

Simcoe's plan was, on reaching the dwelling of Garret Voorhees, which was supposed to be standing at the corner of a crossroad leading into the Princeton Road, to turn to the right and make his way rapidly to the South River, where he hoped to pilot his pursuers into the ambuscade. Both he and his guide kept a bright lookout for the house which was to mark the diverging road. Unhappily for the success of the expedition they were neither of them aware that this was one of the many buildings that the British had destroyed when they retreated from Millstone in 1777. Consequently the Rangers passed this crossroad at a sharp trot without recognizing it, and were within two miles of New Brunswick before the error was known.

During the early part of the march of this command its character had not been discovered, but on reaching Quibbletown someone at the tavern recognized Colonel Simcoe. A messenger was at once dispatched to New Brunswick, whereupon Colonel John Neilson moved with his regiment—the Second Middlesex militia—to Raritan Landing, where the smoke from the burning buildings at Millstone announced the position of the enemy. Had Neilson crossed the river, with but little doubt the raiding column would have been either captured or destroyed; but he, thinking that the Rangers must re-embark where they had landed in the morning, remained on the Middlesex side to oppose their passage of the bridge. Meanwhile he sent forward Captain Moses Guest with thirty-five men to harass the foe on the march. This officer, on reaching a point where the narrow Amwell Road was flanked by thick woods, hid his men and awaited the coming of the enemy.

The British Colonel's situation had now grown distressing. He well knew that his guide was at fault and had missed the crossroad; shots were popping on his flanks, a Captain Voorhees with some militia horsemen was pressing on his rear, and he was in great concern over possible ambuscades in front. When the wood was reached where Guest and his men lay concealed, Simcoe, who was riding in advance with the guide, was fearful that it contained a hidden enemy. On discovering an opening in the fence, he wheeled his horse, intending to lead his men to the right and thus avoid the possible danger. Just then, as he said in his report, he heard the words "Now! Now!" and knew nothing more until he found himself a prisoner in the hands of the Americans. A sudden fusillade had killed his horse with five bullets and stretched him on the ground, stunned by the violence of the fall. His troopers, being on the canter, swept by without discovering that it was intended to leave the highway. The timber was too dense to admit of charging the enemy, so the Rangers pushed on through the woods in open files, receiving a volley from the militia which killed one man and wounded three others and some horses.

The command now devolved on Captain Sandford, who continued toward New Brunswick at an increasing pace. The raiders found themselves in a critical situation. The mounted force hanging on their rear was increasing in numbers, and the militiamen in their front were rapidly multiplying to oppose their further advance. But the desire of the Rangers was to avoid, not to enter, New Brunswick, so Captain Sandford suddenly faced about his squadron and charged the pursuers, putting them to flight. Their leader, Captain Peter V. Voorhees, in attempting to break through a fence became entangled, and was so cut and slashed by the troopers' sabers that he died in a few hours. The killing of this officer was considered by the Americans little less than a murder, as he was wholly in enemy hands and incapable of resistance. Captain Voorhees' death was greatly lamented. He was on leave and was to have been married on the following day—indeed, it is said that he was on his way to visit his fiancée when he came upon a party of militia in pursuit of the Queen's Rangers and put himself at their head.

Captain Sandford's anxiety was now to reach his body of supporting infantry, so in order to delude the enemy in his front he marched to the left as if intending to enter New Brunswick. The Americans in front then pushed to their right in order to check a retreat in that direction. Whereupon the Rangers retraced their steps and with a sharp gallop gained the left flank of the Jerseymen, and thus made their escape in the direction of South River. Before four o'clock in the afternoon Captain Sandford with his cavalry had joined Major Armstrong at the bridge, and that night the combined forces crossed from

South Amboy to Staten Island. Although the expedition failed in drawing the militia into the ambuscade, the exploit reflected great credit on the British arms, and but for the loss of Simcoe it would have been considered brilliantly successful. At least sixty miles of hostile country were passed over with the loss of but few men, about thirty prisoners were secured, much property destroyed, and many bad horses exchanged for good ones taken from the prisoners and the country people.

22

Rivers Firm as Land

A WORK OF THIS CHARACTER necessarily covers periods of time devoid of interest. This particularly applies to those parts chronicling the affairs of the occupants of the Old Stone House. It is hardly to be supposed that their daily experiences could at all times have been so replete with incidents as to add to the weight of this narrative.

During these days of Revolutionary turmoil the current of domestic life in the Old Stone House flowed peacefully on in sober comfort, for within its walls was an orderly and a cheerful household, where love and duty kindly blended, and where each day's busy hours wore away in the homely toils and pleasures usual with farm families.

Aaron's children now numbered five—the final complement—Margaret having been born in 1767 and Maria in 1771. John, who had long ere this been released by the British, was again off soldiering, this time with the Continental Line. Daniel, now a sturdy boy of sixteen, was aiding his father in the tannery and on the farm, and educating himself so as to eventually become an able man of business and his father's partner. Two of the girls were old enough to take upon themselves much of the cares of indoors; and doubtless, as was the custom with farmer's daughters, waited each night at the barn with clinking pails and wooden stools while the motherly brown cows came lowing up the lane. Wartimes naturally brought privations and some discomforts, but there were compensations, not only in the increased value given to farm and tannery products but in the many excitements that ruled the hour, which it is reasonable to suppose must have given added zest to the ordinarily quiet life of the rural community. Later on it was not improbable that we shall find material in the daily routine of this family's existence that will make interesting reading; but before again taking up such homely topics we must wait until camps and their influences have disappeared from the neighborhood. Just now we will turn once more to the Continental Army, which is to spend this winter and spring (1780) on the northeast border of Somerset.

Early in December the army went into winter quarters between Morristown and Mendham, Washington establishing himself at the residence of the widow of Colonel Jacob Ford. Her family gave up all of the building excepting two rooms, but as the General's household comprised eighteen persons he was much inconvenienced for want of space. He wrote to Greene, who was still quartermaster general, complaining of his contracted quarters, saying: "All Mrs. Ford's family are crowded together in her kitchen, and scarce one of them able to talk for colds they have caught." This resulted in a small log kitchen being attached to the east end of the mansion, and a larger log house being erected which furnished offices for the Commander in Chief, his aides, and secretaries. The Life Guard were barracked in fifty rude huts that were set up in a triangular bit of meadow just east of the dwelling, from where in case of alarm the house could in a few moments be reached and surrounded.

The main army was on Kimball Hill about four miles southwest of Morristown. About one thousand acres were occupied, embracing properties then known as the Kimball and Wicks farms. Kimball Hill commands extensive views ranging from Schooley's Mountain on the west to the Short Hills on the east, and from the New York Highlands on the north to the heights above the Raritan on the south. The encampment was pitched on this commanding elevation because of its being a natural watchtower, enabling the army to be ever on the alert against surprise or invasion. During each night men were constantly scanning the horizon to discover the first tongue of flame leaping heavenward from any of the many beacons that were planted on the spurs of the encircling hills between the Delaware, Hudson, and Shrewsbury. During the day, in case of an alarm, signal guns were fired from the beacon-posts. The cannon that oftenest had occasion to shriek warnings from its iron throat became historically known as the "Old Sow"; it was an eighteen-pounder set up at the beacon-post on the Short Hills just back of Springfield.

However advantageous Kimball Hill may have been in a military sense, it proved a very bleak and inhospitable camping ground, and it was not long before some of the line officers of the army were making unfavorable comparisons between this exposed situation and the warm, nearby Lowantica Valley that had sheltered the encampment of three years before. The weather this winter was in extraordinary contrast to the mildness of the preceding one; the cold was the severest ever known in the colonies, and the snow fell almost continuously from the tenth of November until far into March. The Lower Bay, New York Bay, and Hudson River were equally firm as the land, and people crossed Long Island Sound from Connecticut to Lloyd's Neck, a distance of twelve miles, as if on a prairie. The ice of New York Bay was thick enough to enable two hundred sleighloads of provisions, drawn by two horses each and escorted by two hundred cavalry, to cross from New York to Staten Island. The Raritan River was frozen solid for four months, during which time its surface was more used as a thoroughfare for teams than were the highways on its banks.

In January the Somerset militia were called out—not to fight the King of England—this time the enemy was the king of storms, for on the night of the third the greatest body of snow fell known during the war. The whole face of the country lay buried from three to five feet deep; roads, fences, and frozen streams were obliterated and, as the storm had been accompanied by a very high wind, in places the drifts were piled ten to twelve feet high. The army on Kimball Hill suffered severely, as the weather was intensely cold. Thacher [1] tells that officers were almost smothered in the snow because of the collapsing of their tents by the high winds; and, to quote another witness and sufferer: "No man could endure the violence of the storm many minutes without danger of his life." The roads being blocked, great difficulty was experienced in procuring fuel and supplies. So it was that the militia were called upon to break the roads from Morristown to Hackettstown on the north and to Princeton on the south. In addition, the people were requested to come to the aid of the militia with their teams. Greene wrote to Colonel Hathaway:

The roads must be kept open by the inhabitants or the army cannot be subsisted; and unless good people immediately lend assistance to forward supplies the army must disband. The dreadful consequences of such an event I will not torture your feelings with a description of; but remember, the surrounding inhabitants will experience the first melancholy effects of such a raging evil. . . . You will call to your aid the overseers of highways and every other order of men who can give despatch and success to the business.

Nothwithstanding the aid furnished by militia and inhabitants in breaking the roads, such a great body of snow paralyzed all arteries of travel, and the army was soon in an extremity for provisions. Washington was forced to levy on the inhabitants for cattle, flour, and

---

[1] Surgeon Thatcher, *A Military Journal During the Revolutionary War* . . . (Boston, 1827).

grain. He called upon the magistrates of the respective counties to undertake the business of relieving the distresses of the troops, taking care at the same time to notify them that a force had been detailed to impress the necessary supplies should the people fail to voluntarily alleviate the sufferings of the men. The commanders of the forces were directed to show great tenderness toward the inhabitants in case such extreme measures became necessary; care was to be taken that families should not be deprived of their milch cows or of needed subsistence. The necessity for a recourse to severity happily did not arise, as the sympathies of the people were at once enlisted and relief was afforded without delay or indecision.

The distressing situation of the army was not altogether due to the transportation of supplies being obstructed by the uncommon rigor of the weather. The depreciation of the currency had increased to an alarming extent. Congress had made Continental paper legal tender for debts, however contracted; but its value steadily decreased, until by 1780 it was almost impossible to determine how much paper money represented one Spanish milled dollar, which at that time was the unit of value. Credit was thus prostrated and the commissaries found themselves without a current purchasing medium with which to secure adequate supplies. It is interesting to observe the ruling prices in Continental money. A horse was sold at Camp Middlebrook for six hundred dollars currency that had been offered for eighty silver dollars. A year later paper values had so much more decreased that a mare of eleven years sold at a vendue for eight hundred and five pounds; a wood saw, thirty-seven pounds, ten shillings; an old eight-day clock in a walnut case, two hundred and fifty pounds; fifty sheaves of oats, eighty pounds; and other sales in like proportion.

Notwithstanding that at this time the troops were in a deplorable condition as to provisions and clothing, Washington was not willing to let pass an apparently opportune moment for striking a blow at the enemy on Staten Island. The frost had converted the Kills into a solid bridge. On the afternoon of the fourteenth of January a detachment of foot and artillery set out from the Morristown parade on sleds to reinforce the brigade lying at Elizabethtown. Early on the fifteenth the party, twenty-five hundred strong, commanded by Lord Stirling, crossed at De Hart's Point and marched on the enemy's works. The enterprise proved a failure. The British garrison having been strongly reinforced, an assault was not attempted; after some skirmishing the Americans retired, bringing with them a few prisoners, the casualties being not many on either side. Ten days later the British made a return visit to the Jersey shore, their enterprise being crowned with more success. At midnight on the twenty-fifth of January about four hundred infantry and one hundred dragoons, commanded by the Tory Lieutenant Colonel Buskirk, crossed on the ice at Trembly's Point and surprised Elizabethtown. Four officers and about sixty privates were captured, the inhabitants were plundered, and the courthouse and the Presbyterian Church burned. The same night a small party attacked Newark with equal success, burning the Academy.

Human nature is ever the same. Many a brave Englishman prepared for death at Waterloo by dancing the night before at the Duchess of Richmond's ball. So it was with our Revolutionary soldiers—recreation must be had even in the face of the most adverse circumstances. Early in the winter subscription balls, or assemblies, were established at Morristown, Washington and his leading generals heading the subscription list. As was usual with each annual encampment, there was a fair sprinkling of ladies with the army.

A young lady reached Morristown during the winter whose arrival created a flutter in camp society, especially among the young men surrounding headquarters. It was

305

Miss Betsey Schuyler, the second daughter of General Philip Schuyler. She was a beauty and a belle, very small and delicately formed, with an oval face and bewitching black eyes. Colonel Tench Tilghman, on meeting her for the first time, described her as being "a brunette, with the most good-natured lively dark eyes that I ever saw, which threw a beam of good temper and benevolence over her entire countenance." This handsome staff officer was just then proof against her fascinations, being no longer fancy free. It was not so, however, with his brother staff officer, Colonel Hamilton, who succumbed at once to the attractions of this imperious little beauty. Rugged Mars made way for the gentler god, who soon guided the barque of these young people into the safe harbor of matrimony.

On the nineteenth of April the Chevalier de la Luzerne, who had succeeded Gerard as minister from France, and Don Juan de Miralles with their suites arrived at headquarters on a visit. They were received with great honors; salvos of artillery were fired, and an escort of officers and orderlies was sent to meet them at the Somerset County line. Out of compliment to these distinguished guests, on the twenty-fourth four brigades of the army were paraded in review. In the evening there was an exhibition of fireworks, after which the excitements and pleasures of the day terminated with a grand ball.

One of the guests for whom all this display had been prepared was unable to be present. Don Juan de Miralles, the Spanish envoy, was tossing with fever in one of the upper chambers of the Ford mansion. He grew rapidly worse and four days later, to the great consternation and regret of his hosts, died. His funeral was literally attended by thousands of persons, the procession of soldiers and civilians on foot, which included General Washington and several members of Congress, extended for a mile. While the funeral cortège with its vast escort moved with solemn slowness to the music of muffled drums from headquarters to the Presbyterian burying ground, minute guns were fired and every military honor accorded to the remains of the distinguished stranger. A Spanish priest recited the Roman Catholic service for the dead at the grave, the details of the burial being attended with much pomp and ceremony. Lest some predatory soldier should be tempted to dig for hidden treasure, a guard was left in the churchyard. This was considered necessary because of the Spanish dignitary's having been buried in full regalia. He was arrayed for interment in a scarlet coat embroidered with heavy gold lace; a three-cornered gold-laced hat and a well-curled wig were on his head and a costly gold watch, set with diamonds, in his pocket; diamond rings were on his fingers and several rich seals depended from his watch guard. The body was laid out in a coffin covered with rich black velvet ornamented in a superb manner. This leads one to wonder where in so short a space of time such burial magnificence could have been procured.

It is not surprising that the soldiers should have inwardly protested against so much of value being placed underground with the dead, when live men serving their country were in sorest need of the merest necessities. Although the response made by the citizens in January to Washington's appeal had saved the army from the immediate danger of starving or disbanding, it had very far from ended the sufferings of the soldiers. Throughout the winter and spring the privations and want almost equalled the unhappy experiences of the memorable encampment at Valley Forge. For weeks the men were on half rations, often without meat, often without bread, much of the time nearly frozen for need of blankets and clothing. Frequently the horses were destitute of forage, and the hospital had neither sugar, coffee, tea, wine, nor liquors. The military chest was empty and the army was unpaid for five months; even when the soldiers received their

307

pay, owing to the diminished value of government money it was of but little avail. A common laborer, whose wages were in hard money, received four times as much as an American officer.

Under such a tide of misfortunes it speaks well for the discipline and temper of the men that they neither inaugurated a war of plunder on the inhabitants nor deserted to the enemy. At this time the American camp was flooded with circulars calling upon the men to fly from sickness, famine, and nakedness to the British army, where they would be received with open arms, and fed, clothed, and paid. Upon Washington fell the embarrassments and responsibilites of this time. The citizens looked upon him as their protector from the marauding of an impoverished and famished soldiery, while the army relied upon him for provisions. To satisfy both was no small undertaking; but Washington seemed equal even to such an emergency. He not only guarded the interests of the inhabitants but retained the army in service and preserved the affections of his soldiers.

To secure order and subordination great firmness was necessary, and sometimes he was forced to resort to severe punishments. One unhappy day in May eight soldiers, who had been court-martialed for thievery, desertion, and other crimes, were brought in carts to the gallows for execution. After being addressed by the chaplain, they were placed under the fatal beam of one scaffold, halters about their necks, their coffins on the ground before them, and their open graves in plain view. An officer suddenly rode forward and read the Commander in Chief's reprieve of seven of the culprits. Weak and agitated by the excitements of the occasion, it was almost necessary to carry the pardoned from the scaffold. After they had somewhat recovered, the chaplain urged them to remember the awful fate they had escaped by the clemency of the General and begged that their future lives might in consequence be devoted to a faithful discharge of duty.

Before starting on his journey alone, the one poor wretch remaining to be executed addressed the soldiers, urging them to take warning by his fate and to be true to their duties and country. The offense for which he suffered was that of forging discharges, whereby he and over one hundred men had escaped service. When the fatal moment had arrived, he placed the noose about his neck himself and adjusted the knot, at the same time protesting that the halter was not strong enough to bear his weight. When he swung off, the rope broke and the unhappy man was dashed on the ground and much bruised. On mounting the scaffold again, he cried out: "I told you the rope was not strong enough, do get a stronger one!" A new halter was procured, and upon a second attempt being made he was successfully launched into eternity. The admonition of the chaplain had no effect upon one of the reprieved soldiers, for on the sixteenth of June he was hanged for deserting to the enemy.

During the winter Sir Henry Clinton, leaving von Knyphausen in command at New York, sailed southward with a large detachment of troops and invested Charleston. After a prolonged defence, on the eleventh of May the garrison of three thousand under General Lincoln capitulated to a British force of nine thousand men. Including the adult inhabitants of the city, the enemy secured five thousand prisoners, among them seven generals and two hundred and thirty-eight other officers. It was a severe blow to the American arms and added much to the depression of the public mind.

Owing to this loss and to the discontent of Washington's army because of the lack of clothing and pay, the British were led to believe that the whole country, including citizens and troops, would welcome the royal standard and, provided they felt sure of English support, would again give their fealty to the Crown. In order to foster this feeling and encourage disaffection, the enemy landed in force on the sixth of June at Elizabethtown Point, intending to penetrate in the direction of Morristown. The invading troops were six thousand strong, with von Knyphausen in command. It was the flower of the British army, the celebrated Coldstream Guards being in one of the divisions.

Von Knyphausen expected to be met with open arms. Nor was he disappointed—at least not in fact though perhaps in kind. His men were not fairly on the march before arms opened to them on every side. When the head of the column moving towards Elizabethtown reached where the Old and New Point roads divide, a small guard of militia fired and fled. General Stirling, who led the first division, was unhorsed and his thigh fractured. The advance proceeded in good order by way of the Galloping Hill Road to Connecticut Farms.

The welcome that the marching column received was a very different one from what had been anticipated. Puffs of smoke and the spatter of bullets greeted the soldiers from trees and hedges, and the citizens seemed relentlessly alert, ready to make targets of English grenadiers or of Hessian horse and foot. Soon the invading force was fearfully galled and so angered as to be ready to wreck vengeance on all things animate and inanimate. Dwellings, church, and people alike fell prey to the frenzied soldiers; even a weak unoffending woman was not safe from their vengeful slaughter. When the troops passed the parsonage at Connecticut Farms, a red-coat jumped over the fence and, pointing his gun in an open window, fired two balls through the body of the wife of the Reverend James Caldwell of the First Presbyterian Church at Elizabethtown, stretching her dead on the floor. Mr. Caldwell had moved his family to the village, thinking that retired spot to be more secure from chance incursions of the enemy.

The flames ignited by the invaders soon licked up this little village. When von Knyphausen crossed from Staten Island the previous day, Maxwell with his brigade was at Elizabethtown, but on the landing of the enemy he retired to Connecticut Farms. At the same time notice of the enemy's approach was sent to Washington. Colonel Dayton had established a system of fleet-footed scouts, who, running rapidly one to the other, were able to quickly convey intelligence to Morristown. Washington was early on the march and late in the afternoon reinforced Maxwell. But during the day the Jersey brigade and the militia opposed the enemy with great stubbornness; first in the vicinity of the Farm's meetinghouse, where they checked their advance for nearly three hours. The Americans then fell back slowly in the direction of Springfield, where a stand was made, which Maxwell describes in a letter to Governor Livingston:

Never did troops, either continental or militia, behave better than ours did. Every one that had an opportunity— which they mostly all had—vied with each other who could serve the country most. In the latter part of the day the militia flocked from all quarters, and gave the enemy no respite till night closed the scene. At the middle of the night the enemy sneaked off and put their backsides to the Sound near Elizabethtown.

When the American army marched to Connecticut Farms in support of Maxwell, Mrs. Washington was left at Morristown with a temporary guard commanded by Captain John Steele. One night during Washington's absence there was an alarm, and four members of Congress, who were in camp in order to learn the needs of the army, joined Captain Steele's detachment as volunteers. In speaking of them, in a letter to his brother, the young officer expressed a wish that he had a company of congressmen for the next campaign, as it would surely result in the army's being better victualled. To quote him, "The rations they have consumed considerably overbalanced all their services done as volunteers, for they have dined with us every day since, almost, and drank as much wine as they would earn in six months."

Von Knyphausen with his royal detachment did not recross to Staten Island but remained behind entrenchments at the Point. While he was there, Sir Henry Clinton returned from the South; elated by his success at Charleston he determined to reinforce the Hessian General and again endeavor to beat up the American's base of supplies at Morristown. To insure success he first made a feint northward in order to draw Washington from New Jersey. This ruse was successful. The American General, suspecting a design against West Point, moved his army on the twenty-first in that direction, leaving Greene with two brigades to protect the stores and support Maxwell in guarding the lower country.

At five o'clock on the morning of the twenty-third the enemy advanced from Elizabethtown, their numbers increased by a large body of cavalry and fifteen or twenty pieces of artillery. They moved rapidly in two columns, though considerably harassed by Lee's legion and the militia. Greene, collecting all his available troops at Springfield, there met the enemy and opposed their march. The British maneuvered for two hours in a futile effort to flank their opponents, after which a general action ensued lasting about forty minutes, when, as Greene says in his report of the operations of the day, "Superior numbers overcame obstinate bravery, and forced our troops to retire." The American General fell back to the first range of hills, where he advantageously posted himself so as to check any effort of his foes to gain the heights.

The British showed no disposition to advance further but contented themselves with wasting and ravaging the country. In a few hours four houses were all that was left of what had been the flourishing village of Springfield. The British fell back early in the day, their line of retreat being marked by dead and wounded men; the militia were on their rear and flanks for the entire distance, keeping up a continuous fire upon them until they reached Elizabethtown at sunset. At midnight the enemy evacuated the state.

The departure of the British was followed by the breaking up of the camp on Kimball Hill. Among the stories preserved of that time is one about Wicks' daughter, Tempe. This young woman was a fearless rider, and the owner of a valuable saddle horse. When the regiments were on the move some soldiers attempted to steal her favorite, claiming him to be wanted for army purposes. Being scarce, horses were much needed, and this spirited animal, even were this not so, would have been a tempting bait for careless campaigners not over-particular as to the rights of property. Miss Wicks, when mounted and a short distance from home, was surrounded; but with a bold dash she escaped from her captors and rode rapidly up the hill to the house. Springing to the ground she led her steed through the kitchen and parlor into a rear spare bedroom, which had but one window guarded by a closed wooden shutter. The disappointed soldiers repeatedly searched the farm in vain for the coveted horse, but the courageous young lady kept him secreted in the house until the last of the troops had left the neighborhood.

The rest of the year wore away without much advantage to the American cause. The surrender at Charleston was supplemented by the reverse at Camden, where Gates lost much of the prestige gained at Saratoga. With an empty military chest, a barren commissariat, and an army in need of almost everything it was impossible for Washington to engage in an active campaign. The best that could be done was to present a bold front north of New York City and watch the enemy.

On the tenth of July, to the great joy of the country, the long expected succor from France reached our shores. A French fleet with six thousand troops under the command of Lieutenant General Count de Rochambeau arrived at Rhode Island. The expectations of the Americans were raised to the highest pitch, as it was supposed that the co-operating armies would now be able to strike a decisive blow. All such hopes were blasted by the arrival of a superior British fleet, which blockaded the French ships and army at Rhode Island. And so the campaign of 1780 closed in chagrin and disappointment. The gloom of this period was further darkened by the black treachery of Benedict Arnold, which resulted in the necessary sacrifice of that handsome and gifted youth, Major André—a tragedy which brought honest grief to both armies.

23

Heavy Pockets Make Light Hearts

A<small>T THE END</small> of November the army was in winter
quarters, Washington establishing himself at New
Windsor on the Hudson, where the eastern troops were
cantoned. The New Jersey and Pennsylvania lines were
in our state; the former at Pompton, the later on Kemble
Hill, both being under the command of General Anthony
Wayne. In a letter to General Frome, Wayne writes, "The
men are poorly clothed, badly fed, and worse paid, some
of them not having received a paper dollar for near twelve
months; exposed to winter's piercing cold, to drifting
snows, and chilling blasts, with no protection but old
worn-out coats, tattered linen overalls, and but one blanket between three men."

What wonder that such sufferings should have fo-
mented in the troops a feeling of discontent and bitterness? Another case for dissatisfaction was a disagreement
that had arisen between the officers and men as to the
true interpretation of the phraseology of the enlistment
papers. By them the men were bound to serve for "three
years or during the war." Those who had been in the
army over three years claimed that their services were
being prolonged beyond the term of enlistment—contending that the election was with them whether to remain at the end of that time. The officers maintained that
the alternative was with the government, and that the

war not having ended the men could be held until the cessation of hostilities.

The feeling of discontent bred by such a condition of affairs rapidly increased, until on the night of the first of January it resulted in an open revolt. The men of several regiments refused to obey their officers, and declared the intention of marching at once to Philadelphia to demand of Congress the redress of their grievances. A vain attempt was made to arrest their departure; coercion only resulted in a spread of mutiny. Shots were fired on both sides, wounds inflicted, and several of the insurgents killed. They in their turn gave a death wound to a Captain Billings, who was endeavoring to bring them under subjection.

General Wayne found himself powerless to quell the mutiny. With a cocked pistol in his hand he exhorted his men to return to their duty, threatening that a failure to do so would result in direst punishments. They replied through their spokesman with great firmness, saying: "We love and respect you, but you are a dead man if you fire. Do not mistake us; we are not going to the enemy; were they now to come out you would see us fight under your orders with as much resolution and alacrity as ever." Just before midnight the mutineers, thirteen hundred strong, armed and under command of their noncommissioned officers, set off in good order from camp, taking with them six fieldpieces and an adequate number of artillery horses.

Bad news travels quickly. By the next morning the people of Bedminster and the surrounding country knew that the army was in revolt, and much anxiety was felt lest the soldiers commit excesses during their march southward. Nor were their fears without reason, but happily this danger was averted by the sagacity of Wayne. This general, upon consultation with his officers after the rebels had started, determined that if he could not command his men he would at least follow in their wake, and by judicious management and by seeing that they were supplied with provisions prevent plundering and depredation. In the morning, accompanied by regimental Colonels Stewart and Butler, he overtook the insurgents bivouacked at Vealtown and immediately had an interview with the noncommissioned officers. This resulted in a committee of the sergeants being appointed, who drew up a specification of grievances and who made the most solemn promises to preserve good order during the march. Wayne dispatched couriers to Philadelphia announcing the unfortunate condition of affairs and urging that Congress be prepared to treat with the men. Whereupon a committee from that body was appointed, which with President Reed at its head proceeded to Princeton, where the insurgents were met and negotiations were at once entered into for an accommodation of all differences.

The Tories were prompt to carry intelligence of this insurrection to the enemy, who falsely concluded that it would be the desire of the insurgents to make their way to the British lines. Acting on this supposition Sir Henry Clinton collected a number of boats opposite Perth Amboy, and dispatched five thousand troops to the lower end of Staten Island. He then sent a New Jersey Tory named Ogden and a British sergeant to the rebels, telling what arrangements had been made in support of their movement and offering to discharge all debts due them from the United States without demanding military service in return. The board of sergeants to whom the propositions were made immediately turned the bearers, together with their papers, over to Wayne, and eventually these emissaries were hanged as spies. The soldiers were indignant that their loyalty to the government was suspected. "See, comrades," said one of the sergents on reading aloud Clinton's message, "he takes us for traitors! Let us show him the American Army can furnish but one Arnold, and that America has no truer friends than we."

Such spirit on the part of the men had a powerful influence in securing for them a favorable adjustment of their difficulties. A compromise mutually advantageous was effected whereby some of their just demands were complied with and many of the soldiers were discharged, their places in the Pennsylvania line being filled by recruits in the spring. So most fortunately terminated an affair which, had it been managed on both sides with less discretion, might have led to the disruption of the entire army.

So great a breach of disclipline was not without its evil effects upon other portions of the Continental force. In the middle of January some of the Jersey line at Pompton, encouraged by the success of the Pennsylvanians, refused longer to do duty. Washington, fearing further trouble, had already taken the precaution of having a trusted command of one thousand men under arms, ready to march from headquarters at a moment's notice. This detachment made a rapid move on the Jersey camp, and the refractory soldiers were forced to parade without arms and deliver up their ringleaders. Three of the latter who had been at the head of the revolt were at once tried by drum-head court-martial, sentenced, and two of them executed on the spot, twelve of the most guilty of their associates being obliged to serve as the firing party. In such a terrible but effective manner was this second mutiny throttled at its birth.

The next incident of interest in the Revolutionary story of Somerset is the memorable march of the allied armies across the county on their way to the triumphant campaign in Virginia. The achievements of Greene, who was transferred from the quartermaster's department to the command of the Southern army, produced a marked change in the aspect of affairs, for with an inconsiderable and miserably provided army he successfully contended with a regular British force, his efforts culminating in brilliant victories at Cowpens and Eutaw Springs. Before the first of April, with alternate marching and fighting, the opposing armies had crossed the two Carolinas and Cornwallis had entered Virginia. By this time the British General had been largely reinforced and had divided his command. At the Virginia line Greene abandoned the pursuit of Cornwallis and turned back to meet the other division.

The Earl continued to Winchester and to Petersburg where he combined with General Philips, and being there further reinforced by fifteen hundred men from New York found himself at the head of a formidable army, seven thousand strong. He advanced from Petersburg, opposed guardedly by Lafayette, who in February, 1781, had marched to Virginia with twelve hundred men. Cornwallis, deciding to make Virginia the seat of future operations, proceeded to Yorktown, where he strongly fortified himself and awaited the arrival of a British fleet from the West Indies, by which he hoped to prosecute a vigorous campaign. All this time Washington was not unmindful of what was transpiring in the South. Knowing that a French fleet would soon arrive at the Virginia capes, he believed that he saw an opportunity in conjunction with the allied army for striking a deadly blow at the enemy. His preparations accordingly were secretly and effectively made.

During the entire summer of 1781 the British garrison and Tory residents of New York City were in constant trepidation because of the proximity of the combined American and French forces. Early in July Washington's army was encamped at Dobb's Ferry, and by the sixth of that month he was reinforced by Rochambeau from Newport. The enemy had good cause for fearing an immediate attack, and Clinton had grave doubts of the favorable results of an encounter, his force having been much weakened by drafts on him from Cornwallis. Washington was well informed of the fears and apprehensions of the British General, and by a series of feints and movements did what he could to add to his discomfitures and to prolong his anxieties. Clinton learned from his spies and scouts that on the twenty-second of July the Americans and French, five thousand strong, were marching and countermarching on the heights north of Harlem, that on the twenty-third Washington and Rochambeau dined at the Van Courtland mansion at King's Bridge, and that a few days later they were reconnoitering in the vicinity of the British outposts.

Washington and his leading generals kept their own counsels, and the Continental officers generally were as curious as were the English as to what was to be the outcome of the many preparations being made within the American lines. Camps were established, earthworks thrown up, bread ovens erected, and much else done by order of the Commander in Chief calculated to alarm the enemy and deceive his own army. Meanwhile the position of Cornwallis in Virginia was growing perilous in the extreme. Though Clinton had nearly eighteen thousand men on and about Manhattan Island, while menaced by Washington he dared not detach a single company to reinforce the southern army. This explains the American General's masterly maneuvers. He was biding his time.

When the news came that Count de Grasse with twenty-eight ships of the line carrying four thousand soldiers had entered the Chesapeake, he showed his hand —at least to his own force. On the nineteenth of August small detachments were sent against New York and Staten Island to occupy the enemy, while the main allied army broke camp, crossed the Hudson, and hastily marched southward. So sudden and unannounced was this movement that the armies were well on their way before the officers learned that they were bound for Virginia.

The allied armies in crossing New Jersey marched by different routes in four divisions, two American and two French. An old order-book of the Continental light infantry presents some interesting glimpses of the experiences of this column while on the march. Assembly was beat each morning at half after three and the troops were in motion at four. The column was preceded by the commissaries with a drove of cattle, who, on reaching the place of encampment for the night, slaughtered the necessary stock and had the rations of beef ready to be issued on the arrival of the troops. Brigade commanders were ordered on reaching campground to make immediate application to the commissary for fresh beef, "and if it was not killed and ready to serve out They are to demand the Reason and report it." Each regiment was allowed one uncovered and three covered wagons for carrying baggage and tents, which were ordered to fall in between the New York brigade and the rear guard. In addition two empty wagons followed each brigade in which were placed men too sick or lame to march. Wagoners who permitted such persons to ride without written permission from the corps commanders were to be punished at the first halt. The women contingent of this force appear to have caused considerable annoyance. They were inclined to steal rides from the wagons, and evidently were not amenable to military discipline. One of the orders relating to them recites:

Prior to the commencement of our march this morning the commanding officers will inform the women of their respective corps that the General saw many of them yesterday from their proper line of march, strolling in gardens and orchards, an irregularity which must not be repeated. Should any attempt it hereafter they will be denied their rations and prevented farther from following the army.

It was the passage of the French divisions that excited the liveliest interest among the Jersey people. The allies' right column consisted of Lauzun's legion; the regiment Bourbonnais, uniformed in black turned up with red; the Royal Deux-Ponts, in white broadcloth coats faced with green; and the heavy artillery, the men of which were uniformed in blue with white facings. The left column of the French army contained all the stores and baggage, together with the regiments Saintonge and Soissonnais, the men of the former being arrayed in white and green, while the white uniforms of the latter were faced with pink, their grenadier caps being gay with floating pink plumes. Attached to each regiment were companies of chasseurs formed of light active men, and of grenadiers who were always soldiers of good size and appearance. The latter were considered the elite of the corps, being men of long service and acknowledged bravery; they wore high bearskin hats and distinctive uniforms, and always marched at the head of each battalion.

There have been left us numerous notices of the passage of the foreign troops through our country. The Abbé Robin,[1] the chaplain of the regiment Soissonnais, records that the conduct of the men was admirable, there not even being a single instance of one of the soldiers taking an apple or a peach from an orchard without obtaining leave. The Duponceau manuscripts[2] recite: "It was given out in general orders that if a Frenchman should have a dispute with an American the Frenchman should be punished, whether he was in the right or in the wrong." Claude Blanchard,[3] commissary of the French army, found the dwellings of Bernards Township "always unique. They have no gardens, no fruit walls, only some apple trees, some peach trees and some scattered cherry trees, all forming what we call orchard. The road which I took to reach 'Bullion's Tavern' is not disagreeable, but the farms are still middling, they were sown with maize and buckwheat; I also saw a little hemp there." Princeton he called "a pretty village of about

---

[1] Claude C. Robin, *New Travels Through North-America* . . . (Philadelphia, 1783). There were various other editions in French, German, Dutch, and English.

[2] This reference is probably to the papers of Peter Stephen Du Ponceau, now owned by the Historical Society of Pennsylvania.

[3] *The Journal of Claude Blanchard* . . . 1780–1783 . . . (Albany, 1876).

sixty houses; the inns there are handsome and very clean. A very handsome college is also to be seen there, built in the same style as that at Providence."

Another diarist furnishes us with an interesting account of some French officers from one of the divisions having been entertained at John Morton's residence, near the church at Basking Ridge. Mrs. Morton's parents—Mr. and Mrs. Kemper—who had emigrated from Germany early in the century, were at this time visiting their children at Basking Ridge. While all the other members of the household were delighted with the appearance of the French soldiers, and vied with each other in their entertainment, the old gentleman and his wife retired to their chamber. They could not forget the sufferings of their fatherland under Gallic oppression, and were confident that no good would come to the American cause by the employment of such allies.

The foreign troops while swinging through Bedminster on their hurried march made a magnificent appearance. As soldiers the Frenchmen were a revelation to the inhabitants, presenting a marked contrast to the poorly clad and equipped Continentals. The view of such perfect phalanxes, thronging helms, and thick array of waving banners was a new military experience for Bedminster people, and when the *tambour majors*, resplendent in *panache*, aiguillette, and tinsel, flourished their ponderous batons, making the hills and valleys vocal with the melody of the Gallic bands, the acme of warlike splendor seemed to have been reached. The private soldiers in their handsome and varied uniforms appeared as neat as their officers; easy, debonair, and with natures proverbially gay, they were not stern-looking, grim-visaged warriors, as though wielding the offensive blade from love of carnage or eager to sack cities and devastate and raze villages. But do not for a moment make the mistake of thinking that these Frenchmen were mere holiday soldiers. They could fight—and they did fight like gladiators when the time

323

came. On the fourteenth of October one-third of the Regiment Gatenois—afterwards the royal Auvergne—which had landed from Count de Grasse's fleet, fell in the trenches near Yorktown when storming a redoubt.

Heavy pockets make light hearts. Perhaps that is why the French soldiers bore such cheerful countenances, as they were paid regularly every two weeks. They had other causes for being contented with their military lot. One James Tilton, in a letter from Williamsburg, Virginia, in December, 1781, to Captain Thomas Rodney of Delaware, wrote,

> It must be mortifying for our poor devils to observe the comfortable and happy life of French soldiers. They appear on parade every day like fine gentlemen . . . The officers treat the soldiers with attention, humanity and respect, and appear to employ all the means necessary to inspire them with sentiments of honor. Theft is said to be a crime held in universal abhorrence among them. I have not seen or heard of any instance yet of a French soldier being whipped. Their desertions, I believe, have been rare, and their sickness but little. When will our army bear this comparison?

The Jersey people especially marveled at the brave show made by the Duke of Lauzun's legion, a corps of six hundred men, hussars and infantry, the very pick of the French army. These soldiers, especially the hussars, were sparkling with life and activity and seemed to look upon the march as a holiday excursion. Their officers were all tall young men with handsome faces and noble bearing, who made a superb appearance mounted on fine horses, richly caparisoned. Their distinctive characteristics—which were quite new on this side of the water—were the mustaches they all wore. We may easily figure the interest and admiration that these volatile, laughter-loving *beaux sabreurs* must have excited in the hearts and minds of the American girls met during their campaign. It is said that, following the impulses of their gay dispositions, more than once after a day's march their assurance and captivating manners secured for them partners for an evening dance.

The combined armies were quickly beyond the Delaware. It was the thirtieth of August—by which time the French and American generals were being enthusiastically welcomed at Philadelphia—before Sir Henry Clinton, almost wild with anger and humiliation, discovered that his army was again the victim of the superior strategy of the American Fabius. On the eighth of September, while Greene was whipping the enemy at Eutaw Springs, Washington was in Baltimore, and on the evening of the ninth he was at Mount Vernon—his first visit in six years. Here two days were spent in entertaining distinguished guests from the two armies. The generals and their retinues on the fourteenth joined Lafayette at Williamsburg; by the twenty-eighth, all the divisions of both nations having come up, the combined armies moved on Yorktown, and by the fifth of October the place was completely invested.

Shortly after midnight of the twenty-third, people living in the vicinity of High and Second streets in Philadelphia were disturbed by a loud pounding on the front door of the dwelling of Thomas McKean, President of Congress. It was Lieutenant Colonel Tench Tilghman, who had ridden express from General Washington bearing dispatches, announcing that on the nineteenth seven thousand British and German soldiers had laid down their arms, and that with them Lord Cornwallis, the King of England's ablest general, was a prisoner. Soon booming cannons, clanging bells, and loud-voiced watchmen carried the glad news to every quarter of the city. When the morning light was breaking, couriers were flying in all directions conveying intelligence to the country that the darkness was disappearing—that Britain had forever loosened its hold on America.

The fall of Yorktown virtually closed the Revolutionary War. Three months had not gone by after the cap-

ture of Cornwallis became known in London before
Parliament concluded to abandon offensive operations.
Negotiations for peace began at once and continued until the thirtieth of November, 1782, when a provisional
treaty was signed.

24

Up Goes Huddy

THE ONE EVENT that distinguished the closing year of
the war, and in which the people of Somerset were
much concerned, was the sad condition of a young English officer, who in the autumn of 1782 was confined in
the huts of the Jersey line in Chatham Township, Morris
County, awaiting execution. The knowledge of his approaching fate harassed Congress, disturbed two European courts, and agitated the society of London and
Paris. His unhappy predicament was brought about in
this wise.

Of all the sad Revolutionary chapters contributed by
Monmouth County, none is more dismal than the one
narrating the tragic death of Captain Joshua Huddy,
who was hanged by refugee Jerseymen at Gravelly
Point, about one mile north of the Highland lighthouse
and opposite the southerly portion of Sandy Hook.
Huddy, who was an active patriot, had commanded one
of the two batteries of artillery of state troops that had
been organized by an act of the legislature in 1777. This
militia captain was especially vigilant in suppressing the
incendiary acts of Tories and refugees, of whom there
were many in Monmouth County, where he was stationed. The terror he inspired among these people was
such as to make him a marked man and the object of their
vengeance whenever an opportunity presented itself.

In the summer of 1780, while in his house at Colt's Neck, five miles from Freehold, he was attacked by sixty men headed by Colonel Tye, a mulatto who generally roamed the country with a mongrel crew of Negroes and Tories. With the exception of a colored servant girl about twenty years old, Huddy was alone in the house; but fortunately he had a number of muskets belonging to the members of his absent guard. Together these two made a brave defence; the girl loaded while he rapidly fired from different windows, giving the impression of their being a strong force inside. Several of the assailants were wounded, including their leader, who subsequently died. Finally the house was set on fire, and the captain agreed to surrender provided the enemy would suppress the flames. Tye's men were greatly exasperated on entering at finding so few defenders. As the militia were now collecting, they hurriedly put out the fire and carried Huddy off to their boats at Black Point on the Navesink River. The troops, which were in close pursuit, appeared on the bank soon after the refugees had shoved from the shore. A lively fusillade ensued, during which Huddy sprang into the river and swam boldly to his friends, though reaching them with a bullet in his thigh.

In the spring of 1782 Captain Huddy commanded twenty-five men who were garrisoning a rude fort, or blockhouse, which stood north of the bridge at the village of Tom's River in Ocean County. This fort was attacked by the enemy, the expedition for that purpose being composed of forty refugees. They embarked at New York on whaleboats manned by Lieutenant Blanchard and eighty seamen. It was not until after midnight that the entire party landed at Coates Point on the north side of Tom's River. They were joined by a detachment of Ocean County refugees. Securing a guide, the force stole silently through the woods in the direction of the village, and at daylight suddenly charged the fort. Captain Huddy and his men made a gallant defence with swivels, muskets, and pikes, but the blockhouse was finally carried by assault after the garrison had exhausted its ammunition, one-third of the men being killed.

The commander was conveyed to New York and subsequently to Sandy Hook, where he was confined, heavily ironed, in the hold of a guard ship. Six days after Huddy was taken, a refugee named White, a Shrewsbury carpenter, was captured by a party of county light-horse. He was placed in charge of three men, the father of one of whom had been murdered the year before by some Loyalists, White being of the party. The wheel of fortune had made an unhappy revolution for this Shrewsbury carpenter. When his guard was relieved he was found dead, the explanation being given that he had been shot while endeavoring to escape. Though this occurred after the capture of Huddy, the refugees, eager for a pretence whereby his death could be encompassed, charged him with being privy to the killing of White. Without listening to a defence or even going through the form of a trial, a band of sixteen Loyalists under one Captain Lippencott hurried poor Huddy to Gravelly Point, and there hanged him on a gallows hastily formed of three fence rails and a flour barrel. It is said that he died with extraordinary firmness, and that with a serene mind and a steady hand he drew up his will on the head of the barrel from which, a few moments later, he was forced to spring into eternity. His murderers left a label affixed to his breast upon which was written an attempted justification of their act, ending with: "Up goes Huddy for Philip White."

This murder filled the country with indignation, and urgent demands were made that immediate punishment should be visited upon the murderer. Thereupon the authorities insisted that the British commands should deliver up Lippencott, threatening that otherwise one of the English officers in their hands must die in his stead. In furtherance of this retaliatory measure eight captains and five lieutenants who were on their paroles in Pennsylvania were directed to report at Lancaster in order that the victim might be selected. They assembled on the morning of the twenty-fifth of May in a room of the Black Bear Tavern—twenty mounted dragoons waiting in the inn yard to bear away the unfortunate who should be chosen.

The names of the thirteen British officers were written on separate slips of paper and placed in a hat; another hat contained thirteen slips of the same size, all blank but one which was inscribed, "unfortunate." Two drummer boys simultaneously drew the papers. When the one was reached on which was written "unfortunate," it appeared with a slip containing the name of Captain Asgill, who was the youngest officer present; he was a youth possessing many graces of mind and person, and was of high connections in England. At once, upon the result of the drawing being known, the brigadier turned to the dragoon officer, saying, "This gentleman, Sir, is your prisoner." Asgill left Lancaster for Philadelphia, escorted by the dragoons. From there the unfortunate British officer was sent to the Jersey line at Chatham, the place assigned for his execution, and put in charge of Colonel Elias Dayton.

At first it appeared as if nothing could avert Asgill's execution. Washington was deeply afflicted by the unhappy fate menacing the young officer, but after deliberation his determination had been firmly fixed on retaliation as the only means of preventing a continuance of refugee iniquities. The sympathies of America and Europe were aroused in behalf of Asgill, who was but little more than a boy. Sir Guy Carleton, who had succeeded Sir Henry Clinton in the command of the British army, successfully appealed to Washington for delay. Later he submitted the result of a court-martial, whereby Lippincott had been exonerated on the ground that William Franklin, ex-colonial governor of New Jersey and the then president of the "Board of Associated Loyalists," had given verbal orders for the execution of Huddy because he had been a persecutor of the King's faithful subjects in New Jersey. Sir Guy, who was a man of broad views and great humanity, broke up this "Board of Loyalists," and in a communication to Washington declared that notwithstanding the acquittal of Lippencott he "reprobated the measure" and gave assurances of prosecuting a further inquiry.

Meanwhile, the Commander in Chief and Congress were besieged with communications and memorials praying that the life of the proposed victim might be spared. Finally the sympathies and good offices of the French were enlisted, and Count de Vergennes, representing the Court of France, made a strong appeal to Congress in behalf of clemency. This, together with the prospect of a speedy peace rendering avengement as a preventative of future murder unnecessary, materially changed the situation of affairs.

There was another circumstance that powerfully influenced Congress and the country regarding the fate of the young soldier. Asgill was among those who had surrendered with Cornwallis. The fourteenth article of the capitulation expressly excluded all the prisoners from liability to be used as hostages in subsequent reprisals, and the British Major Gordon on the twenty-seventh of May had protested strongly in writing against a violation of the terms of surrender. Washington in a letter to the Secretary of War on the fifth of June acknowledged being sorely embarrassed by the possible infringement of the article of surrender, and begged that the Secretary would transmit to him his views and those of members of Congress with whom he had talked on the subject. As the days went on, public feeling grew stronger that even if Huddy was unavenged good faith demanded that retaliation should not be visited on the British in the person of Captain Asgill. On the twenty-fifth of August General

Washington ordered Colonel Dayton to leave his charge on parole at Morristown, and on the seventh of November Congress, recognizing the altered sentiment of the country, directed that the prisoner should be unconditionally set at liberty.

Of all the general orders issued by Washington to the army during the war, none was received with more profound satisfaction than the one dated, "Head Quarters, Chatham, April 18th, 1783," which directed the cessation of hostilities. It further ordered that an accompanying proclamation of peace should be read the next evening at the head of every regiment of the army, after which the brigade chaplains were to render thanks to Almighty God for "overruling the wrath of man to his own glory, and causing the rage of war to cease among the nations." At the same time an extra ration of liquor was to be issued to every soldier to drink "Perpetual peace and happiness to the United States of America."

On the third of September the final treaty of peace was signed at Paris and definite treaties entered into with other countries whereby the liberty and independence of the United States were fully acknowledged and the country was received among the great family of nations. There was nothing left for the patriot army to do but to disband. Furloughs were freely granted to the soldiers, who upon going home were not required to return. On the third of November the entire army was discharged, and thus a force of nearly ten thousand men were dismissed and dispersed over the states without, with but one exception, tumult or disorder. The officers received five years' full pay in money, or, at their election, half pay for life. The case of the privates was indeed hard. The general government found itself powerless to procure the necessary funds for paying the large arrearages due the army. The men who had stemmed the tide of British oppressions were obliged to content themselves

332

with the immediate recompense of four months' pay, and promises well intended but poorly carried out.

It was at first feared that the distribution throughout the country of so many men who had good reasons for grievance would cause disturbances and lawlessness. Happily the strength of the government was not to be tried by such a condition of affairs. The army melted away; and, peaceably laying down their arms, the privates as a rule betook themselves to honest labor and became absorbed among the farmers, planters, and mechanics. The one exception to such a peaceable disposition is to be found in the action of the Pennsylvania levies, who in the last of June in defiance of their officers surrounded the State House in Philadelphia, and threatened destruction to Congress unless their demands for redress were immediately gratified. The national legislature succeeded in escaping from duress with dignity and retired to Princeton, convening in Nassau Hall.

Our Revolutionary chronicles are now ended. War with its attendant horrors no longer stalks over the land sowing discord, hatred, and vengeance and trampling under foot human affections and the happiness of communities. In its place, peace, an honorable peace, securing all the great principles and demands for which the country has been contending for eight long and doubtful years. The effusion of blood and all the terrible calamities incidental to civil strife are now to be matters of the past. The future is made bright by the revival of hope, and the anticipation that the toils and dangers, the stern resolves and active endeavors, the tears of sorrow and the moans of despair of the years now happily bygone are to be followed by an era of national prosperity—an era when trades will again flourish, business activities once more prevail, and the people prosper in the tranquil possession and enjoyment of the liberties they have wrested from the hand of oppression.

333

But all these beneficent results were not so immediate as might be supposed would have been the case. With the close of the war unreflecting persons had anticipated the enjoyment not only of the repose and safety of peace, but of a period of instant and unbounded prosperity. Such buoyant natures soon discovered that the poverty of the people was almost universal. With the exception of some of those engaged in agricultural pursuits and the few who had grown rich from privateering or who had fattened on dishonest gains in government contracts, almost everyone was deeply in debt, and insolvencies, prosecutions, and legal embarrassments of all kinds became common. Order, industry, and contentment were not the flowers that first bloomed on the Revolutionary plant; they came later after the disappearance of the factions, clamors, bankruptcies, and distresses that were bred by financial depressions and the political doubts and uncertainties prevailing as to the relative rights of the different states.

The generation whose sacrifices had achieved independence must first eat the bitter fruits of strife. The land was full of widows and orphans. The impoverishment of estates was the rule rather than the exception. The financial demoralization of the entire country hampered all efforts at trade. Another bar to the complete enjoyment of peace was the division of families on political lines, for patriots and Loyalists no longer possessed a common country.

The occupants of the Old Stone House did not altogether escape from the evil. At the outbreak of the war William, the elder son of Godfrey Moelich, was not in sympathy with the Revolutionary movement and joined the British army, serving as a sergeant in a regiment of foot. He saw much active service and was wounded by a musket ball, which he carried in his shoulder till his death. In 1784, in company with thirty-five thousand other Loyalist Americans, he was forced to emigrate to Canada.

334

With him went his younger brother, John. The latter does not appear to have been an active enemy of his country, and in leaving the United States was probably actuated by the natural love and affection he bore his brother William.

Of the many untoward circumstances connected with the Revolutionary War, none were more particularly calamitous than the divided sentiments among honest citizens as to the policy of rebellion. Civil war involves cruelties and hardships that are unknown when civilized nations contend with each other. Every man is forced to actively take sides in the contest; this, of course, greatly aggravates the miseries of strife, as neighbors and friends are thus made antagonists. The American Whigs were naturally greatly exasperated against those of their fellow-citizens who upheld the course of Britain, and felt toward them a resentment much greater than that harbored against those of their European adversaries. The desertion of their countrymen in the hour of trial, early in the war, filled them with angry hatred, and as the years went on this rancor was increased by the feeling that the prolongation of the conflict and the asperity with which it was carried on were largely due to the aid and information furnished to the enemy by the so-called renegade Americans.

Among the Loyalists were many worthy persons who in adhering to the Crown were merely living up to their honest convictions. Of such, some like William Melick, braving their lives and fortunes for their beliefs, entered the English army. Others, like John Melick, loved peace and justice, and were content to stand aside and take no active part in the controversy. But there was a third Tory element whose conduct throughout the contest has fastened a stigma upon the name Loyalist that will last as long as the pages of history remain open for inspection. Humanity shudders at recounting the atrocities committed by these fiends, whose rapacious and ingenious cruelties toward those among whom they had been born and bred were often such as would never have occurred to a foreign soldiery. All Tories were forced to suffer for the dastardly acts of these inhuman Americans, and so it was that the hatred for these people dated from the very beginning of the war. Throughout the entire time that the prolonged contest continued, patriot and Loyalist may be said to have had each other by the throats.

Dominated by their sympathies, historians too often perhaps have been prone to dwell and enlarge upon the overt acts of the King's American adherents, but to the dispassionate student of history evidence abounds that Tory and Whig were alike intolerant of each other's convictions, and ready to fall one upon the other as opportunities occurred. The following strong language is taken from the minutes of a meeting of the General Committee of Observation and Inspection for Middlesex County held on the sixteenth of January, 1775, and is quoted as showing the feeling animating the Whigs even at that early date:

Resolved—That we think it our duty publickly to declare our contempt and detestation of those insidious scribblers who, with the vilest views, enlist themselves in the cause of ministry, and by the vilest means endeavor to effect a disunion among the good people of the colonies, that they may become a prey to the oppression against which they are so laudably and unanimously struggling; who skulk behind prostituted printing-presses, and with the assistance of the prostituted conductors of them labor to circulate their pestilent compositions through the land, under the show of friendship and a regard to the publick good; who, with the most unexampled effrontery against the sense of every man of the least information and impartiality, will persist in retailing the rotten, exploded, and ten thousand times confuted doctrines of a passive acquiescence in the measures of government, however distempered and tyrannical.

The New York *Journal* of the ninth of February, 1775, defines a Tory as a thing whose head is in England and its body in America, with a neck that ought to be stretched. This not only fairly expressed the sentiment with which they were regarded, but suggests, also, the mode of treatment they had too often dealt them. In 1778, after the British had evacuated Philadelphia and retreated to Sandy Hook, both Pennsylvania and New Jersey brought to trial such citizens as had given aid and comfort to the enemy. Of those convicted in Philadelphia two were hanged; but Governor Livingston pardoned seventeen, being the entire number found guilty in New Jersey.

It has always been difficult to estimate the number of disaffected in any one state, or even to determine how many entered the English service. No record can be obtained of those who enlisted in regular regiments, but the muster rolls of the provincial corps have been preserved. Sabine, the historian of the Loyalists,[1] estimates the latter to have been at least twenty-five thousand, and Tory documents claim that between the years 1781 and 1783 the King had more American soldiers than had Congress. It is undoubtedly true that at that time disaffection was much more rife in neighborhoods where the British had long quartered than it had been at the outset of the war.

At the close of the war Congress was bound by the English treaty to urge the states to abstain from persecuting those who had been faithful to the Crown. It was found impossible for the general government to influence the states in furtherance of this pledge. Now that the people had in their power the violent oppressors of those who had been of the patriot cause, they would not brook any interference with what they considered their just rights of retaliation. Notwithstanding the recommendation of Congress vengeance was visited on the "Fawning Spaniels." The following from a Massachusetts paper may be accepted as a fair exponent of the feeling prevailing at that time:

---

[1] Lorenzo Sabine, *Biographical Sketches of Loyalists of the American Revolution* . . . (Boston, 1864). 2 vol.

As Hannibal swore never to be at peace with the Romans; so let every Whig swear by his abhorrence of slavery, by liberty and religion, by the shades of departed friends who have fallen in battle, by the ghosts of those of our brethren who have been destroyed on board of prison-ships and in loathsome dungeons, never to be at peace with those friends the refugees, whose thefts, murders, and treasons, have filled our cup of woe.

There was nothing left for the Loyalists to do but fly the country. Consequently thousands were forced to emigrate to foreign shores. The English government did much for its faithful American subjects besides insisting upon the stipulations regarding them being entered in the treaty of peace. For those who feared facing the resentment of their countrymen, vessels were provided to bear them to the Bahamas, the West Indies, and to the bleak shores of Nova Scotia. In 1782 a committee was appointed by Parliament to take in consideration the claims made by Loyalists for indemnity. This resulted in large sums being for several years annually paid for their comfort, until a permanent board of commissioners was established, whose labors brought about the distribution by the English government of nearly fifteen millions of dollars. Sabine mentions this as "an unparallelled instance of magnanimity and justice in a nation which had expended nearly one hundred and sixteen millions in the war."

Among the American Whigs not all cried persistently for vengeance against the Loyalists. There were notable and honorable exceptions, and as a rule they were found among those who had been the most active and prominent in the patriotic cause. Of these, Alexander Hamilton, from the very cessation of hostilities, pursued a policy of leniency toward Tories, and pleaded that their mistaken course during the war should not inevitably result in their losing citizenship and property. Early in 1788 he by his eloquence, aided by the efforts of Schuyler, succeeded in passing a bill which repealed the "Loyalist Disfranchising Act." Tyler, in his life of Patrick

338

Henry,[2] avers that while the war lasted no man spoke against the Tories more sternly than did this patriotic Virginia statesman. The war being ended and its great purposes secured, no man, excepting perhaps Alexander Hamilton, was so prompt and so energetic in urging that all animosities of the war should be laid aside, and that a policy of magnanimous forebearance should be pursued respecting the baffled opponents of American independence.

However much good these earnest men accomplished by preaching the doctrine of returning good for evil, it could not inure to the benefit of such Tories as had already suffered attainder and confiscation. Among these was William Melick, against whom proceedings were instituted as early as 1778. It is a sad commentary on the bitterness existing at that time between those closely allied in blood that the name of Captain Andrew Malick— William's cousin and Aaron's brother—was among the jurors on the inquisition.

---

[2] Moses Coit Tyler, *Patrick Henry* (Boston, 1887).

339

25

Dragnet of History

THE DRAGNET of history brings to the surface both big and little fishes. Our seine no longer sinks into deep or troubled waters but explores peaceful shallows, and we must be content with such catches as these lesser fishing-grounds afford. The remaining chapters must necessarily be devoted to the sober chronicles of the ordinary incidents in the lives of the members of a simple country family. Possibly those readers who remain with the writer to the end will find that their time has not been altogether misspent. Perhaps such ones may feel the satisfaction that often comes to those few favored kinsmen and neighbors who, when the guests have departed and the lights are low, linger with their host about the fire for a parting glass and pass a final hour in social sympathy and intercourse. Such a time always opens the sluices of the heart and brings that comfortable enjoyment of each other that can only exist between those bound by the ties of intimate friendship.

As we occasionally look upon the miniature world revolving within the narrow horizon of the walls of the Old Stone House, it ever presents a different aspect. With each successive season, with each decade and generation, changes are always to be noted. Children grow to be men and women. Familiar faces alter as their lines deepen, tracing where tears have flowed, where mirth has lurked, where sunshine and shade have chased each other across their owners' lives. As we turn again in the year 1788 to survey the Bedminster household, we discover little tremulous tones in Aaron's voice which tell of the seventy-two years that have over him gone. We find that the tide in the current of his family life, which swelled with the birth and growth of each child, now, having passed the flood, is on the ebb. Children grown to be men and women soon find homes of their own, and Aaron's offspring were no exception to this rule. His generation, like the one it succeeded, is making way for the one that is to follow, for four of his children have taken husbands and wives, and a second Aaron is playing about the hearth of the deep-chested fireplace in the living room.

Catharine, the oldest daughter, married Peter Perine, a fellow-campaigner of her brother John. Peter Perine and Catharine Malick moved to Salem, Washington County, New York, in which vicinity numerous descendants of their seven children are still living. Margaret, Aaron's second daughter, married Joseph Gaston. They moved to Northumberland County, Pennsylvania, where they had seven children. Daniel, Aaron's second son, had married his playmate from over the brook, Margaret Gaston, in 1785, their first child, Aaron, having been born in April, 1786. Before this time he had entered into partnership with his father in the tannery, and their books and papers show them to have carried on at that time a large and prosperous business. Daniel spent his life on the Old Farm. His twelve children were born in the stone house, five of them making it their home for their lives.

Before the time of which we are now writing Aaron had come into possession of the entire tract of land originally purchased by his father from George Leslie. It will be remembered that Aaron's brother Peter inherited that portion of the land lying on the Lamington Road. This property he conveyed to Aaron as early as 1772, but does not appear to have given possession until several years later. Sometime during the war Peter left the neighborhood, living for awhile at Perth Amboy. Ultimately he settled in the vicinity of Martinsville in Somerset County.

Aaron's eldest son, John, celebrated the advent of peace by taking unto himself a wife, Jane Coriel, a Somerset maiden eighteen years old. Three years later his father established him in business by building for him on the corner of the Peapack and Lamington roads the first Bedminster tavern. Large barns and sheds were erected on the opposite corner. We may readily imagine that while comfortably seated before his taproom fire he shortened winter evenings by refighting his battles for the benefit of friends and admiring neighbors. In those old days, when all travel was in the saddle or on wagon wheels, the innkeeper was a man of much consequence in the community.

So it was that not only the chance traveler, catching sight of John's swinging sign, found rest and comfort at his little hostelry; here, on the sanded floor of his old-fashioned bar in cold weather, or on the long benches flanking the front porch in summer, were to be found all grades of rural society, from the village magnate to "boots" and the hostler. Here came Federalist and Republican to dispute and argue over their glasses on politics and party; here came old soldiers to tell over and over again how the day was won at Princeton and at Monmouth; here came the gossiping doctor to bait horse and only too ready to disseminate the news gained in his daily peregrinations; even the ministers thought it no sin to go out of their way in order to stop for a chat with John and his wife; nor did they consider that they were putting an enemy in their mouths to steal away their brains, while enjoying honest libations of liquor that had mellowed within their host's oaken staves.

That some of the doctor's visits to Bedminster Tavern were professional is shown by the following bill, which

342

is an interesting exhibit as to the generous doses prescribed by old-time physicians:

Mr. John Melick

1787		To Wm. McKissack	Dr.
Feby 26	Child	To Anthelmintic Powders	£ 0 1 6
		" Vermifuge Decoction with Senna	0 2 0
April 17		" A visit, 3 Doses Pectoral Drops	0 3 6
		" Emetic & ½ oz. Liquorice Juice	0 1 6
19		" 1 oz. Febrifuge Julip	0 1 0
29	Self	" Zx Mercurial Ointment and Box	0 2 0
	Family	" 1 oz. Alterative Powder & 3½ ozs. Itch Ointment	0 7 3
May 21	Daugr	" An Emetic	0 1 0
Novr 12	Mrs. Melick	" Cathartic Powder	0 1 6
14	Do	" 1½ dr. Camphor	0 1 0
1788			
May 11	Do	" 2 dr. Essential Oil & 2 Anodyne Pills	0 2 6
			£ 1 4 9

Doctor William McKissack was at that time a resident of Pluckamin, but he subsequently removed to Bound Brook. He enjoyed an extensive practice and was widely known and esteemed for his professional judgment and skill. Most of his waking hours were spent in riding long distances over bad roads. He was obliged to be hail-fellow-well-met with every one in the county, for on his popularity largely depended his professional success. In those toping-days there was always something on the sideboard for the doctor, of which he was rarely loath to take advantage; consequently, he generally mellowed with the years, grew rotund in person, and, like Hawthorne's middle-aged Englishman, "his legs abbreviated themselves, and his stomach assumed that dignified prominence which justly belonged to that metropolis of his system." His eye contracted a merry twinkle, a chuckle lurked in his full throat always ready for use, and gradually he grew to be known as a peripatetic story-teller, and often the best gossip in the county.

So it was with Doctor McKissack. At the time of his visits to John Malick's family he was already a large, burly man with an expansive girth. Owing to his great popularity he was welcomed by everyone, and being a generous liver, it is said that sometimes he too frequently accepted the invitation of his friends and patients to recoup himself after arduous hours on the road. Dr. A. W. McDowell, in writing of old times in Pluckamin, says that on one occasion Doctor McKissack drove from that village to Somerville. Starting for home after nightfall a little exhilarated, he mounted his horse, forgetting that there was a sulky behind. On the way back, disturbed by the noise of the wheels, he continually cried out, "Turn out! Turn out behind! Don't run over me!" Still the rattle of the wheels continued, and in constant fear he journeyed on. It was not until he reached Pluckamin that the discovery was made that he was astride of a harnessed horse hooked to his own empty sulky.

The gradual growth of medical knowledge in New Jersey is an interesting study. The beginning of things for the healing art may be said to date after the year 1670, for it was of then that Oldmixon, the ancient historian, wrote that the province had no lawyers, physicians, or parsons.[1] To have been without a curer for soul, body, or estate suggests a society in its most primitive stage. At that time, wherever a church was planted there was apt to be a fair physician in the minister, but the people generally were obliged to doctor themselves, or, what was worse, to rely upon the services of ignorant old women and their herbs. Even up to the middle of the eighteenth century in the sparsely settled portions of the country the healing art was almost wholly in the hands

---

[1] John Oldmixon, *The British Empire in America* . . . (London, 1708). 2 vol. There was a second edition in 1741.

of such persons. The basis of most of their remedies was sassafras and other simple roots and herbs from which decoctions were made, infused with much ignorance and not a little superstition. Professor Kalm makes mention of medical women among the Swedes of West Jersey in 1748, and Winterbotham [2] as late as 1796 reports that in Cape May County it was only in the most extraordinary cases that women were not called upon as doctors.

In the practice of obstetrics, even in the large cities, the entire reliance was upon women, and very generally upon ignorant old women. Doctor Stephen Wickes [3] states that it was not until the close of the first half of the nineteenth century that any intelligent effort was made to educate men in this branch of the profession. It met with great opposition, as ignorance, prejudice, and female modesty combined in making the belief general that it would be impossible to use the services of men in such cases. Before the Revolution, one Doctor Atwood is said to have been the first physician who dared to scandalize the feelings of the community by offering his services as an *accoucheur*. It was due to Doctors William Shippen of Philadelphia and V. B. Tennent of New Jersey that the science of midwifery assumed its place among the regular branches of medical education. Doctor Shippen advertised in the *Pennsylvania Gazette* on the first of January, 1765, the notice of his first course of lectures. In it he takes occasion to condemn the practice of calling upon the services of unskilful old women, whereby great suffering and loss of life were caused. The medical school of New York established a professorship of midwifery in 1767, Doctor Tennent being appointed to the chair.

In New Jersey, up to the close of the French and

---

[2] William Winterbotham, *An Historical, Geographical, Commercial, and Philosophical View of the United States of America* . . . (New York, 1796). 4 vol.

[3] *History of Medicine in New Jersey, and Its Medical Men to* A.D. *1800* . . . (Newark, 1879).

345

Indian War, the main reliance of the people for medical attendance was upon the pastors of the churches. It was the custom for those who came from the old country to have taken a course of medical study as a preparation for their duties in the New World. The native ministers, also, even up to the close of the century, on being educated studied both professions, and often, not content with two, mastered so much of the law as would enable them to draw wills, conveyances, and other legal instruments. John Wesley, the founder of Methodism, not only like many other parsons prescribed and supplied medicine, but published a book called *Primitive Physick*, which went through thirty editions.

The ignorance of the times and the extraordinary remedies in use can best be exemplified by quoting a few prescriptions contained in this precious medical volume. For a violent bleeding of the nose a piece of white paper was recommended to be placed under the tongue. Treatment for cancer in the breast was to swallow in a pint of warm ale an infusion distilled from warts taken from a horse's leg; goose dung was also to be applied externally. Consumptives were directed to breathe for fifteen minutes each morning in a hole cut in fresh turf. The sovereign remedy for apoplexy was a pint of salted water; for cuts, poultices of toasted cheese; for a cold in the head, orange peel thrust up the nostril.

As the century grew older men began to appear throughout the Middle Colonies who could properly claim some medical knowledge, but still they, like their predecessors the ministers and old women, relied mainly upon herbs and roots for the curing of diseases. Doctor Wickes quotes Salmon's *Herbal* as a standard work on such remedies. This book of twelve hundred pages was issued in England in 1696 at a cost of sixty pounds per volume. It was the textbook for many New Jersey doctors up to the time of the Revolution. It must not be supposed that at this time New Jersey stood alone within the black belt of medical ignorance. Like all other colonies she reflected the customs of the home country. England was still wanting in almost all the present advanced knowledge of *materia medica* and its manner of practice. Lord Colchester narrates in his diary that up to 1754 no London physician ever visited the wards of a hospital, and only on rare occasions met any of his patients. The healing was attempted through the medium of the apothecaries, who would visit the doctor at his home and describe the symptoms of the sick under their care. The celebrated Doctor Meade, who died in 1754, used to go to Batsson's coffeehouse in the city and there consult with and prescribe for all the apothecaries.

Medical progress in the Middle Colonies can be said to date from the French and English wars; this was certainly so in New Jersey. That province furnished a quota of one thousand men; the surgeons and surgeon's mates attached to these troops were thrown in contact with medical men connected with the British regulars, who had received much better education than had those of the colony. The result was a recognition on the part of a few Jersey doctors of their own inferiority, which bred a natural ambition to emulate the attainments of their brother officers. They learned much by this association with cultivated physicians, and to a certain extent ignorant presumption and self-sufficiency retired before a more general diffusion of knowledge.

The small knowledge of the country doctor was generally gained by what he could learn while serving as an apprentice or general assistant to some more or less well-known town practitioner. Indentures for the year 1760 bound apprentices for four years and eight months, for which they paid one hundred dollars, entitling them to board, lodging, clothing, and such tuition as could be obtained through observation and experience. The indenture bound the apprentice to serve his master faithfully, "his secrets keep, his lawful commands gladly

347

everywhere obey." He was forbidden to incur debts, play cards,. or "contract matrimony" during his term. Nor could he "hant ale-houses, taverns, or play-houses."

Of course books were few, and observation, memory, and an aptitude for the profession constituted the best means of obtaining a practical knowledge of *materia medica* and. surgery. In those days a majority of those seeking to become practitioners were without the benefit of medical schools and colleges, and public sentiment was much opposed to autopsies and dissection. Postmortems were condemned by the ignorant public as but little better than grave-stealing. The uneducated masses were in full accord with George Eliot's Mrs. Dollop in thinking that such slashing of the dead was a poor tale for a doctor, who, if he was good for anything should know what was the matter with you before you died and not want to pry into your insides after you are gone. Subjects for anatomical study could with difficulty be obtained except by robbing graves. We learn from Mc-Master that when the medical school at Harvard College was started, a single body is said to have been the only one furnished for a whole year's lectures.

In the year 1750 Doctors Bard and Middleton succeeded in obtaining the cadaver of an executed criminal, and used it in dissection before the first anatomy class in America. In 1752 Surgeon Thomas Wood advertised in a New York paper a course of medical lectures to be concluded with "performing all the operations on the dead body." Dr. Chovet, well-known in Philadelphia during the Revolution, gave notice through the press in 1778 that on the seventh of December he would begin a course of lectures on anatomy, to be demonstrated by the use of skilfully constructed wax figures. Lectures so demonstrated, we may imagine, left the student with but a slender acquaintance with the delicate mechanism of the human body.

Oldtime practitioners being without scientific culture,

and having no notion of what is termed the philosophy of medical evidence, were totally ignorant of the initial treatment of cases, and consequently were forced to start off with a new patient guided by intuition, conjecture, and experiment rather than a correct and accurate diagnosis. The necessary sequence of such darkness was mistakes of deplorable frequency. At that time, as a general thing, chemists and druggists had not yet been educated and established on the most prominent corners of the towns. The apothecary shop of the neighborhood was usually where the doctor's saddle-bags happened to be at the time.

Up to the middle of the century, and even later, a physician's profit and support lay for the most part in the quantity of drugs he administered, his charges not being made for professional visits, but for the medicines prescribed and furnished. In consequence he must either starve or dispense drugs; his saddle-bags, therefore, were in constant requisition, and the stomachs of his poor patients paid the penalty of the unwise custom. Drugs were thus not only taken in large doses, but their use was not by any means confined to the sick. Purgative compounds were administered to the hearty and strong each spring, and it was deemed necessary that at that season of the year the blood of both old and young should be purified by the use of generous doses of noxious mixtures. Rhubarb and molasses were forced down the throats of healthy children as a fancied preventive of disease, and mercurial medicines were used to such an extent as often to result in the falling out of the patient's teeth. Powerful tinctures, loathsome infusions, and bitter barks were prescribed in such quantities as would hardly be credited by physicians of the present day.

Gentlemen of the profession, when at a loss to know what to prescribe, were always ready to pull out the lancet and relieve the patient of copious quantities of blood, often at a time when such a weakening and de-

349

pleting treatment increased the malady and hastened death. Blood-letting was even resorted to in cases far gone with consumption, and by the old-time physician was considered the alpha and omega of all practice. During the prevalence of yellow fever in Philadelphia testimony was taken as to its manner of treatment. Mc-Master quotes from the published report showing that one patient was bled twenty-two times in ten days, losing one hundred and seventy-six ounces of blood. From another of the sick one hundred and fifty ounces were taken in fifteen bleedings; several lost over one hundred ounces, and from one child but six years old thirty ounces were drawn. The Reverend Doctor Ashbel Green writes in his autobiography [4] that when a lad of but nineteen and without any medical knowledge he used to be called upon by his father—the clergyman, physician, farmer, and distiller—to prepare medicines, let blood, extract teeth, and inoculate for smallpox.

At the beginning of the eighteenth century smallpox was still the enemy of mankind. It was annually committing fearful ravages—as many as four hundred thousand dying in Europe in one year. The East, as if desirous of compensating the world for originating this terrible scourge, gave to suffering humanity its initial knowledge of how to check its spread, for it was in Turkey that inoculation first became known. This manner of fighting the disease was introduced in the American colonies in 1721 by Doctor Zabdiel Boylston of New England at the earnest instigation of Cotton Mather, who had learned of the success in the Ottoman Empire of such treatment. In the face of great opposition the doctor's first experiments were made on his son, a lad of thirteen, and on two Negro slaves. The result was such as to warrant his extending the operations, and during the year two hundred and forty persons were inoculated.

For a time Doctor Boylston stood alone. Physicians,

---

[4] See footnote, page 252.

people, and the press were intense against this new manner of combating the smallpox. Even Franklin, who was generally far ahead of the times in his appreciation of what was valuable for the community, wrote strongly in condemnation of the practice. He altered his views in later life, although long before that time the treatment had conquered opposition and was generally accepted as a true preventive of this terrible scourge of the colonists.

It was not until the close of the century that this fell distemper was robbed to a great extent of its terrors. Jenner in 1798 put into practical use his wonderful discovery made some years before, that milkmaids who contracted a mild eruptive disease from handling cows' udders never suffered from the smallpox. Thus commenced the beneficent era of vaccination, which, when after much opposition it had been accepted by the medical fraternity, placed this terrible disease almost completely under control and largely relieved the world from a fear of its ravages.

Let us abandon medical talk and turn again to the Old Stone House. There was a wedding in its best room in the autumn of 1788 which attracted much attention and caused considerable comment in the neighborhood. It was the marriage of Aaron's wife's cousin Barbara Margaret Gibbs to Daniel Cooper. Many guests were invited—at least we may so conclude, as traditions all concur in speaking of lavish hospitality on such occasions at the Old Farm. The bidden relatives and neighbors did not find a timid or a blushing bride, for the Widow Gibbs was seventy-seven years old and had been married twice before. The lusty groom was in his eighty-ninth year and was well acquainted with marriage ceremonies, this being the fifth time that he had deliberately placed the matrimonial noose about his neck. We are led to believe, however, that Charlotte opened her house and made the occasion one of as much festivity as if the contracting parties were entering the bonds of wedlock for the first time. Father Graff came over from New Germantown to perform the ceremony and affix the seal of his blessing to the extraordinary connection. Charlotte's cousin did not journey with her new husband to the end, but like her four predecessors fell by the way. The aged Mr. Cooper, however, was not discouraged; evidently he was fond of the sex and gave to the marriage relation his full countenance. Before receiving his final summons to relinquish wives and all mundane affairs he again led to the altar a blooming bride—his sixth wife, whom, when he died in his one hundred and first year, he left a disconsolate widow.

Daniel Cooper was born at sea late in the seventeenth century while his parents were emigrating from Holland. On reaching man's estate he settled on Long Hill in Morris County, becoming a farmer and a large landowner; at one time he was high sheriff of the county and for many years sat on the bench as magistrate. This inflexible judge—"a second Daniel come to judgment"— had the unhappy experience of sentencing his own son to be hanged. On the nineteenth of August, 1773, over a thousand persons were assembled in the old courthouse at Morristown, which probably had never held a more interested audience nor one that exhibited a deeper sympathy with the course that justice had taken. They were there to hear the dread sentence of death pronounced upon four remarkably fine-looking men who were arraigned before the bar of the court. Among them was the son of Daniel Cooper, one of the magistrates sitting on the bench in judgment.

In all Mr. Cooper had eleven children. One of them, Benjamin, was interested with Lord Stirling in the Hibernia iron works. In 1773 a great number of forged bills began to circulate in Morris County; this led to the arrest and conviction of Doctor Barnabas Budd, Samuel Haines, David Reynolds, and Daniel Cooper's son Benjamin, they confessing to having received the bills from one Ford, a

clever counterfeiter. This principal, who was also arrested, managed to effect his escape, but his accomplices
were not so fortunate. Only one of them, Reynolds, who
seems to have been the least guilty of all, was executed.
The influential connections of the others bore with great
weight upon the pardoning power, resulting in a reprieve
on the very morning set apart for the executions.
Cooper's escape was largely due to his having furnished
information regarding the robbery of the treasury of the
eastern division of the province of six hundred pounds in
the year 1768. For this confession, together with the influence exerted by Lord Stirling, the son of the upright
judge and venerable bridegroom was subsequently pardoned.

26

The Flying Machine

Spread upon the table at which I am writing lies a mass of interesting manuscripts. Dating from the days of Johannes Moelich, they are as varied in form, appearance, and original purposes of use as they are in age and color. These papers have at odd times been discovered in different corners and crannies of the Old Stone House. In handling them we are seemingly not only grasping the hands of all the men, women, and children who have ever lived on the Old Farm, but are also looking into the eyes and listening to the words of a by no means small minority of the Bedminster residents, as well as of worthies of reputation of the county and state.

Let us take up at random some of these yellow, time-stained papers and hear the story they have to tell. We will begin with a large, important-looking document that fairly smells of authority. It announces in the most dignified and old-fashioned phraseology that the Council and Assembly, in consideration of the especial trust and confidence reposed in Guisbert Sutphen, have, by the command of "His Excellency, the Governor," appointed him one of the justices to aid in the conservation of the peace in Somerset County. Guisbert Sutphen's official robe seems to have descended in the line of his family, for here is another commission of thirty years later appointing his son, Peter, justice of the peace. Peter Sutphen's honors were not confined to the judiciary. We now come upon a third commission, dated in September, 1797, appointing him to the captaincy of a troop of horse in a Somerset battalion commanded by Major James Henry.

The close of the Revolution left the military instincts of the American people most actively alert, and, there no longer being a standing army, it was necessarily considered important for each state to have a thoroughly equipped militia. In New Jersey all able-bodied men of proper age were enrolled, and the rural citizen-soldier cut a splendid figure before the eyes of his friends and neighbors. For the country people, about him centered the acme of everything that was grand, magnificent, and ostentatious, and the "trainings" of the militia were always important occasions and insured a great number of spectators. "General training days," that is, when the entire troops of the county were drilled, were considered holidays, and high carnival was held, attended often by license and disorder. At such times all grades of society, white and colored, flocked to witness the grand doings, and everywhere was flourish, pomp, and ceremony. The importance of the country lad, arrayed in a ranger's or cavalryman's uniform as he strutted before the admiring glances of his sweetheart, was only surpassed by the magnificence of the mounted officers, who curvetted on their caparisoned horses in all the splendor and glitter of epaulettes of bullion and cocked hats with red, white, and black feathers.

At the present time there are no public rural gatherings that approach to the old "general trainings" in prominence or glory—the flaunting banners and the martial array of men in their starch and frippery; the acres of people all dressed in their Sunday best, before whom the troops deployed, marched, and countermarched to the inspiring music of drum, fife, and bugle. Booths were set up for the sale of cakes, pies, beer, and rum; huckster wagons, laden with like goodies, were distributed about the field, and eating and drinking were by no means an unimportant portion of the business of the day. When the drills and ceremonies of the militia were concluded, all kinds of shows and games were instituted for the amusement of the people; gambling and horseracing were frequent features of the occasion, and, as the hours wore on, too often the power of rum asserted itself, and the day came to a close in turbulence and riot.

Lieutenant William Fulkerson purchased from Aaron Malick on the eleventh of April, 1800, the Bedminster Tavern, with thirty acres of land extending to the North Branch of the Raritan River. By this time Aaron's son John had grown tired of keeping a "public"; a few years later he removed with his family to Schoharie County, New York, where he died at the age of seventy-five. Captain Fulkerson, as he was afterward known, continued to be the Bedminster tavernkeeper until his death. On infrequent occasions he had seasons of intemperance, lasting a week or ten days. At such times his mind ran very much on his military experiences, which had comprised Revolutionary as well as militia service; his habit was then to talk of himself, using often a favorite expression which he applied to any and everything that met his approval: "I honor the movement." He used this phrase to such an extent that in later life the Cross Roads boys dubbed him "the Old Movement."

Our next old paper treats of tending flocks. Instead of the tramp of horse accoutred for war, we hear the multitudinous clatter of little hoofs, and view spacious meadows where foolish sheep with bent heads and necks flaked in soft yellow wool are "nibbling sharp-toothed the rich, thick-growing blades." But here is the paper referred to; it leads us to believe that Aaron's flocks were too great for this pasture supply:

Articles of Agreement made this twenty-ninth day and the year of our Lord one thousand Seven hundred and Eighty

356

four with Elisha Lowrance that is to Let him have twenty one sheep valued at Nine shillings per head, all said sheep the above mentioned Lowrance is to have for four years from this Date and he Doth Agree to give unto Aaron Malick one pound of wool per head yearly, and Return the sheep at the Expiration of four years as Good as when he Received or the money if said Mealick Chuses, as witness my hand this twenty Ninth day, 1784.

ELISHA LOWRANCE.

In turning over these old papers one finds among them a great number of bonds, notes, and due bills, their amounts varying from a few shillings to several hundred pounds. The people of Bedminster in the last century did not need much money. Bank bills were of course unknown. Before 1781 the nearest place of deposit was at Baltimore, Maryland, then a place of ten thousand people. It was in that year that the Bank of North America was established in Philadelphia, and three years later the Bank of New York and the Massachusetts Bank in Boston opened their doors for business. One of the earliest financial institutions in our state was the Bank of New Jersey at New Brunswick, charted in 1807. In Somerset County the cost of living was but little; land and taxes were low, ministers' salaries were small, farmers raised enough to supply their table and feed their stock and made much of the clothing needed by their families. For what they had to buy at stores, blacksmith shops, and vendues, they were all in excellent credit, and notes and barter served as cash.

The members of the family in which we are interested were not infrequent purchasers at the country stores. This is evident from the multifarious paid bills to be seen among these relics of the quill. We will examine a few of them, choosing several of various dates in order to learn the prices that prevailed, and that we may know for what manner of goods farmers went to the country merchant. We will begin with one of a store at Pluckamin.

357

Mr. Jacob Puyderman
For John Boylan Dr.
1785

	To Sundries	£0–2–1
Ap 26	To ¼ lb. Tea 1/B. & 1 lb. Sugar . 8d .	. 1–8
28	To 1 Qt. Rum	. 1–4
May 4	To 1 Lb. Coffee	. 1–6
27	To 1 Qt. Mols	. 9
31	To 1 Lb. Sugar	. 7
June 13	To 1 Lb. Ditto	. 8
July 29	To 1 Lb. Coffee	. 1–6
	To 1 Lb. Sugar	. 9
	To 1 Qt. Mols	. 8
	To ¼ Tea	. 1–0
	To 1 Chamber Pott	. 1–3
		£0–13–9

This storekeeper is the same "Captain Bullion" whom we found standing behind his counter when Washington and his soldier lads, fresh from Princeton and Trenton, encamped at Pluckamin. John Boylan was a man of substance, and in 1788 was one of the Somerset county judges. He carried on an extensive mercantile business, having besides his Pluckamin store stands at Liberty Corner and at Vealtown.

About the year 1790 this Revolutionary storekeeper disappears from view, and for a number of years thereafter the leading merchant of the vicinity was George I. Bergen. By his energy and perseverance he developed in his capacious Pluckamin store a very large trade which extended over a wide area of country, overriding competitors and causing several storekeepers in the neighborhood to go out of business. After 1800 he dealt largely in pork and provisions for the European markets, the great armies at that time creating a brisk demand and high prices. Owing to the embargo of 1808, followed by the Non-Intercourse Act, he became financially embarrassed, and a few years later was obliged to close up his business. Subsequently, in company with other New Jersey families, he settled in Illinois.

358

The Flying Machine

Aaron and Daniel Malick did not confine their purchasing to nearby stores. The sale and shipment of the products of their tannery and farm required their making frequent journeys to tidewater at New Brunswick. This city was at that time and for many years later the center of an active trade, and possessed numerous large general stores. We may be sure that the women of the Old Stone House had plenty of commissions to be filled when their husbands went "to town." That the visitors did not return empty-handed is evidenced by the bills that have been preserved, dated at New Brunswick. Here is one that is interesting, as showing the great variety of goods that could be bought under one roof:

New Brunswick, Nov. 4th, 1800.

Mr. Melick
Bought of Sarah Brush.

		£		
½ Dozen China cups & saucers		0	12	0
1 Tea pot, 4 6, 1 Sugar Bowel, 3 6, 1 Cream p. 2		0	10	0
½ Doz. Supe plates	3 3	0	3	3
½ Doz. Blue edge Do	3 3	0	3	3
1 Oval Dish	2	0	2	0
⅝ of Swansdown		0	5	6
⅔ of Flannel	2 9	0	1	10
1 Stick of twist		0	0	6
1 Doz. Small Buttons	1d	0	1	0
2 Bandannah Handkerchiefs	6 6	0	13	0
8 pains of 8 By 10 Glass	10d	0	6	8
1 lb. Hyson Skin tea		0	8	0
½ Doz. 7 By 9 Glass	8d	0	4	0
Sundreys of wood ware		0	9	9
To 1½ Bushels of Coarse Salt		0	12	0
		£ 4	10	9
To Cash		2	0	0
		£ 6	10	0

Commencing with the year 1785 New Brunswick experienced a remarkable era of prosperity. It continued until 1834, when the opening for business of the Delaware and Raritan Canal and the New Jersey Railroad paralyzed industries that the inhabitants of the city had hoped were to be perpetual. It prospered not only from the fact of its being in the heart of a rich agricultural, long-settled country, but because, being located on the Raritan near the head of navigation, it was the terminus of several business thoroughfares, some of which extended all the way to Pennsylvania. The traffic across the state between these years was something enormous. Great Conestoga wagons painted blue from Pennsylvania, and others almost as large from Hunterdon County, passed daily over the Amwell Road to New Brunswick, many of them drawn by four and six horses, all heavily laden with flour, flax, grain, and other produce. The wagons conveying the productions of Sussex, Warren, Morris, and Somerset counties came by way of Bound Brook, and so on down the Raritan Valley. It is said that at one time on an account being kept of the teams passing through Middlebrook in one day they were found to number five hundred. Hence, probably no place in the Middle Colonies outside of New York and Philadelphia contained busier storekeepers, mechanics, and tradesmen of all kinds than did this Middlesex city; every one had employment, and its wharves were scenes of busy activity.

The merchants and forwarders of New Brunswick occupied broad lots extending from Burnet and Water streets to the river. Their retail stores and dwellings, which were often in one building, faced the streets. In the rear their warehouses fronted a continuous wooden wharf, or bulkhead, broad enough to admit of the passage of teams; frequently the wharves and streets were connected by a private alley. Here on this river front a lucrative trade was carried on which amassed for not a few merchants considerable fortunes. All of these merchants owned sloops—some of the larger dealers owned two or three—so at all times there was a very respectable fleet of small craft moored along the Raritan River front. These vessels carried the produce of the back country to

New York and returned with cargoes of salt, plaster, barrelled fish, and other general merchandise which were sold from the Burnet and Water street stores to the farmers and country storekeepers.

Up to the time of steamboats, many sloops that were built for that purpose served as packets for carrying passengers. When we accompanied Johannes to Perth Amboy in 1752, we learned something of the sloop navigation of that period. As the century waned many improvements had been made that added to the comfort of traveling by water, until "a cabin fitted up with a tea-table" was no longer considered so luxurious an appointment as to warrant its being advertised to attract passengers. The year 1788 saw a great revival of business throughout the Middle Colonies, and the era of stagnation which had continued since the close of the war gave way to one of activity and enterprise. In New York City, in the few months of the open and mild winter of 1778–1789, the change was both sudden and extraordinary. Houses and stores sprang up in every direction, and the country roads north of Chambers Street began to take on the aspect of a town.

With the return of prosperity came a marked increase in the number of travelers, and from this time dates the introduction of large passenger sloops with much heavier tonnage and greater breadth of beam. Often a vessel of seventy tons burden and less than sixty feet in length would be twenty-two feet wide; as the cabin occupied much of the space below deck the passenger accommodations equalled those found on a full-rigged ship of three hundred tons built for crossing the ocean. When wind and tide served, these short, broad, and shallow sloops could make the passage to New York within about four hours, but with adverse winds and bad weather the voyage was often prolonged for two days.

It would appear that the comforts of sloop travel on the Delaware at the beginning of this century were much less than what travelers experienced on the New York end of the journey. From 1800 to 1810, on what was known as the Amboy and Burlington route, the water passage from the latter place to Philadelphia was by the little sloop, *Mayflower*, owned and commanded by the then celebrated taciturn Captain Jacob Myers. Often twenty-four hours were consumed between the two places, though no provision was made to supply the passengers with food and light. No certainty was ever felt by travelers as to the hour of starting. They were generally required to be on board at seven in the morning, but when ready to cast off the lines, did a load of apples or country produce appear on the wharf, the sailing was postponed until the new freight was on board and until it was very sure that no more was in sight. Thus it was often midday before the *Mayflower* hauled out in the stream and her passengers commenced bobbing and dodging to keep their heads clear of the ever-moving boom. If the comforts of the voyage at the New York end of the route were greater, so owing to the open water were the dangers. The *New Jersey Journal* recites that on Saturday the tenth of November, 1798, one of the Elizabethtown and New York packet sloops capsized off Bergen Point, drowning eight passengers.

In the year 1807 Fulton astonished the world by paddling in the *Clermont* from New York to Albany, averaging five miles an hour irrespective of winds and currents. A few years later John R. and Robert James Livingston established a steam line from New Brunswick to New York. They constructed at a cost of twenty-six thousand dollars a boat one hundred and thirty feet long and twenty feet beam, which they named the *Raritan* and ran as a packet between those places, touching at Elizabethtown Point and at other landings on the Jersey and Staten Island shores. For two years she was operated at a loss, but eventually the enterprise became profitable.

This induced Colonel Aaron Ogden to build a steamboat called the *Sea Horse*, about one-third the dimensions of the *Raritan*, which he ran from Elizabethtown Point, from which he had been operating a sloop ferry for a number of years. As Colonel Ogden had no right to ply in New York waters, the trips of the *Sea Horse* ended off Bedloe's Island, where passengers were transferred to a boat propelled by horsepower, which conveyed them to the city. Thomas Gibbons, an eminent lawyer and planter of Georgia, was the owner of an undivided half of the ancient ferry upon which the *Sea Horse* was running, Colonel Ogden being the owner of the other half and the lessee for a term of years of Gibbons' moiety.

Upon the expiration of this lease Ogden and Gibbons quarreled as to the conditions of a partnership to which Gibbons insisted upon being admitted. This resulted in Gibbons bringing out a new boat, the *Bellona*, which was soon plying to New Brunswick in connection with the "Old Union Line" to Philadelphia. The company operated two lines of transit between that city and New York. The first was by post-chaise, one leaving 145 Broadway each morning at five o'clock, proceeding to Whitehall Ferry, crossing the Delaware at Bristol, and arriving in Philadelphia at five o'clock the same evening. An old advertisement of the second route of this "Union Line" dated in 1819 announces:

The Vice-President's steamboat *Nautilus* will leave New York every day (Sundays excepted) from Whitehall Wharf, at eleven o'clock A.M. From her the passengers will be received without delay into the superior fast-sailing steamboat *Bellona*, Capt. Vanderbilt, for Brunswick; from thence in Post Chaises to Trenton, where they lodge, and arrive next morning at ten o'clock in Philadelphia with the commodious and fast-sailing steamboat, *Philadelphia*, Capt. Jenkins.

Doubtless, travelers by the "Old Union Line" considered that the height of comfort had been reached in the transit from the Hudson to the Delaware. The *Bellona* was a small single-decked, plainly finished steamboat, but together with her sister boat the *Thistle*, put on the route soon after, was considered a marvel of speed and beauty. Her cabin accommodations were meager, being confined to a small saloon abaft the wheel on the main deck. No soft cushions, upholstered chairs, or curtained windows added to the comfort of the passengers. Ladies sat on hard-backed benches, while men were well content with round wooden stools. The speed of "the fast sailing and superior steamboat *Bellona*" did not exceed from ten to twelve miles an hour, but this her passengers thought exhilarating as compared with the slow and uncertain transit of the sloops of a few years previous.

Her captain was the father of William H. Vanderbilt —the "Old Commodore"—then a long, lank youth of twenty-four years of age. As the commander of this fine vessel he was looked up to by the traveling public, and he enjoyed the princely income of fifty dollars a month for his services. The wife of "Captain Corneel," as he was called—whom he had married when he was but nineteen —kept "Bellona Hall," a small tavern on the steamboat landing at New Brunswick, where she proved to be a most popular and capable hostess. She saved much money, which later contributed to assist her husband in putting on the river opposition boats whereby he laid the foundation of his great fortune.

In the sloop age the New Brunswick masters did not secure all the passengers. Like vessels sailed from Elizabethtown Point, to which some stages ran, and from early days there had been a stage line across country to the Hudson. In 1772 John Meserau's "Flying Machine" was advertised to leave Paulus Hook thrice weekly for Philadelphia. This "Machine" was still a country wagon, but it had four horses, with changes, and was supposed to fly over the ruts and stumps at such a high rate of speed as to reach the Delaware within two days. In the same year an act of the Assembly authorized a lottery to raise one thousand and fifty pounds to pay for graveling the causeway over the Newark meadows. Previous to this improvement being made, the passage of this bit of road was attended with both delay and danger. Passengers by the "Flying Machine" were forced to cross from New York to Paulus Hook the night before starting, which counteracted to a considerable extent the advantage of flying overland instead of sailing leisurely by sloop.

Elkanah Watson, who journeyed from New York to Philadelphia in 1784, recorded his experiences in a journal.[1] He crossed the Hudson on a cold winter's day in an open ferryboat, and the Hackensack and the Passaic on the ice. The first night was spent at Newark. The next journey was by stage-sleigh as far as Princeton, and on the third day Philadelphia was reached. Another traveler just ten years later made some interesting notes on his journey. He recites that after spending an hour and a half on the Hudson ferry he left Paulus Hook by the coach "Industry," paying five dollars for his seat. In crossing the cedar swamp before reaching Newark, he made the acquaintance of New Jersey mosquitoes, "which bit our legs and hands exceedingly; where they fix they will continue, if not disturbed, till they swell four times their ordinary size, when they absolutely fall off and burst from their fullness."

The Passaic River was crossed by the "Industry" on a "scoue," propelled by pulling a rope which was fastened to the further shore. The Raritan bridge had been carried away by a storm, but the coach and six horses were ferried in a "scoue" in six minutes. Our traveler's stagecoach did not go beyond New Brunswick, a wagon without springs being used as far as Princeton. The road was so full of deep holes and rolling stones that on reaching the college town the passengers had been so badly shaken that many of them were sick and could hardly stand.

---

[1] *Men and Times of the Revolution; or, Memoirs of Elkanah Watson* . . . (New York, 1856).

Coaches at that time were yet few, being the exception rather than the rule. The public conveyances generally were long-bodied stage-wagons without doors, windows, or panels. Leathern curtains were let down to keep out the rain, and entrance was had over the whiffletrees and front wheels, the passengers clambering back over the intervening benches. After the nineteenth century came in, land travel was made more expeditious and the discomforts much lessened. Heavy English mail-coaches, swung on huge leather springs, were introduced, and more frequent changes of horses greatly diminished the time between New York and Philadelphia. The traffic so rapidly increased that how to carry the many passengers became a problem.

In the palmy days of road and steamboat travel the hour that heralded the arrival of the southern coaches was the most important one of the day for New Brunswick citizens. As the time drew near, a crowd gathered where the taverns clustered in Albany Street. Presently the eager cry, "Here they come! Here they come!" passed from mouth to mouth. Then with loud huzzas the six-horse coaches, piled with luggage, topped with people, and coated with dust, came swinging around the corner of George into Albany Street. With much clatter of hoof and rumble of wheel, cracking of whip and blowing of horn, the long line of lurching vehicles often numbering thirty rapidly approached, until with a final flourish of whip and blast of bugle their drivers drew rein in front of the City Hotel and the White Hall and Bell taverns. To the New Brunswick people it meant more than the arrival of passengers; with them came letters, papers, and news from the outside world. The Albany Street arrival was a scene witnessed only during those months when the steamboats were not running. When navigation was open, the coaches on entering town turned down New Street to Burnet Street, thence to the landing, where the steamboat was waiting to continue the journey.

The last stop made before reaching New Brunswick was at Enos Ayres' well-known tavern, five miles south of the town at Dunham's Corners. Regular travelers by the road were for a time much interested in this hostelry because of its landlord's daughter, who before she was twenty-eight years old had had four husbands. She is said to have been very beautiful, and to have secured her numerous consorts by physical rather than mental perfections. Her conversational powers were limited, but through the daily scanning of over two hundred coach passengers she probably acquired the habit of "looking unutterable things."

27

Old Yombo

ALADDIN, STANDING in the cave of the magic lamp, could with difficulty decide into which glittering pile of gems his hand should be thrust. We, too, feel this *embarras de richesse* in the presence of our heap of interesting manuscripts on the table. At a venture we will take up a package of narrow papers that time has tanned to the hue of old gold. Ah! on looking through them we find that they do not belie their color, as they all treat of money. They are receipts for salary given by the Reverend John Duryea, the third clergyman of the Bedminster Dutch Reformed Church. They extend over a period of several months and are issued to the church treasurer and to individual members of the congregation, in some instances being but for a few shillings. The Domine evidently in part collected his own salary and often had difficulty in doing so. Even the treasurer was not always on time in his payments.

This collecting by the minister from members of the congregation must have been attended by much inconvenience, as his parishioners were widely distributed and their subscriptions were often exceedingly small. They were not inclined to pay even these meager sums. A writer in the tenth number of the Somerville magazine, *Our Home*, narrates that, when the invitation to preach was extended to Mr. Duryea, the call was conveyed to him by John Vroom, an explanation being made that there was but little money in the congregation but that all his temporal wants should be provided for. He preached several months without any payment being made, whereupon, after a regular morning sermon, he thus addressed his people: "You made certain promises to me if I would preach for you. Several sermons have been given and I have performed my part. A bargain thus made becomes a sacred contract. If you refuse, you are a congregation of story-tellers; and you, John Vroom, are the biggest liar of them all." While this preacher was under the sounding board, restful sleep did not unbidden "creep from pew to pew."

In the eighteenth century it was not usual for farmers in Somerset County to own carriages. As a rule they were content with their white-covered farm wagons, the bodies of which on Sundays were strewn with clean straw, while chairs from the kitchen served as seats. Aaron Malick appears to have considered himself well-enough-to-do to warrant his riding in a four-wheeled carriage, and to warrant his paying the government a tax for the privilege, which at that time was a necessary consequence of such a luxury:

THIS IS TO CERTIFY, THAT Aaron Melick of Bedminster in the County of Somerset—hath paid the Duty of two Dollars upon a four Wheel Carriage called a Light Waggon owned by him, Having Framed Posts & a Top, &, Resting on Wooden Spars—to be drawn by two Horses—for the Conveyance of more than one Person; for the Year to end on the 30th Day of September 1797.

Samuel Annin

September 19, 96.   Collector of the Revenue
 Receid Sept. 1796.   10th Division of New Jersey

This carriage tax was imposed by Congress in the general impost bill of 1794. It created much dissatisfaction, especially among the Republicans. The carriage-makers claimed this tax to be unconstitutional and carried the question to the Supreme Court; but the government was sustained, and the law remained in force until Jefferson and the Republicans came into power. The impost on pleasure wagons was removed in 1802, together with many other obnoxious impositions; the effort caused a bitter contest in Congress between the Federalists and Republicans, the debate lasting for five days. The result was considered a great triumph for Jefferson's administration, and of course was bitterly deplored by the Federalists; they urged that the carriage tax had been only paid by the rich, and quoted in proof the fact that Virginia had six hundred and sixty-six coaches paying tax while Massachusetts had but ninety-nine.

There were in New Jersey neither almshouses nor poorhouses in the eighteenth century. In some counties it was the custom to sell the paupers at auction to the lowest bidder; the amount bid was paid to the buyer by the overseers of the poor, which bound him to mend the pauper's clothes, to furnish him with a good bed, with washing, lodging, and victuals for one year, during which time the pauper was to work for the buyer as much as he was able. All new clothing was supplied by the county.

The Old Stone House for three generations furnished overseers of the poor for Bedminster Township. After the justices of the peace had passed upon the application of a pauper for maintenance, it was the duty of the overseers to provide for the impoverished one a comfortable home, generally with a farmer. The amount paid for a year's support varied considerably, depending somewhat upon the condition of the paupers and their ability to aid the families with whom they were living. On the twenty-fifth of January, 1797, James Wintersteen received from "Daniel Melick, one of the overseers of the poor," forty-two shillings "in full for keeping Widow Mahew"; while on the eighteenth of March of the same year Simon Hagerman, Jr., received seven pounds, ten shillings, "for

370

keeping Leaney Rush a pauper on s'd Town." On the twenty-third of December, 1803, Elizabeth Castner was paid "Twenty Dollars in full for the support of Salley for the year Ending next Town meeting Day."

It was the duty of the overseers not only to secure comfortable homes for their charges, but to clothe them and to furnish them with extra necessaries. Thus we find that on the seventh of January, 1804, John Demund was paid "$2.50 for making a suit of clothes for Gideon Berry, a pauper." We may suppose that this charge did not include the cloth. On the twenty-sixth of April the same year, Levi Sutton, a farmer living near the lower lime-kiln on the Peapack Road, was paid "One Dollar and twenty-five cents for 10 lbs. of pickle pork for Joseph Richardson last fall." A bill of Doctor Robert Henry, dated the twentieth of September, 1756, "For medicine and attendance done for Mrs. Biderman, one pound," shows that the paupers when ill were not neglected.

Our old papers do more than tell us how the Bedminster poor were cared for in sickness and in health; they bring us to the paltry bed of the pauper when his death has burst the prison bars of his poverty.

Sir:
    Please pay the Bearer hereof Mr. Derrick Young or order the sum of ten shillings it being for a shirt that Thomas Carey was buried in from your Huml. Servant Robert Gaston June the 5th 1790
Mr. Aaron Melick Late
    Overseer of poor.

Poor Thomas Carey! "Rattle his bones over the stones, only a pauper that nobody owns." We suspect that he had but little honor while living, and when dying perhaps no friendly voice spoke comfort to his soul or gave him the melting tear of pity. But now, after being many years dead, his name at least shall be rescued from oblivion. Whatever immortality it may be insured by appearing

371

on these pages can be charged to the fortuitous circumstance of its having been necessary to buy a robe that he might lie down decently to his long night's sleep.

Although the buying and selling of Negroes had been common throughout the century in Somerset County, Aaron Malick was an old man before he became a slaveholder. He had often desired to purchase a few hands to work in the tannery or on the farm, but had refrained in consideration of the wishes of his wife, who had always strenuously opposed the introduction of bondspeople into her household. Charlotte was a descendant of a Quaker family and had inherited that hatred of the institution which has always distinguished the peace-loving Society of Friends. But in the year 1786 Aaron's brother-in-law, Jacob Kline, offered to sell him his Negro man Yombo, who was a master-hand at tanning, currying, and finishing leather. This offer came at a time when Aaron was sorely pressed for help, and the opportunity seemed too good to be passed by. After much urging on the part of the husband, the wife finally stifled her scruples and acquiesced in the purchase.

So Yombo was transferred from the Hunterdon tannery on the Rockaway River to the Bedminster tannery on the Peapack Brook, where he soon proved himself a most valuable workman. He was a Guinea Negro, having been brought from Africa when a boy, where, as he claimed, his father was a "big man." Yombo was stout, coal black, club-footed, and very bow-legged. At first his appearance quite terrified Daniel's little children; he rarely wore a hat, always chewed tobacco, rings hung from his ears, and his language was a mixture of poor English and a jargon peculiar to himself. In addition his disposition was not in any sense agreeable, and his perverseness always displayed itself when he was not under the immediate eye of his owner and master. But being an excellent workman, his peculiarities were passed over,

372

and for many years he was a conspicuous feature of life at the homestead.

Yombo had a slave wife living at Elizabethtown. It was Aaron's custom to permit him occasionally to visit her, for that purpose putting money in his pocket and lending him a horse and chair—as the two-wheeled gigs of that day were called. Notwithstanding his master's goodness the darkey was treacherous, and, when he was ready to start on the journey, Aaron was always particular to look under the seat of the chair, where he not infrequently found a wallet stuffed with finely finished calf-skins with which Yombo had hoped to improve his fortunes at Elizabethtown.

A short note written to Aaron Malick by Oliver Barnett on April 22, 1797, presages the advent of the second slave—or rather a whole family of slaves—on the Old Farm: "I have not any objections to your purchasing the negro man, Ballod [?] Dick from General John Taylor." General John Taylor was a well-known resident of Hunterdon County, who had been an active militia officer in the war. At the time the note was written he had become financially embarrassed, and finding it necessary to sell some of his slaves had offered Dick and his family to Aaron. General Taylor's principal creditor was Doctor Oliver Barnett of New Germantown. Aaron, knowing this, was unwilling to entertain the idea of purchasing these chattels until the doctor's permission had been obtained.

So now for the second time we behold Aaron and Charlotte facing the question of the wisdom of buying slaves. The matter was given much serious reflection and provoked warm and earnest discussions in the living room of the old house. We may imagine that Daniel urged the purchase. His parents were growing old; their children were married, and all but himself had left home. His son, little Aaron, had grown to be twelve years old, his second child, Elizabeth, was ten, the third, Charlotte, eight, and the youngest, Rozannah, but six. The care of these children and the old people, and the oversight of the household generally, was largely on his wife's shoulders, and he doubtless thought that so unusual an opportunity of procuring efficient help should be embraced. Everyone said that Dick was a "most likely nigger." Charlotte was at last induced to give unwilling assent to the purchase, which was finally consummated in the spring of 1798.

In fancy we see these colored people as they reach their new home and stand a little abashed and nervous while receiving welcome from their new mistresses. Dick is of a good dark color, heavy set and dignified in appearance, courteous and quiet in demeanor, while Nance does the talking and laughing for the family through thick lips which partially cover a full set of white teeth. She is lighter in color than her husband, and very short—not to say fat. You know where her waist is because you see her apron strings, but with that feminine badge removed, to locate her zone would be like establishing the equator —a matter of calculation rather than visual certainty. Her breadth affords a good cover for her three frightened children, who peer shyly from behind her ample skirts at the new "white folks," at the same time taking curious note of Daniel's flock who form a background to their mother and grandmother. Diana the oldest is seven and large for her age, Sam is four, Ben the youngest is a little pickaninny of two—all pretty black, and each one well ivoried. A few pleasant words, emphasized with cookies, soon calm their agitation, and it is not long before parents and youngsters are at their ease and taking kindly to their new surroundings. The children proved to be quiet and obedient and quickly found themselves possessed of a happy home; they had playmates in Daniel's boys and girls, mutually kind feelings existed almost immediately, and white and black lived happily together.

Nance was duly installed in the outer kitchen at the

east end of the house, and Dick was made general farmer. Both husband and wife were devout Christians and regular attendants at church, greatly to the satisfaction of Charlotte, whose affections soon went out to these worthy bondspeople, causing her prejudice against slavery to wane daily. Nance became her devoted attendant, cook, and skilful housekeeper, while Dick met his master's expectations as a farmer and trusty servant. In a few years he had nearly the entire control of the farm, which he managed with great prudence and intelligence; being always faithful to the interest of his master, he was rewarded with a leniency and trust that few white people in the same situation would have enjoyed. In March, 1800, a fourth child, Joe, was born.

Two years later the current of home life was unhappily disturbed by the sudden death of Charlotte. It was the result of an accident which occurred in February, when she and her husband were returning from a visit to some friends living near Rockaway. Owing to the breaking of the harness, the gig in which they were riding was overturned, and its occupants were thrown violently to the ground. Aaron escaped with a few bruises, but Charlotte was so injured that for five weeks she was on the "verge of Heaven." Then came the thirteenth of March, an unhappy day for those who loved her. While sitting in a rocking chair at the window of the best room looking out on the familiar meadows with their tree-fringed river, suddenly for her the world grew dim. The grief of Nance at the loss of her mistress was as deep and sincere as that of any other member of the household, but to Daniel's wife as sole mistress she was equally faithful, and to Aaron in his old age and loneliness she gave the most devoted care.

The slaves on the Old Farm had their indulgences and enjoyments. The Christmas season was one of great festivity, of some pomp, and not a little dignity. During the week between Christmas and New Year's Day they generally gave a party, when the older colored people of respectability were invited. In those days the slaves were known by the family names of their masters, so on such occasions in the living room and outer kitchen, which were given up to the entertainment, were to be seen the Gastons, Klines, Linns, Van Dorens, Van der Veers, and such others from near and far as attended the same church and mingled in the same colored society. There was much style and a profuse use of large and heavy words, each person being addressed as Mr., Mrs., or Miss. At the supper, after a lengthy grace fervently uttered by the one supposed to be the most gifted, even staid Dick Melick, who took upon himself the service of the table, displayed airs quite foreign to his generally modest deportment. This supper was, of course, entirely under Nance's supervision, and in quality and quantity was creditable alike to her as cook and to her old master as showing the liberality and kind feeling he extended to his slaves. ("No, Sah, Sarvunts, if you please.") Although whiskey, cider, and metheglin were always furnished to the lowly guests, a too-free indulgence would not have been countenanced by the hosts, nor was it ever known, the whole party always conducting themselves most decorously and politely, endeavoring as far as possible to be "jes like white folks." The pleasures of the Christmas season were not confined to this one festivity; but little work was expected of the blacks during the entire holiday week, for, dressed in their best, their whole time was devoted to visiting and pleasure.

Another great day for the Bedminster colored people, always celebrated by Dick and Nance, was "general training," usually occurring in the middle of June. Then it was that Dick took the big wagon and put on its tow and linen wagon cover, tying up the sides so that from within an unobstructed view could be had of the martial array. Nance and the children were placed on chairs in front, and behind was a barrel of root beer of Dick's own manufacture and a corn basket full of large round ginger cakes —they called them bolivars—baked by Nance the day before. In addition there was a plentiful supply of new-mown grass from the bleach patch in the garden, which was always mowed at that time, to keep the beer cool and to give the horses a bite during the day. Dick, in his Sunday clothes and displaying a most conspicuous nosegay, would then seat himself on the foreboard, seize the reins, and with the stalk of a long whip against his shoulder and the lash hanging behind would set off with his happy family and join the procession of teams that from early morning had been slowly moving up the long hill in the direction of Pluckamin.

On reaching the grounds, the horses were taken out and tied to a fence, and the business and pleasures of the day commenced. As long as the barrel and basket held out, beer was to be had for two cents a glass and cakes for a penny a piece. Between customers the sable merchants had plenty of friendly visitors, the children meanwhile playing about the wagon or sitting quietly in round-eyed wonder at all the glories of the day. With the approach of night Dick "geared" his horses and drove slowly home, his spirits lightened by the pleasures he had experienced and his pockets full-weighted with big copper pennies. He would now have pocket money for all his needs for months to come, and some to drop in the black bag each Sunday morning at church when the deacon passed it in the gallery, which Dick always did with a most reverential bow.

Not only were the bodies of the dusky toilers clothed, but their minds were not neglected, for here is a bill of Christopher Logan to the "Estate of Aaron Melick Dec'd," dated the twenty-third of March, "To Schooling Negro boy Joe 61 days $1.39." I find another bill of two years later for one of Daniel's children in which "William Hambly teacher" charges "$4.16 for 159 Days' Schooling."

377

Slavery on the Old Farm was not altogether an un-
mitigated evil. For a number of years much happiness in
their mutual relations came to both bond and free; their
lives moved on with but little friction, excepting an occasional outbreak from Yombo, which was met by a few
earnest words of reproof from Aaron, who even in extreme old age retained the spirit of mastery. But on the
seventh of April, 1809, the peaceful calm of home life
was rudely arrested by the death of the head of the household, who succumbed to an attack of apoplexy in his
eighty-fourth year. Then Dick and his family knew what
trouble was. Not only did they honestly grieve at the loss
of a good master, but they sorrowed because they knew
they must be sold and possibly separated. A fifth child,
Ann, had been born since the manumission laws had gone
into effect; she, consequently, could be sold only for
service until reaching twenty-five years of age, but the
other slaves had no reason to expect anything but servitude for life. What to do with the Negroes had been a
serious question with Aaron, and a subject of much anxious thought on his part; but the decision he had reached
could not be known until his funeral was over and the
will read. His death occurred on Monday, the funeral
being held at half past ten on the following Thursday.
The intervening days offered but little opportunity for
sorrow, owing to the busy activity of the household in
brewing, baking, and in generally preparing for the obsequies, as in that age the occasion was made one of
feasting as well as of grieving.

The morning of this all-important day found the Old
Stone House full of friends and neighbors, for Aaron had
been widely known and greatly beloved. Daniel, aided by
other relatives, received the people, at the same time
listening to their words of greeting and sympathy. Pastor
Graff came over from New Germantown to conduct the
services. As the hour approached for the service, the
immediate friends and relatives gathered in the darkened

378

best room. In one corner on a table were several decanters containing rum, applejack, and madeira, while before the looking-glass, which was covered with a sheet, the plain, almost rude, coffin rested on two chairs. There were no caskets in those days, nor much if any of the multitudinous paraphernalia now attendant upon funerals. Farmers of the olden time, as a rule, supplied their own burial cases and accessories. It was not uncommon for them to put aside, years before the death of any of the household, suitable boards for making coffins. These primitive shells were, of course, roughly fashioned, the interior trimmings and decorations furnished by members of the family being of the plainest character.

On this funeral morning all the other rooms and the hall were filled with neighbors, who overflowed through the open doors on the front and rear porches. In fancy we can see the aged and feeble rector, robed in his Lutheran vestments, standing at the foot of the stairs — before him a little mahogany table upon which rest the big family Bible and the pastor's well-thumbed prayer book. At his side the tall clock ticks in solemn unison with the slow, measured, and sad tones of the holy man, who speaks from the heart, for he is bidding a last adieu to dust that is dear to him. His voice grows husky as he dwells on the virtues of the departed, and points out to the sorrowing hearers how the common walk of the good man of the house had been beyond that of ordinary everyday life. He cannot refrain from speaking of his own bereavement as he remembers that during his thirty-four years of ministrations over Zion's congregation he who now lies before him shrouded for the tomb had been not only a parishioner but a friend and counsellor as well. In fancy we see the simple country folk in their Sunday garb as they gather about the bier — we hear their low tones and the noise of their feet scraping along the sanded floor. Through the rear door comes the sympathetic murmur of the dam below the hill, borne on the

379

soft April wind, which as it draws through the house
carries with it to the outer air a faint mingled odor of
cake, varnish, and spices.

The burial was at Pluckamin, and it was a large
funeral cortège that slowly toiled up the long hill. The
hearse was an ordinary farm wagon, as indeed were
nearly all the vehicles that followed after, although a few
one-horse chairs, with quite a number of neighbors in the
saddle, offered a little variety to the funeral procession.
After the interment, as was the fashion of the time, very
many of the people returned to the house, where much of
the rest of the day was taken up with eating and drinking, a succession of dinners being spread in the living
room. The appetites of all being satisfied, the relatives and
immediate friends gathered in the best room to listen to
the reading of the will.

It was soon known as to the manner in which Aaron
had partially solved the problem of what to do with his
Negroes. The will ordered that Nance's children should
be sold under indenture to serve until the boys reached
the age of twenty-eight and Diana twenty-five, when
they were to be manumitted. This was evidently a compromise by the old gentleman between his children and
his slaves. Had he freed his Negroes it would have meant
pauperism for them, and an incubus for his estate, as
they would have had to be supported. This plainly had
seemed to him to be the best way out of the difficulty,
and as no mention in the will was made regarding Dick
and Nance there probably was an understanding between
him and his children as to their disposal.

The auction, or vendue, was to be held on the twenty-
second of May. The intervening weeks proved a serious
time to both whites and blacks, and the hours wore heavily on, though only too fast when the thought of separation and the loss of a happy home confronted the poor
slaves. The fateful day at last arrived, and with it came
a large assemblage of people, as at that time an auction

sale of this character was always made a festive occasion. We can judge of the numbers present by the following extract from a bill of Levi Sutton showing the amount of applejack that was consumed in their refreshment. "1809 May 20th To 27 gallons Cyder spirits for vendue and settling a'cts at 69 cents—$18.63." William Cummins, well-known in those parts as an auctioneer, cried the sale, and Nicholas Arrosmith's son William acted as clerk, each charging two dollars a day for their services. The sale commenced at the barns, when, after the hay, grain, and other property had been disposed of, the people were invited to the house to buy the "niggers."

The dark cloud had a silver lining: Sam and Diana both went to Elizabethtown to prominent men well known to them, and who had been old friends of their late master. They were to be well cared for and to have good homes. Mr. Smiley who purchased Ben was also intimately known to, and respected by, the household. Joe was carried off to New Germantown by Jacob Kline, Daniel Melick's uncle, which was next to being at home; but above all Dick, Nance, and the little Ann would stay in the Old Stone House. The old home was still theirs.

Then came under the hammer poor old Yombo, bending under the weight of his seventy years. Here is the record of his sale. "One old Negro Man, Yombo, sold a slave to John Hastier—$50." It is my impression that this purchaser was the owner of Yombo's wife; at any rate he was a tanner and currier doing business at Elizabethtown. The sale over, Yombo goes contentedly to his new home; the old bark mill and currying shop and the seat by the fireplace in the outer kitchen know him no more. Nothing more was heard of him by the Bedminster people until several years afterwards word came from Elizabethtown—"Old Yombo is dead."

28

Like Leaves on Trees

INTEMPERANCE in the use of liquor has been the gradual growth of many hundred years overindulgence, but the culmination of its baleful influence may be said to have been during the close of the eighteenth and the beginning of the nineteenth century. Six hundred years ago alcoholic drinks were confined to malt liquors, wines, ciders, and metheglin. It is only within three centuries that brandy and whiskey have been recognized generally as beverages; earlier they were used principally for medicinal purposes. The great impetus to intemperance came in about 1640 with the introduction of West India rum, and in this country sixty years later intoxicants were powerfully reinforced by the beginning of the manufacture of Medford and other rums by Puritan New England. The next period in the increase of drinking followed the French and Indian War, when the soldiers, who during the campaigns had been furnished with regular rations of spirits, acquired habits of drinking "strong water" which they introduced on their return home into their families and communities. Then came the Revolution, when the government considered it as necessary for the troops to be supplied with rum as with bread.

In the Middle States during the last quarter of the eighteenth century many new devices arose for concocting stimulants. In New Jersey the most important of these innovations was the production of applejack from apple pulp, and the distilling of cider-brandy from cider. Peaches, too, were converted into a sweet, rich brandy, and the same strong liquor was made from cherries, plums, persimmons, and pears. The last, known as perry, was considered the most delicate and appetizing of the stronger drinks. But in Somerset and Morris counties applejack sprang at once into favor. Morris soon became the banner county in the production of this seductive compound; to one of its citizens, Richard Kimball, is given the honor of introducing "Jersey lightning" in the neighborhood, he having in 1773 imported from England a twelve-gallon copper still and commenced its manufacture.

Plentiful drinking was the feature of every occasion. It was not uncommon for a father at the birth of a son to lay in two pipes of wine or two barrels of rum. As the boy grew toward manhood, he frequently surveyed these two packages with both a lively and a melancholy interest, for one was to be broached at his marriage, the other at his funeral. At christenings, if not the baby, at least the event was always baptized in copious quantities of liquor. The seeds of intemperance were literally sown in the cradle, for while yet little toddlers the male children learned to love the spirit-soaked sugar reserved for them in the bottom of their parent's tumblers.

At home and abroad, in summer and in winter, in prosperity and in adversity, in the house of mourning and in the house of feasting, a free circulation of rum, applejack, or fiery madeira was invariably the rule. At public vendues "a dram to the next bidder" was a frequent announcement of the auctioneer. At the stores where the farmers sold their produce, a big brown stone pitcher full of water and a teapot of whiskey usually stood at the end of the counter, and all customers were invited to take a cup of tea. That New Jersey farmer who refused each hay or harvest hand a daily portion of one pint of rum was considered a mean man. Did neighbors assemble to aid in raising a barn, to shear sheep, or to draw and stack the minister's winter supply of wood, the bottle was deemed requisite to give strength to arm and will and to restore flagging energies.

An old gentleman of my acquaintance, of Connecticut ancestry, informs me that his grandfather always kept in the cellar a hogshead of New England rum. It was his custom on summer mornings to draw a pitcherful, and then go to the garden and obtain from a bed kept for the purpose a bunch of tansy, with which he would mix a bowl of punch. Then calling together his wife, children, and servants, he gave each one a drink, whereupon they had family prayers. After this came breakfast, all feeling conscientiously satisfied with the day's beginnings, for the rum punch would warn off fevers, miasmas, and fluxes, while the prayers insured the family virtue for twenty-four hours to come.

In all households of any substance a tankard of punch was mixed each morning and placed on the sideboard for the use of the family and chance visitors. In fact, almost everybody drank, and the majority of people in good society thought it no shame to become tipsy at table; it was the manners of the world, not only of one country or of one state. Even a noble English lord of that time, an exponent of virtue, though opposed to "the habitual soaking of port wine or whiskey punch," expressed himself in his autobiography favorably toward "an occasional booze" as having "a tendency to excite the faculties, to warm the affections, to improve the manners, and to form the character of youth." This scion of nobility probably thought, with Coleridge, that men were like musical glasses—to ring their best they must be wet.

Even when death entered the door and friends and neighbors assembled to pay their final tribute of respect to the departed, copious libations were considered necessary, until it was not unknown for persons to reel in

funeral processions or even to stagger on the brink of the
grave. Hawthorne, in describing the obsequies of a colonial governor, recounts that the minister's nose glowed
like a ruddy coal of fire, and the aged bearers staggered as
they endeavored to solemnly uphold the coffin, for all
day "many a cask of ale and cider had been on tap, and
many a draught of spiced rum and aqua-vitae quaffed."
At the funeral of Joanna Nevius in 1735 the bill of expenses paid by her son Wilhelmus shows that while the
coffin cost fifteen shillings the outlay for wine, beer, rum,
spices, sugar, and pipes was nearly five pounds. When
Philip Livingston, the father of New Jersey's first governor, died in 1749, funerals were held both at his Hudson
River mansion and at his city residence on Broad Street in
New York. At each place a pipe of spiced rum was consumed, and to the eight bearers were given gloves,
mourning rings, scarfs, handkerchiefs, and monkey
spoons. These spoons had a shallow, circular bowl, with
the figure of an ape carved on the end of the handle.

Even the ministers were unable to withstand the alluring vice and occasionally overindulged without forfeiting
the respect of their people. In the Memorial Hall at Deer-
field, Massachusetts, is an oblong flask with a round hole
in the top just large enough to admit the small end of a
goblet. For a long time it was a matter of conjecture as to
what original use this curious article had been put. After
abandoning various theories it has been proved that the
purpose of the flask was to keep the parson's glass of
toddy warm on a winter Sunday morning. We have been
told by Doctor Lyman Beecher that clergymen at con-
sociation meetings always had something to drink, and
though not intoxicated there was among them on occasions a considerable amount of exhilaration. Doctor
Leonard Woods has recorded that he could count at one
time among his ministerial acquaintances forty pastors
who were immoderate drinkers, and that he saw at one
ordination two aged ministers literally drunk and a third

indecently excited. Of course there were instances of clergymen becoming habitual drinkers to an excess that necessitated their deposition from the ministry, but such cases were happily rare. The reverend Samuel Melyen, one of the early pastors of the First Church of Elizabeth-town, was obliged to sever his relations with the congregation owing to intemperance. The unfortunate example of a minister's lapse from virtue does not seem to have proved a warning to the officers of the church, for we are told that at the ordination and installation of Mr. Melyen's successor, Jonathan Dickinson, then barely twenty-one, "great quantities of toddy was consumed."

Well-authenticated traditions are current that when the temperance question began to be agitated in New Jersey, it was not uncommon for ministers who were conscious of their own failings to urge the people, saying, "Do as I tell you, not as I do!" At the time of the installation of Doctor Leonard Bacon over the First Congregational Church of New Haven, free drinks were furnished by the society at an adjacent bar to all who chose to order them. The spiritual shepherds were not only consumers but producers. Not content with furnishing themselves as examples to their flocks in the habit of drinking, at times they set up stills and supplied their followers. The Reverend Jacob G. Green of Morris County was equally learned in law, medicine, and theology, and engaged largely in secular pursuits. Although so pious that he would not permit the members of his family on Sunday to converse on any but religious subjects, he did not hesitate to own and operate a distillery. In the year 1790 the Reverend Nathan Strong, pastor of the First Congregational Church of Hartford and the author of the familiar hymn, "Swell the Anthem, Raise the Song," engaged with a member of his congregation in the distilling business. The enterprise failed, and the financial straits brought upon the minister prevented his appearing in public life for some time excepting on Sundays, that being the only day on which he could not be legally arrested. This circumstance did not operate against his receiving the degree of Doctor of Divinity from Princeton College in 1801.

It is to our old friend whose acquaintance we made at Pluckamin some time ago, Doctor Benjamin Rush of Philadelphia, that the honor must be given of being the pioneer in the temperance movement. While connected with the army he had become impressed with the error made by the government in so plentifully supplying the soldiers with rum. In 1777 he published a pamphlet addressed to the army protesting that the frequent use of spirits by the men wore away rather than supported their bodily powers, and laid the foundation of fevers, fluxes, jaundice, and other ills common in military hospitals. But it was in 1785 that this father of temperance reform gave to the world what soon exerted a powerful influence. This was his celebrated essay, "The Effects of Ardent Spirits on the Human Body and Mind," a treatise which was the germ from which grew the great temperance movement.

Though the seed fell into ground that was rank from the decaying weeds of many years of excess and indulgence, it did not at once develop; but containing the potentiality of great results it eventually became quick with life and forced its way above ground up into the sunlight and public endorsement, until it grew into a great tree bearing rich fruit. Doctor Rush, armed with this essay, commenced an individual crusade. Religious societies, general assemblies, and other bodies were visited, stirring appeals were made in support of the tract, thousands of copies of which were distributed; leading men of the country were extensively corresponded with, Quaker yearly meetings and Methodist conferences were besieged, and wherever this earnest doctor went, his voice could be heard crying aloud, beseeching ministers of every denomination to aid him with all the weight and

387

influence of their sacred offices in saving "fellow-men from being destroyed by the great destroyer of their lives and souls."

The fight of Doctor Rush was not against wine and beer—these he accepted as nourishing and healthful—but against distilled spirits. He declaimed against not only the abuse but the use altogether of "hard liquor," excepting in cases of sickness "when," he said, "it is better applied to the outside than to the inside of the body." His continuous agitations resulted in enlisting the sympathies of many prominent men; among them the Reverend Doctor Lyman Beecher, who after reading Rush's essay, "blocked out" six powerful temperance sermons which, it is said, went echoing around the world. In 1808 Saratoga County in New York gave America its first temperance society. Other like organizations were soon established in the same state and in Connecticut and Massachusetts, and within a few years the movement had extended through all the Middle and New England states. The fight was against distilled, not fermented liquor, and it was the moderate use of the former, rather than abstaining from it, that was advocated. It is on record that after the organization in a tavern of one of the earliest societies, the officers, in return for the honors conferred upon them, treated the members at the bar. The president, raising a glass of liquor to his lips, said to his associates—"Now, brethren, let us show to the world that we can drink in moderation."

For a number of years the progress of reform was exceedingly slow. The breaking up of the army at the close of the Revolution had distributed throughout the country men whose appetites for liquors had been developed by the great quantity of free rum furnished the troops by Continental Congress. The government, notwithstanding the protest of Doctor Rush, had acted under the delusion that the soldiers, owing to their privations and hardships, needed a plentiful supply of stimulants in order to preserve their health and spirits. Throughout the war rum, when it was to be had, was the feature of every occasion, and double quantities were always served to the men on high-days and holidays.

A letter written by Major Barber to Mr. Caldwell on the seventeenth of the same month informs us how the news of independence was received by Colonel Dayton's New Jersey command—then at Fort Stanwix. After the Declaration had been read, cannons fired, and huzzas given, the battalion was formed in a circle with three barrels of grog in the center. The Colonel took a cup and drank the toast—"God bless the United States of America." The other officers followed, drinking the same toast, as did afterward the battalion, accompanied by loud hurrahs, shouting, and other signals of approbation. So it was to the end, when on the announcement of the cessation of hostilities barrels were broached in every camp—rum seemed to be considered the one thing needful, either as a panacea for evil days or as an aid in rejoicing over success.

The period between the Revolution and the War of 1812 was a singularly unpropitious time in which to endeavor to inculcate in the public mind the idea of restrictive habits and controlled appetites. The people were but little inclined to brook any interference that tended to check their individual liberty in thought or conduct.

We have used the old farm as a cord or chaplet upon which to string our historical pearls. That cord, having been cut for the needs of a single century, is now full. It remains for us, therefore, but to tie the ends together and to modestly lay our votive gift at the feet of Clio—the fair muse of history. Of books in her honor there have been no end. Many, like luminaries in the literary heavens, have thrown floods of light over vast areas of the globe and have embraced long eras of time, but it is hoped that the work we are now concluding will also serve her cause.

389

All cannot be suns, yet a modest torch or candle can throw light and reveal what has before been hidden. Thus would we fain believe that this book will find a welcome because of the little it contributes to our fund of knowledge of times and ways long bygone. Of course it falls far short of what was hoped for when planned, but the ideal is rarely realized in execution. Content must come with the consciousness that the preceding pages embody an honest endeavor to faithfully and truthfully preserve unrecorded facts and traditions, which meteor-like, had they once fallen to the ground, could never have been rekindled, but now, so far as this book may be considered a repository of information, they become fixed stars in the firmament of history.

Someone has said that the two most engaging powers of a historical writer are to make new things familiar and familiar things new. Thus as we have turned over the pages of the past, blurred and often indistinct though "rich with the spoils of time," an effort has been made in retelling an oft-told tale to increase the interest in the narrative by correcting some errors, by adding a little that is new, and by throwing the light of the most recent research on much that is old. Care has been taken, meanwhile, to follow the injunction of Johnson not to lie on the watch for novelty and great things, for such cannot have escaped former observation, but rather to follow the quiet undercurrents of life of both ordinary and extraordinary folk, and thus fill in many interstices left by greater historians. The writing of these pages has not been in vain if they influence their readers, especially their youthful readers, to turn their minds from the present and carry their sympathies and interest back to the early days of the country's inception and growth, and fill them with a desire to become more and more familiar with its gradual advancement from primitive beginnings to its present state of high civilization and importance among the nations of the world.

And now it is time to say farewell to the Old Farm. We found it an unrecognized indefinite part of an indefinable wilderness. We have traced its emergence from such a condition into definite boundaries and individual possession. We have followed the gradual growth of its surrounding country from barbarism to a state of progressive refinement and cultivation; we have witnessed the introduction of religion and noted the increase of population; we have seen our forefathers leading contented lives subjects of a king; we have learned what a poor thing is a king when he tries his power against freemen. An Old World's kinsman has crossed the seas and established himself on our ancestral plantation. With interest we have watched in him, in his children and descendants, the gradual transformation of German subjects into American citizens. Three successive generations of occupants have peopled the Old Stone House, and now we leave it with others playing their simple parts therein. Like their predecessors they will make their exit, following that behest of nature, as inexorable in their day and in ours as it was in that remote age when time was measured by Olympiads instead of centuries, and when Homer wrote:

> *"Like leaves on trees the race of man is found,*
> *Now green in youth, now withering on the ground,*
> *Another race the following spring supplies,*
> *They fall successive, and successive rise;*
> *So generations in their course decay,*
> *So flourish these when those have passed away."*

Index

Adams, John, 162, 387.
agriculture, 4, 15–17, 66, 74, 75, 79–80, 114–17, 118–20, 123, 139–40, 146–47, 163, 300–01.
Alexander, James, 79.
Alexander, Lady Kitty, 288.
Alexander, William. *See* Stirling, Lord.
Allenton, 261.
Amwell Presbyterian Church, 73.
Amwell Road, 129, 236, 295, 297, 360.
André, John, 314.
Anne, Queen, 90, 101.
Armstrong, Richard, 294, 298.
Arnold, Benedict, 228, 314, 317.
Arrosmith, Nicholas, 381.
Arrosmith, William, 381.
Asbury, Francis, 184.
Asgill, Capt., 330, 331.
Assunpink Creek, 203, 256.
Atlee, William, 108.
Atwood, Dr., 345.
Axtell tract, 129.
Ayres, Enos, 367.
Ayres, Obadiah, 107, 108, 111.
Ayres family in the Revolution, 178.

Bailey, Jane, 148–49.
Bailey, Peggy, 148.
Bancroft, George, 102.
Baptist church, Morristown, 220.
Bard, Dr., 348.
Barnett, Oliver, 373.

Basking Ridge, 11, 67, 165, 189, 231, 288, 323.
Beach, Abraham, 184.
Bedminster, 3, 6, 10, 13, 20, 130, 136, 372, 381.
Bedminster Dutch Reformed Church, 7–10, 130, 136–39, 245, 247, 248–51, 253, 254, 257–58, 274–75, 368–69.
Bedminster school, 11–12.
Bedminster Tavern, 10, 342–43, 356.
Bedminster Township, 6, 20, 42–43, 53, 65, 67, 69, 77, 114, 129, 155, 156, 164, 180, 188, 189, 210, 216, 218, 240, 242, 244, 247, 254, 258, 316, 323, 341, 354, 357, 370, 376.
Beecher, Lyman, 385, 388.
bees. *See* frolics.
Belcher, Jonathan, 86–87, 290.
Bell Tavern, 366.
Bendorf, 23, 24, 126, 199.
Berger, Caspar, 55–56.
Berkeley, Lord John, 47.
Bernard Hills, 185.
Bernards Township, 66, 67, 68, 322.
Bernardsville, 11, 68, 164, 317, 358.
Bethlehem Presbyterian Church, 67.
Blanchard, Claude, 322, 326.
Blue Anchor Inn, 108.
Blue Hills, 5, 209, 239.
Bodine, Peter, 73.

393

Index

394

Index

Index

Index

Index

400

NOTES ON THE DESIGN
OF THIS BOOK

This book was designed by Warren Chappell. The two woodcuts and the repeating ornament used on the binding were made by Fritz Kredel. The book was set on the linotype in Janson, and was composed, printed, and bound by Kingsport Press, Inc., Kingsport, Tennessee.